DEDICATION TO HUNGER

DEDICATION TO HUNGER

The Anorexic Aesthetic in Modern Culture

LESLIE HEYWOOD

UNIVERSITY OF CALIFORNIA PRESS
BERKELEY   LOS ANGELES   LONDON

University of California Press
Berkeley and Los Angeles, California

University of California Press, Ltd.
London, England

© 1996 by
The Regents of the University of California

Library of Congress Cataloging-in-Publication Data

Heywood, Leslie.
    Dedication to hunger : the anorexic aesthetic in modern
culture /
Leslie Heywood.
        p.   cm.
    Includes bibliographical references and index.
    ISBN 0-520-20117-5 (alk. paper)
    1. Literature, Modern—History and criticism.   2. Anorexia
nervosa in literature.   3. Women in literature.   I. Title.
    PN771.H43   1996
    809—dc20   95-729
                                                                      CIP

Printed in the United States of America
9 8 7 6 5 4 3 2 1

The paper used in this publication meets the minimum
requirements of American National Standard for Information
Sciences—Permanence of Paper for Printed Library Materials,
ANSI Z39.48-1984.

"Dedication to Hunger," from *Descending Figure,* is reprinted by
permission of Ecco Press, © 1980 by Louise Glück.
"Anorexic" is reprinted from *Introducing Eavan Boland: Poems*
(Princeton: Ontario Review Press, 1981), © 1981 by Eavan
Boland.

To the Hillaries

Touching, at fifteen,
the interfering flesh
that I would sacrifice
until the limbs were free
of blossom and subterfuge: I felt
what I feel now, aligning these words —
it is the same need to perfect, . . .
        Louise Glück, "Dedication to Hunger"

Contents

Preface

> This is it. Next would be her arm, her hand, a toe. Pieces
> of her would drop maybe one at a time, maybe all at
> once. . . . she would fly apart. It is difficult keeping her
> head on her neck, her legs attached to her hips when she
> is by herself. Among the things she could not remember
> was when she first knew that she could wake up any day
> and find herself in pieces. She had two dreams: exploding,
> and being swallowed.
>
> Toni Morrison, Beloved

What do anorexia, high modernist literature, and one woman's personal narratives about sexual harassment, rape, and eating disorders
have in common with the exploding body of a reincarnated slave?
What do these issues share with *The Silence of the Lambs,* Nike,
Freud, Plato, Joseph Conrad, Hegel, women's bodybuilding, Descartes, early twentieth-century suffragettes, T. S. Eliot, male identification, "high theory," Jean Rhys, the contemporary academic scene?
Dedication to Hunger traces a system of connections between these
phenomena as complicated as it is dense. Beloved's ghostly body
brings together the disowned fragments of a cultural logic that rejects,
condemns to silence those pieces of the Western self constructed as
feminine, dark, and despised. A precarious collection of frightening
pieces thought to incarnate the opposite of reason, of the sufficient
and centered rational man, Beloved harbors a hunger there is no ap-
peasing. She is the feminine darkness, the chaotic emotion that the
rationalist tradition most struggles to keep in. Instead of loving her,
as Morrison argues we must if we are to survive as human beings
rather than ghosts, if there are to be substantive forms of political

change, we are taught to hold the world's Beloveds in contempt. Beloved stands for those features that the anorexic, like the cultural fathers she follows, devalues in herself and directs the symptoms of her disease against.

I call that set of assumptions that fragments an "anorexic logic." I am interested in how this logic contributes to the different ways, informed by our race and class positions, we disfigure ourselves. In the movement from individual lives to the larger cultural context that informs them, *Dedication to Hunger* asks why so many of us are dedicated to an anorexic logic—that set of assumptions, crucial to the logic of assimilation, that values mind over body, thin over fat, white over black, masculine over feminine, individual over community.

This book comes out of a desire to make connections between literary theory and criticism, analysis of popular culture, and feminist politics from an engaged subject position that is above all personal: the need to understand the sometimes violent divergence of those aspects of my life, to form an intelligible narrative that could help me understand why at certain moments I have felt—as I believe others have felt—as if I would "fly apart." Although the stories I tell are often my own, the response of self-inflicted disfigurement informing so much of my life is frighteningly similar to the stories of other women who share different experiences, so vividly evoked by the Morrison passage, of social inequalities and trauma that contribute to our devaluation.

In coming to terms with anorexia and the cultural logic that informs it, I have been struck by the resonance between the body images and sensations of anorexics, whose symptoms mark an attempt to keep the "pieces" together, and the body image described by Morrison, which refers specifically to black female experience within slavery. In describing so clearly this sense of fragmentation, a body as a formless chaos, an assemblage of detached parts, Morrison points to ways in which bodies racially as well as sexually coded are affected by what I call the anorexic logic, and how bodies of whatever color experience fragmentation in response to trauma. We are not the same, but the anorexic logic affects us all.[1] There are reasons why a ripple of fat tissue over the ribs or the protrusion of a stomach is the source of anxiety, self-loathing, unreasonable fear. As the following pages will show, the logic I discuss invokes intimate, immediate questions of cultural value, who is and who isn't granted the right to love themselves, to *be*.

In writing this text, I have brought more of my life to it than is the case in most criticism. I started this book as an attempt to bring together parts of my experience that often seemed in violent opposition: writer and academic, competitive athlete and woman, and to make connections between myself and the lives of other women affected by the same logic of fragmentation. When, in "Dedication to Hunger," the poem from which I take my title, Louise Glück describes "the interfering flesh/that I would sacrifice/until the limbs were free/of blossom and subterfuge: I felt/what I feel now, aligning these words—/it is the same need to perfect," she brings some of those oppositions together. The convergence between "perfecting" the body and perfecting a structure of words marks a dense set of cultural assumptions about language, gender, subjectivity, and identity that stand as a constitutive problem in the lives of many women who struggle to keep "legs attached to ... hips" while living with the awareness that they "could wake up any day and find [themselves] in pieces." The act of writing has given me some freedom from the grip of anorexic cultural scripts, and I will feel this work is successful if it inspires others to write their own versions.

In a postliterate, postfeminist, postmodernist culture, I would like to make a claim about why it is still important to read and analyze the work of "dead white males" like Joseph Conrad, William Carlos Williams, or Franz Kafka, who so clearly articulate the anorexic tradition, as well as literature that offers alternative perspectives like the writing of Louise Glück, Eavan Boland, and Jean Rhys, or even why it is important to analyze literature at all. My claim is part of a committed, embodied feminist perspective that comes as much from literary and cultural theory as it does from personal experience. Although in each chapter I have tried to bring together methodologies sometimes kept separate, readers more interested in an analysis of popular culture may be particularly engaged by chapter 1 and parts of chapter 4. Those interested in literary analysis may turn to chapters 2 and 3, and other parts of chapter 4. Throughout, *Dedication to Hunger* is an attempt to create connections between "high" and "low" culture, the contemporary and the modern, and to show why doing so is as much a personal necessity as a political philosophy, a pedagogical imperative for reading the texts of contemporary lives. My motivation in doing so is to construct a ragged pattern, stitching together work and life, mind and body, masculine and feminine, white and black, thin and fat, individual and community in such a way that their bifurcation may cease to disfigure, and that their manifestations, like anorexia, may become part of our collective histories.

Acknowledgments

There are many who have contributed to the making of this book. I would like to thank my colleagues at Binghamton and elsewhere who have read the manuscript and offered me so much support: Susan Bordo, whose vitality and work on the body, feminist theory, and eating disorders are so healing and influential to my own thinking and that of others; Suzette Henke, whose example as a reader of modernism is unparalleled; Nancy Armstrong, whose comments on the early version helped me to rethink and revise; my dear friend Liz Rosenberg, the poet whose friendship and moral conviction helps me to stand up, think straight, and face the day; Susan Strehle, whose smiles and unwavering support enable me to continue working; David Bartine, whose love, patience, and line-by-line suggestions made this a much stronger book; Constance Coiner, for her early encouragement; and my graduate students at Binghamton, whose work has reinforced my belief in the importance of cultural studies to intellectual, personal development. I would also like to thank my graduate professors and friends at Irvine who were there at the formative stages, and whose insights and support were foundational: Jacques Derrida, without whose work my work would be unthinkable; J. Hillis Miller, for his patience and trust; Barbara Spackman, for her friendship and intellectual toughness; John Carlos Rowe, for his incisiveness; and Robin Harders, Jeff Niesel, Marc Geisler, and Alice Crawford, for their support and dedication. To my earliest influences: Charles Sherry, who made me believe I could think (even if I was a girl); Pat

O'Donnell, whose enthusiasm about my work gave me confidence to continue; and Jerrold Hogle, who introduced me to feminist theory and a whole new way of reading, thinking, and living. Last but not least, many thanks to Doris Kretschmer, my editor at the University of California Press, whose enthusiasm for and helpful suggestions about my book made its publication possible, Dore Brown, who shepherded *Dedication* through its final stages, and Rachel Berchten, whose perceptive copyediting brought clarity to a sometimes muddled prose.

Chapter One

Clarice Got Her Gun
Tracking the Anorexic Horizon

To write "clearly," one must incessantly prune, eliminate, forbid, purge, purify; in other words, practice what may be called an "ablution of language.". . . Women . . . wallowing in confessions and in personal, narcissistic, or neurotic accounts, are held to be hopelessly inept for either objective, subjective, or universal—that is to say accurate—thinking. Remember, the *minor*-ity's voice is always personal; that of the *major*-ity, always impersonal. Logic dictates. Man *thinks*, woman *feels*. The white man knows through *reason* and logic—the intelligible. The black man understands through *intuition* and sympathy—the sensible. Old stereotypes deriving from well-defined differences (the apartheid type of difference) govern our thought. . . . To write well, we must either espouse [the white man's] cause or transcend our borderlines. We must forget ourselves. . . . The danger in going "the woman's way" is precisely that we may stop midway and limit ourselves to a series of reactions: instead of walking on, we are content with opposing woman('s emotion) to man('s abstraction), personal experience and anecdotes to impersonal invention and theory.

Trinh T. Minh-ha,
Woman, Native, Other

I'm learning to fly, but I ain't got wings
Coming down is the hardest thing.

Tom Petty,
"Learning to Fly"

I. Personal Bodies. Struggles.
Contexts. Legends.

Walking into the women's locker room at the fitness center one Satur-
day afternoon, I found it deserted with the exception of two young
girls who were discussing whether they had worked out long enough
or if they should keep going. I smiled to hear what is so often my own
internal dialogue spoken out loud. I went to a locker, and as I was
pulling off my sweatshirt and substituting my bra top and weight belt,
one of the girls turned to me as if she had recognized a kindred spirit
and said, "Tell me the truth. The real truth. I want to know. Look at
my body. I'm fat. I need to lose weight, don't I?" My response rang
hollow as I tried to reassure her that she looked beautiful just the way
she was (and indeed from one perspective she did, with her smooth
body barely breaking into the curves of puberty, the rounded hips
and stomach defining a female shape), hollow because her frenzied
questioning and tone of voice sounded all too familiar to me. I had
asked the same pointed question of dozens of people countless times,
never believing their reassurances as now she did not believe mine:
"But I know. Tell me. It's okay. Just say, 'Hillary, you weigh too much.
Lose some weight.' Just look at my butt." I already had, and at her
stomach too, my internal response divided between the old "Yes, you
could lose some weight. You're not quite linear, not quite a straight
line. Getting some unsightly bumps and bulges there," and a more
sympathetic, politically committed "NO, you are FINE!" After trying
to say something nonacademic about the pressure of distorted cultural standards on women and repeating the usual line that weight
doesn't matter, that muscle weighs more than fat, I asked her how old
she was. Shyly, braces gleaming, she told me, "Thirteen." Trying to
quiet the voice in myself that is so much like her own and to present
the "older and wiser" perspective that could "save" her from self-
condemnation and self-mutilation, I told her she should value herself
the way she is. All the while I cringed inside at the familiar tone and
the insistence with which she returned to her object of horror, her
own flesh. I was a poor savior, for I could only half believe what I was
saying myself.

   In Jonathan Demme's *Silence of the Lambs* (1991), the film's heroine, the FBI trainee Clarice Starling, acts as a different kind of savior. She is trying to save female victims from a male serial killer who wants to be a woman, and who starves women in a walled-in pit in order to be better able to remove their skins, which he makes into dresses he wears himself.[1] An apprentice, Clarice needs the help of the notorious prisoner Hannibal Lecter, known for his cannibalism, in order to find the killer and save the women. She is granted the authority of the father through Lecter at a price: that she reveal painful psychosexual details about her life. Clarice resists this sexualization, preferring the professional mask. Her mask is the face of a woman with something to prove and is all too familiar. Eyes set, teeth clenched, jaw tensed, focus forward, Clarice conquers the FBI obstacle course at least partially to overcome the doubts that this male-dominated institution has about her competency, her ability to perform as well as a man. Here, in the beginning of the movie, Clarice's mission is to prove that she has as much value as "one of the guys," and her toil over the obstacle course in this opening sequence is to gain recognition of her abilities, her purpose, her worth as a human being and as a prospective member of the FBI. The grim determination etched into her face, distorting her lips, curling the edges of her nostrils in a desperate quest for recognition of her mettle, defined as the capacity for steely hardness, is that of an outsider who has a series of nonphysical obstacles to overcome as well: namely, the cultural traditions that equate female bodies with softness, lack of capability and lack of physical and mental toughness. Furthermore, as Hannibal Lecter (played by Anthony Hopkins) reminds her, Clarice's working-class origins also make her an outsider to the inner circle of white male privilege and power. Her discussions with Lecter serve as her price of admission, and Clarice discloses one painful detail.

Her revelation functions as a parable for the systematic sexual violence the rest of the movie explores: At ten, Clarice tried to stop the slaughter of a lamb because she couldn't stand the animal's screaming. She ran with the lamb half a mile from the farm before she was stopped. Clarice's later work is an effort to stop the screaming of those lambs, metaphorically displaced onto the female victims of the serial killer. She is trying to track down and put a stop to a source of male violence against women.[2] The film goes to great lengths to create parallels between the "aberrant" violence of a single killer and the misogynist violence of the other cultural institutions that frame Clarice. Her work is an attempt to recover the part of herself that was split off when she faced the senseless slaughter, the part of herself that was slaughtered, the part of herself that still screams inaudibly when she suffers sexual harassment: from her FBI trainer to wardens and inmates of the prison where she goes to interrogate Lecter.[3] Clarice functions paradoxically in the film as the agent/mind attempting to rescue women who have been literally reduced to flesh while she herself is continually vulnerable to the same reduction.[4]

Aspects of Hillary, aspects of Clarice. As in *The Silence of the Lambs,* in my narrative what started as a "singular" act of male violence repeated itself in several cultural forms that contributed to and intersected with anorexia and related eating disorders. Facing the sources of my own fragmentation, I remember splitting off from myself and watching fragmentation happen, the body carried into the room and entered while it lay wooden and dead, when, at sixteen, I was raped by my track coach. For a long time after, I screamed in silence, displacing the anger onto the body that had made me vulnerable to attack, and declaring myself separate from it. I was at war with that body, starving it, punishing it by running intervals on the track every evening until I couldn't stand, running ten miles hard each morning and doing half an hour of situps on the back lawn under the apricot trees before breakfast, then making it vomit anything taken in. For two years I lived on spinach and toast during the week, binging on the weekends. With only 6 percent body fat, all I could see was the "fat" on my stomach and legs, this remnant of a feminine, bodily presence that had been vulnerable to attack, a body I desperately denied. And it wasn't just me. Whether or not their dis-ease had its origins in sexual violence, all the women I knew behaved the same way.[5] Running on a university track team on scholarship, I had *chosen* to situate myself within an external regime that demanded self-annihilation of a very literal kind in the guise of self-discipline, as had every other member of the team.

Once a month I and my teammates were submerged underwater in a tank to determine our body-fat percentages. The medical establishment says a "normal" percentage of body fat for a woman is between 22 and 25 percent; our coach wanted us all under 10. It would make us run faster, he said. To ensure we would achieve this, we were weighed twice a week in the university training room, where the trainer was asked to call our weights out loud. In our Bill Rogers shorts, single file, we paraded by closed circles of football players sitting, getting their knees taped, their arms bandaged, watching us as a diversion. We felt ourselves eyed, each inch of flesh scrutinized, our worth summed up, and resigned, we trudged toward the scale as if it were a hangman's noose, waiting for the public exposure of our failures. "One hundred and ten. One hundred and fourteen. Ninety-five. One hundred and two." We all thought we were fat. Every one of us, twenty in all, were anorexic, bulimic, or both. Although I did not recognize it at the time, the violence I had experienced earlier was repeating itself, this time with my wholehearted dedication and consent. The athletic program, which promises to give women a "healthy" sense of our own value and power, functioned, with our enthusiastic cooperation, to make us destroy ourselves instead. Like a flu, the logical strain that unites eating disorders and forms of violence against women had mutated, repeating itself in a different pattern.

So far, I had encountered this violence in the physical, empirical, more easily identifiable dimensions of experience. The next mutation surfaced in what might seem an unlikely place: academia. Like the university athletic program, in postfeminist America the academic curriculum, the ideal of "higher education," also promises to provide women with a sense of subjectivity, dominion. Yet, even here, in the "higher" domain of abstract thinking, of figurative language that does not concern itself with the body, the pattern reappeared.

At about the same time I was eating spinach and toast, running workouts such as twenty repeated half-mile intervals, and parading past football players to the scale, I was an English major reading modernist literature. Like Clarice in her FBI training, running under the signs Hurt, Agony, Pain, Love-It, love it I did. Coaches in the early eighties, including mine, still frequently employed the maxim No pain, no gain. This echoes the signs, nailed to the old pine tree in the opening obstacle course sequence of *The Silence of the Lambs,* where the love of pain and agony is etched into hard wood as if a testament to its permanence. Clarice trains under such a regime: you love your agony and pain because they are designated as the price of admission to the upper reaches of white male high culture, the realm of individual achievement, power, and precedence. Through your self-sacrifice, your willingness to offer yourself up to agony, you are given the opportunity to use your mind to discipline your soft body, overcome its limitations, vulnerability, and needs, and to become the self-sufficient male icon offered in American culture as the embodiment of selfhood. Hurt, Agony, Pain, Love-It becomes the symbol of opportunity, the chance to prove your worth. Running under the signs of the dominant cultural logic, Clarice and I were motivated to push ourselves beyond the limitations usually inscribed on the female body and, in doing so, gained respect.

Reading and running, running and reading. Every so often I would pause in my reading, struck by a similarity between longings expressed in these texts and my obsession with food and flesh, my urgent denial of the feminine, and my desire to "get rid of my body." My aesthetics and my longing to transcend this vulnerable body that I was stuck with and that wasn't mine were circulating through those texts, and I read this similarity as an affirmation of my "superior" world, which was, after all, like that described in these "great books." In my junior year I had to stop competing, for the body I had been trying to get rid of broke down instead, grinding to a halt like a rundown machine. My immune system, taking the cue from my mind, had become self-consuming, attacking my connective tissue and swelling my joints until I couldn't turn myself over in bed. But no matter. It was easy enough to transfer the physical drive, that single-mindedness, from the track and endless running to those "great books" and my study of them. I traded in the under-10-percent-body-fat coach for others, "coaches" in books who could promise me no body at all. Books were clean. Pure. Hard. Masculine.

There is a reason why it was so easy for me to slide from one discourse to the next. The very logic I had applied to my body for so many years was articulated in the premises of literary theory, of criticism, in the ways we were expected to write. It was an easy transfer. The similarity of logics made it, for me, a long apprenticeship, longer than Clarice's, since one form blended so easily into the other. It took me a long time to unlearn what the "great books" said, to discover what I was trying to do—"save" my body—because I identified with what I read. I had to forget everything my "coaches" had told me, or like Clarice, I had to twist what the "masters" had taught to serve my own purposes. Trying to combine the cold, clean abstraction of "theory" with my driving concern to find a way of existing, of justifying the embodiment I denied, I explored the "third space" of gender. Following the academic theories current at the time, I took an indeterminate position, which oscillates between the polarity of masculine/feminine, that promised a subjectivity free from gender, a conceivable space as long as it remains theoretical. "But what about the body?" a professor of mine asked me. My body was precisely what these particular forms of theory allowed me to leave behind once again. I had been forgetting or suppressing the emotional sources of my will to theorize: my flesh. Yet, it's not quite so simple: theory also enabled me to think differently, to articulate the relationship between literal and figurative, text and life, of which this book is a result. It was not theory per se that led me to avoid the problems of my embodiment but rather the way theory can be practiced in some circles: as abstract, "higher" thinking detached from or replacing the "real world."

Once I stopped forgetting I had a body, I found others forgetting the same thing. I found I was still silently screaming every time I sat quietly in the seminar room, listening, not speaking, thinking "No, that's not it. You're leaving it out. You're cutting out the body again. And women." Women, bodies; bodies, women—the two always seemed to appear in tandem. So I started to look for those bodies—what had made them disappear?—my body, the body of another woman on the track team who ate only carrots and drank the water from her boiled spinach, the bodies of all of us who look in the mirror every day and see anathema, despair, the horror of a female flesh. Like Clarice, I am trying to find the bodies before it is too late. The bodies we starve in the walled pit of our souls, voluntarily serving our cultural masters, the bodies sacrificed to textual models, televised images, to airbrushed displays. To linear argumentative structure with its clean, hard lines, the kind I had written in so easily, so well, while I stolidly excised any feeling. I want to salvage those bodies, extricate them from some of those nipple-ringed modernists and poststructuralist theorists who, like the serial killer in *The Silence of the Lambs*, would starve them to death in order to cut them away: attraction, repulsion, torturing the feminine in order to try it on. I want the bodies to breathe, I want to heal but not unite the split between spirit and flesh that's been cutting us in two at least since Plato began flinging embodied women off his transcendent ladder toward flying. Like Clarice, I feel compelled to confront the sources of my fears: "It was screaming, some kind of screaming, like a child's voice. I was so scared to look inside, but I had to."[6] Under the guise of the Feminist Bureau of Investigation, this text culminates my apprenticeship. It is my feeble attempt to fly while firmly grounded in the "ponderous prison" of my flesh.

Stylistically, logically, structurally, there are difficulties with flying when the material—language—you use for wings is an intrinsic part of the problem. For the most part, "good writing" as it is defined academically cuts away all thought and impulse that would lead one astray from the pure linearity of argumentative form. No emotion. No reference to the personal, lived experience of embodied women in late capitalist culture, who are negotiating career expectations and Nike ads, along with the religious right, MTV, and Cindy Crawford. No revelation of underlying motivations, of feelings, of compulsions, of the passions where my interests lie, of the space where I combine theoretical insight with my personal narratives every day.

Yet, with an ear turned toward its screaming, the body I had attempted to forget remained. I couldn't get away. I ended up with a project about precisely that process of cutting away, the mode of thought, the privilege given to rationality, the process of elimination that I have named "anorexic" for its similarity to the logic of the disease. Anorexics enact with their bodies the process that Western logic inscribes: they physically demonstrate its subtext, the horror of the female flesh that is often the unconscious of discourse. Anorexics, as Morag Macsween has shown, "attempt to solve at the level of the individual body the irreconcilability of individuality and femininity in a bourgeois patriarchal culture."[7] The real of anorexia is the residue of discourses about it. To write about it, I found that my old ways of writing wouldn't fit. I found I had to resurrect the personal, the creative, the feminine, the emotion I had been so busy murdering according to the dictates of the culture I had accepted and used, quite literally, to shape my flesh. In my "personal" life, textually constituted and bodily lived, anorexia intersected with at least three cultural institutions—athletics, academia, and consumer culture—as a form of violence imposed from inside that is the institutional by-product.

The internal violence that becomes anorexia is dependent on three fully functioning bodies: the ghost body (body image, what we perceive our bodies to be); the real body (biological); and the ideal body (the body image we hold in theory as an ideal that we would like our bodies to become). Like anorexics, in the "construct your body" ethos of contemporary culture, we privilege our ideal bodies over the real to create the ghost.[8] In so doing, we repeat the haunting within language, the privilege often given in critical discourse to the figurative over the literal, the theoretical over the empirical, even though these are intricately related, rather than opposed. In a reversal of the usual logic about the disembodied nature of the postmodern, the utter detachment of signifier from signified, and the constant slippage from one signifier to the next, what was figurative in the modern has become literal in the postmodern. If we are complicit with dominant culture, we now act out the same hierarchy of figurative over literal on our bodies through the rejection of our existing body and our acceptance and pursuit of an ever-receding figurative ideal.

A striking ad that appeared in British *Vogue* plays to the developing cultural awareness that we are chasing ghostly ideals. As such, the ad seems to affirm the female body as it is, appealing to a sensibility, like my own, that is tired of constructing the self for the gaze of the other according to the other's terms. The ad (see Fig. 1) shows a line of women, arm in arm, wearing seemingly little makeup, dressed only in light cotton loincloths reminiscent of the Greeks. Their breasts, of strikingly different sizes, are exposed, and the bold text reads, "It's not the shape you are, it's the shape you're in that matters." In smaller print, followed by the Nike logo, the text reads: "Where is it written that unless you have a body like a beauty queen you're not perfect? You're beautiful just the way you are. Sure, improve yourself. But not in the pursuit of an impossible goal. A synthetic illusion painted by the retoucher's brush. Get real. Make your body the best it can be for one person. Yourself. Just do it."[9] Presumably, the women in the ad are individualist heroines defying "beauty queen" standards, stalwart

it's not the
shape you are,
it's the shape
you're in
that matters.

1. This Nike advertisement appeared in British *Vogue* in spring 1994. Its cynical adoption of a feminist rhetoric, which suggests disruption of the gender status quo while reaffirming it, is characteristic of sophisticated advertisements today.

in their self-acceptance. The butch figure on the far left who looks into the camera with sarcastic defiance, her large breasts in contrast to her short, dark hair and her boyish features, seems particularly in opposition to the standard type her body most resembles—the buxom Loni Anderson blonde that Dolly Parton pushes to parody. No false eyelashes here, the woman seems to hold to her own terms, anchoring the line of women defiantly in the "real." Not "illusion[s] painted by the retoucher's brush," these are "real women," the ad claims, naked, honest, unadorned. They don't have to change themselves to please anyone—except themselves: "Make your body the best it can be for one person. Yourself." Here, however, is where the ad betrays its best intentions.

The ad is constructed with the assumption of bodily plasticity and change. You may be "beautiful just the way you are," the ad tells women, but that every woman wishes to "improve herself" is something this advertisement counts on. From this premise, it then offers them a seeming diversity of body types for identification or as models of "improvement." Yet these bodies have two things in common: they are all thin, and they are all white. Even the woman on the end, whose body structure could be described as "heavyset," has no extra meat on her bones. "The shape you are" is fine, as long as your skin is white and "the shape you're in" is thin. Under the guise of diversity the advertisement offers the tyranny of uniformity: a white, thin female body. A woman isn't supposed to desire a body that is "a synthetic illusion painted by the retoucher's brush." She is supposed to "get real" in her desires by "mak[ing her] body the best it can be for one person. [Her]self." The ad claims to invoke individual desire and choice for each woman as to her bodily configuration, while it offers a monolithic thinness as the standard for that "choice." Even though the ad openly confronts the idea of the figurative ideal, it cynically reinstitutes that ideal while seeming to question it. As this sophisticated advertisement so strikingly shows, our ideal body is a figure. Like the precedence given to figurative speech over common vernacular, that ideal body is more "artistic," more worked upon, than the "raw material" of the body that doesn't work out. In giving privilege to that figure by constantly working against the real body to transcend it, to change it, to overcome it by shaping it into the figurative ideal, we literally inscribe the methodology of modernist critical thinking into our flesh.

A confusion of the literal and figurative? Perhaps. Such accusations have been made before. But these terms were always "confused," implicated in each other, bound together. In view of my subject matter, I can no longer repeat the privilege given to the figurative in my own text. Like many new forms of writing currently gaining wider acceptance, the "original" work that I was expected to produce could not be clear, hard, linear, pure, uncontaminated by the network of concepts coded "feminine." Traditionally, a "feminine" style has been the name given to writing that shows some form of passion, and prohibitions against it are evident in commonplace injunctions against emotion or "the personal" if you are engaged in critical, analytical writing.

And any half-dead *corps,* starved for a long time, begins to walk again with tiny steps. The fissures, gaps, discontinuities, as well as the inordinate structural employment of the very logics I criticize, are all part of my clumsy attempt to restore the starved female text/*corps* and return to her the emotion and validity of a personal, embodied life that is intuitive as well as logical, emotional as well as analytical, part of lived experience as well as theoretical speculation.[10]

Like the thinking of many writing today, mine is informed by post-structuralism. I believe in splits. I believe that the terms paired in the previous paragraph are intricately related, rather than opposed. I believe that the subject is primordially divided, formed in relation to acquisition and lack, at least at this moment in history. I believe that the "masculine" and "feminine" are subject positions not necessarily referring to biological male and female bodies, and that these terms are positions constructed, taken up, and occupied in relation to the dominant cultural logics characterizing a specific historical period. I believe the body is a cultural construction, as much a product of cultural forces and discourses as it is biological, and that any biology is culturally mediated. I believe these things because without a notion of the constructedness of the body and gender, no change in configurations would be possible. But I also believe that a subject position is necessary to facilitate political action, however divided, and that theory in and of itself does not constitute political action but rather a point of departure. And I believe the "choice" of subject position is always mediated through a culture that on some level still imposes—including increasingly complex manipulations like the Nike ad analyzed above—a determined polarity between masculine and feminine, white and black, despite the fictiveness of those determinations, and despite, particularly in our current montage-style, little-of-this and little-of-that culture, what looks like radical indeterminacy. As soon as we are articulated as a male or female body, a raced, classed, or sexed body in the context of the larger culture, a subject position construed hierarchically is not far behind, due in part to that means of articulation, our language. We take up a position according to a dialectic of presence and lack in terms of our relative proximity (still generally connected to our biological bodies) to the monied white male as signifier. If we are in the position of lack, we try to find ways of formulating another choice. We try to find a way out or to attain that which we "lack." Anorexia is a failed attempt to create an alternative, to avoid lining up on one side of the male/female, rich/poor, white/black, heterosexual/homosexual divides.[11] Because it is an attempt to articulate a different space and so clearly a failed attempt, anorexia is an object of fascination in a culture uncertain in its polarities, boundaries, differences, uncertain even as that culture definitively imposes boundaries and differences in specific configurations of power.

Anorexia, once a disease of the few and known only to a few, is now a disease of the many. Recent work that is attentive to a multicultural context, like Becky W. Thompson's *A Hunger So Wide and So Deep*, has focused attention on working-class women, women of color, and lesbians previously absent from consideration.[12] Analysis continues to grow more complicated and multidimensional. Among others, Susan Bordo's *Unbearable Weight* and Morag Macsween's *Anorexic Bodies* have contextualized the debates by providing connections between philosophy, popular culture, sociology, and psychology.[13] Although anorexia is no longer a hot media topic, and there is some indication that beauty ideals are shifting to larger, more voluptuous women, this is not an indication of political progress or that anorexia is a thing of the past but that history is repetitious.

From the size fourteen Guess? model to the character Valerie on *Beverly Hills 90210* to the New York cafés opened by supermodels, body ideals in the midnineties and the politics those ideals reflect seem to repeat the reactionary political history of the 1920s and 1930s that is a context for anorexia. As Ellen Wiley Todd writes, "[T]he revised 1920's 'feminist' emphasized individual rather than collective goals and embraced female and domestic occupations" (131), and this revision corresponded to a revised body image of the anorexic flapper to the more matronly, voluptuous siren. Todd describes how journalism of the period advocated the abandonment of "the boisterous energetic behavior practiced by the flapper because all her rights were now won. The siren was to renew her covenant with femininity and strive to nurture and please men rather than competing with them" (145).[14] The pages of *Cosmopolitan* and *Vogue* make similar arguments today, and the more voluptuous body ideal corresponds to those arguments. The demonized character in the January 1995 movie *Disclosure,* played by Demi Moore, is a successful career woman who works out on the StairMaster and claims to have only "oranges and champagne" in her refrigerator. By contrast, the "good guy" Michael Douglas has a "good wife," who is a lawyer but is only shown at home, and references to her well-stocked refrigerator are paired with references to the weight she never lost after the kids. Her refrigerator and her body are represented as sustenance for the Douglas character, giving him the kind of stability that, according to the movie's logic, we all need. The underlying assumptions readable in contemporary cultural texts like *Disclosure* about body weights, gender roles, and social power are an integral part of the anorexic logic this book traces.

The backlash against feminist advancement and what looks like a correspondent shift in body ideal does not mean that cultural values have significantly changed or that anorexia is forgotten. From a recent front-page article in the *Los Angeles Times* to documentaries (*The Famine Within*) and novels (*Lifesize*), eating disorders like anorexia and bulimia have entered the mainstream of popular culture.[15] Perhaps due to overexposure or the cultural fascination with the new, eating disorders have come to seem somewhat passé. Like alcoholism or drug addiction, these once hidden afflictions are now part of an everyday vocabulary, part of the discourse of disorder that seems to characterize so much of late twentieth-century cultural phenomena. But anorexic values, today as well as in the past, are everywhere. More widely than in the fin de siècle culture of the previous century, anorexia has emerged as a point of convergence between the literal and the figurative; between the artificiality of gender constructions that mark an unstable cultural system and a medical discourse that appeals to an essential "truth" of the body to shore up weaknesses in the cultural model of gender. Like anorexia, medical discourse is an attempt to establish control that simultaneously demonstrates a lack of control. As the historian Thomas Laqueur has shown, in its instability the Victorian ideology of separate spheres turned to biology in an attempt to solidify its constructions of gender; thus, the medical discourse provided a kind of control over a construction that had proved itself too malleable, too indeterminate for comfort. That this indeterminacy required control called attention to the artificiality of con-

structions that claimed to be based in "nature."[16] Similarly, the anorexic's gender confusion or conflicted gender identity is symptomatic
of her feeling that she lacks control over her life and body, a confusion
inextricably linked to the raced, sexed, classed discourses that produce it.

Anorexia has recently been read as everything from a prototype for
the discourse of liberal humanism (Gillian Brown) to a feminist strategy of resistance to a still-patriarchal culture (Sandra M. Gilbert), and
perhaps because of its malleability as a trope, it still remains, in the
words of Hilde Bruch, an "enigma."[17] Bruch, still the most influential
medical doctor and therapist to write about the disease, was the first
to connect anorexia to its cultural and historical context, thus raising
issues that, from a late twentieth-century feminist perspective, make
the disease intelligible. While anorexia cannot be pinned down to one
determinate meaning or function, one can isolate some of the ways
the disease functions culturally to express a set of antagonisms central
to the often contradictory construction and performance of female
bodies in the late twentieth century.

I attempt to negotiate the critical and analytic impasse between the
bodily and the textual. I will argue that anorexia and the related eating
disorder bulimia have developed as diseases that affect large numbers
of women as the result of at least four interrelated cultural factors:
the Western philosophical, religious, and literary tradition that defines femininity and materiality as its principal "others"; the ways in
which gender "otherness" is compounded by a sexual orientation or
race or class position that is deemed "other" by the dominant culture;
the beauty industry and its central position within a consumer economy; and the "first and second wave" feminisms of the early twenties,
late sixties, and early seventies, in their relation to a popular culture
that co-opted their discourse through the presentation of androgyny
and masculine identification as ideals for women attempting to rewrite the restrictive roles related to traditional conceptions of "femininity"—a presentation many of us, myself included, swallowed
whole. Furthermore, cultural ambivalence toward women's professionalization situated a paradox that requires women not to choose
between traditional femininity and "progressive" professionalization
or masculinization, but that they enact both simultaneously. Stretch-
ing across the historical divide that separates those two waves of femi-

nism and levels of discourse between high and low culture, I further argue that anorexia functions figuratively to structure the unconscious logic of a number of male-authored high modernist texts, establishing a field of discourse within which the ideals of high modernism are traceable to those levels modernism most tried to distinguish itself from: the personal, historical, emotional, and feminine—the unaesthetic body and materiality (always gendered feminine) of everyday life. Anorexia can be read as a figure for modernism's engagement with its social and historical context, as one of the ways "high art" served to structure the very registers of discourse it tried to erase.

What is at stake in this reading is an understanding of the ways in which a series of common oppositions—such as art and life, the political and the personal, the figurative and the literal, the masculine and the feminine, the discourses of literature and those of the body—can be read in indissociable relation. These oppositions provide a context for rethinking the function and importance of gender within literary modernism, and the importance of literature in creating, reinforcing, or reflecting cultural norms. Because these norms are presented in the guise of the literary universal, they seem unquestionable when encountered by the reader who searches for a ground for identification, for the formation of a raced, gendered, and sexed subjectivity, a set of principles by which to "shore up the ruins" of a fragmented culture/self/discourse and to stabilize a universe where everything, including seemingly unquestionable categories like the body, present themselves as questionable. Contemporary readers, perhaps particularly the women who negotiate the paradox of individuality and femininity in relation to race and class positions, still look to the "great books" for the answers they seek. Those answers, I will argue, are based on a logic no different from anorexia's own.

II. Historical Contexts. Limits.
Positions. Anorexic Philosophy:
Descartes, Plato, Hegel, Freud.

The term *anorexia nervosa* became a part of medical discourse in 1872. Concurrently, Charles Lasegue in France and William Withey Gull in England described a condition that afflicted "the female sex, and chiefly between the ages of sixteen and twenty three" in which there was "complete anorexia for animal food, and almost complete anorexia for everything else. . . . the condition is one of simple starvation."[18] The etiology of the disease, like hysteria, was baffling, since it seemed to have no physiological cause. Instead, Gull reported, "The want of appetite is, I believe, due to a morbid mental state" (310). Initially interpreted as a rare condition that results from a "moral" failure in which the rebellious female subject defies her "natural" status as a woman by refusing to "grow up," today in the United States and Britain the disease affects one woman in ten.[19] Anorexia nervosa is a common part of our cultural vocabulary and has gained a kind of currency among young women, who openly ask each other how you can "catch" the disease.[20] Every semester students tell me that "three-fourths of the women on my dorm floor have anorexia or throw up," and agonized women with eyes like extinguished lanterns and bodies dwindling to ghostliness ask for a help I can't give them. Largely because of its mass popularization and because it is seen as a feminine "beauty preoccupation" that concerns adolescent girls, anorexia is not given the serious attention it deserves as a public health problem. According to the American Anorexia and Bulimia Association, each year 150,000 American women die of anorexia, 17,024 more than the number of deaths from AIDS throughout the world.[21] While AIDS is on the rise and certainly a major concern, the comparative trivialization of anorexia is striking.

Anorexia is, according to one source, "a structure of facades constructed to hide a central hole of non-being."[22] It is a disease characterized by the following psychological complexes: a simultaneous refusal to eat and incessant preoccupation with food (attraction to and repulsion from food); a lack of independent personality structure—the anorexic self-image is a black hole, a cavernous nothingness; a disruption of the sense of linear time, so that the present becomes a synecdoche for past and future and all of lived experience; an experience of the mind and body as radically split, with the mind struggling to control the body; an increasing isolation, a sense of superiority to and lack of emotional contact with others; a complete suppression of sexuality, as well as loss of secondary sexual characteristics; and a marked identification with the masculine and simultaneous rejection of the feminine, along with a paradoxical attempt to accede to beauty standards of thinness.[23] In one sense, anorexics are paradigmatic Cartesian subjects, and in another, they are exemplary postmodern subjects, the vanishing point where the two discourses come together. To some extent the anorexic is the literalization of the fragmented postmodern subject who has no autonomous self but is the product of a range of heterogeneous discourse, since her inability to establish boundaries between herself and the rest of the world is arguably postmodern. Yet, anorexics also experience themselves very like Descartes, who in his first meditation writes, "I will consider myself as having no hands, no eyes, no flesh, no blood, nor any senses," in order to properly think.[24] They place a similar value on mind, or "soul," which Descartes does not distinguish between, over the body: "The first and principal thing required in order to recognize the immortality of the soul is to form the clearest possible conception of it, and one which is entirely distinct from all the conceptions one can have of the body. . . . we cannot conceive any body except as divisible, while the mind or soul of man can only be conceived as indivisible" (13–14).

Entirely separate, privileging the one over the many, the unified over the disparate, universal over the particular, for Descartes like Western philosophers before and after, the mind in its "indivisibility" has domain and control over the unruly, disunified body. As a means of achieving that detachment and control, Descartes desires that "the minds of the readers should be as far as possible withdrawn from the use of and commerce with the senses" (15), and finds that he can "think" and write his meditations only because "I feel myself, fortunately, disturbed by no passions" (17). "Commerce with the senses" —the bodily, the material, the emotions—establishes a sense of fragmentation that must be controlled or fixed through a split or separation from that body. In this paradigmatic Western philosophical tradition, the "mind" is gendered masculine and the disunified and deceptive senses, feminine. As Kim Chernin puts it, "[A] woman's body . . . stands for all that is inscrutable, unpredictable, and uncertain in life."[25] The "senses" are the body and the body is female. The senses that Descartes distrusts, all that he labels "uncertain" and therefore casts aside, are the "deceitful mistress." The body, gendered female, can't be trusted in its inscrutable feelings, needs, and desires: "I have learned by experience that these senses sometimes mislead me, and it is prudent never to trust wholly those things which have once deceived us" (*Meditations*, 18).[26]

Anorexics are "Cartesian" in the sense of experiencing (male) mind and (female) body as entirely distinct, with the mind set up as the "dictator" of the deceitful flesh;[27] Descartes's thought is "anorexic" in that its basic tenets are characterized by the same logic: "I doubted the people around me," an anorexic who was a patient of Bruch's says. The patient continues, "I was unsure whether they truly existed."[28] "My body became the visual symbol of pure ascetic and aesthetics," she explains, "of being sort of untouchable in terms of criticism. Everything became very intense and very intellectual, but absolutely untouchable. . . . you feel outside your body. You are truly beside yourself."[29] Untouchable, invulnerable, certain, intellectual, aesthetic and pure—this description begins to elucidate the conceptual field characteristic of anorexic thinking, and of the Western literary and philosophical tradition. This field becomes particularly focused in the literature of the modernist period.

While "philosophical anorexia" is perhaps expressed most clearly in Descartes, one of its first written instances can be seen in Plato's *Symposium*, where women, defined by their bodies, are uniformly equated with the "material" that it is the project of men to transcend. Transcendence is necessary in order to escape the plurality, temporality, and division associated with the material, the "particular" forms inherently subordinate to "universal" Forms or Ideas as Plato articulates them. Perhaps this particular dualism, which equates the female with the transient material and the male with the universal atemporal spirit that has transcended or has the possibility to transcend that material, pervades history and informs and structures paradigms of gender and discourses on the body more than any other.

Plato's theory of Forms is predicated on the idea of a fixed, permanent essence, of which materiality is a copy. The manifold, changing phenomena of the world of sense, as in Descartes, are feminine, deceptive, unreal. The task of the true philosopher is to pass from the "shadows" of the sensible world that are reminders of the Forms to the contemplation of the Forms themselves, and through this process

the material realm is transcended. Love is one of the primary agencies
of this process, a mediatory link between the material and eternal
world. The mind finds its way toward "truth" through love and
through a transcendence of the body. In stages, "love" ascends the
"Platonic ladder" that establishes the hierarchy of thought over sense,
mind over body, masculine over feminine, and it is this ladder that is
the first systematic articulation in Western philosophy to subordinate,
if not sacrifice, the feminine flesh. The first step on the ladder is the
passage from love of particular examples of physical beauty to the love
of physical beauty in general. Individual attachments are important
only in that they facilitate the apprehension of this universal beauty.

In *The Symposium,* the lover is to pass from "one instance of physical beauty to two and from two to all" in order to "relax the intensity
of his passion for one particular person, because he will realize that
such a passion is beneath him and of small account."[30] Once he has
transcended physical love, the lover is free to experience the love of
the soul of a particular individual; he is to "reckon beauty of the soul
more valuable than beauty of body" (92). Materiality and particularity
have been transcended on one level. The third step involves another
purgation of particularity, for the love for a particular soul must
change to a love for all beautiful souls, the love of moral beauty in
general. Throughout this process he becomes freer yet, having liberated himself from materiality and particularity, "no longer . . . the
slave of a base and mean-spirited devotion to an individual example
of beauty, whether the object of his love be a boy or a man or an
activity" (93). The fourth step involves the passage to the contemplation of the ultimate Form, to the beauty of knowledge, a beauty that
"is first of all eternal; it neither comes into being nor passes away,
neither waxes nor wanes" (93). This final stage is "the region where a
man's life should be spent, in the contemplation of absolute beauty"
(94). Contemplation is attainable only after the lover has entirely
emancipated himself from the "bonds of sense," an emancipation that
allows traffic in or with the immortal.

In its insistence on the need to "liberate" oneself from the "bonds"
that both the material and the particular impose, bonds that would
conceivably constrict and destroy the spirit, Plato's theory necessitates

the kind of interchangeability of objects late feminists such as Luce Irigaray discuss in "Women on the Market," specifically, the "masculine" construction and appropriation of the "feminine," as well as the material male and female bodies that participate in these transactional constructions.[31] For Plato, love "objects" logically are male since the pervasive correlation of the female with the material (the non-Ideal) excludes her from any "progress" up the ladder since she *is* that very particular materiality that needs to be escaped and transcended. Traffic in the feminine is unthinkable. Plato's theory of love presupposes this exclusion, and women are mentioned only once in reference to the process of transcendence.

Having stated that all men are "in love with immortality," Socrates mentions in *The Symposium* that procreation is one possible avenue for the achievement of immortality. Men for whom the "creative instinct is physical have recourse to women, and show their love in this way, believing that by begetting children they can secure for themselves an immortal and blessed memory hereafter for ever" (90). These men are of a lower order; they are the nonphilosophical sort. The higher category comprises those "whose creative desire is of the soul, and who long to beget spiritually, not physically, the progeny which it is by the nature of the soul to create and bring forth" (90). That "progeny" is said to be "wisdom and virtue in general" and, to the extent that this "progeny" explicitly involves writing, the production of poetry, as well as the even better progeny of political and philosophical tracts "concerned with the due ordering of state and families," the question of authorship and who is able to "beget spiritually" in this manner is also raised (90). Here is one of the first metaphors of "literary paternity," the spiritual production of texts. Spiritual production transcends the base form of material production that is consistently associated with women. Material production of texts is the only form of production possible for women (and slaves). Excluded from a theory of love that serves as a vehicle of transcendence of particular materiality, women are excluded from the province of spiritual production as well.

The sacrifice of female flesh on the alter of high philosophy continues in the idealist tradition. Hegel's theory of love, for instance, con-

nected to his theory of the body and its relationship to gender, represents a paradigmatic shift that retains the element of female sacrifice:
instead of love as the vehicle that facilitates a progression toward
higher things, it becomes the object that must be transcended in order for man to attain full self-conscious spirit. In Hegel's theory love
is associated with the feminine, the body, and the family—which
must be subordinated to and transcended by the imperatives of the
masculine, the mind, and the state. Hegel conceives of "male" and
"female" as fixed, given essences that have differing ethical contents.
The family for Hegel is a "natural ethical community" in that it is the
concept that expresses the ethical sphere in its immediacy or simple
being. The family is the "unconscious, still inner notion" of the ethical
order, its "state of nature" or base material, and stands opposed to the
actual, self-conscious existence and achievement of the ethical order.
An individual cannot attain full self-consciousness and being until he
has separated himself from the family, for "it is only as a citizen that
he is actual and substantial, the individual, so far as he is not a citizen
but belongs to the Family, is only an unreal impotent shadow . . . in
truth the calm and universality of a self-conscious being do not belong
to Nature."[32] Since the family is affiliated with nature, the attainment
of universality and self-consciousness that is Hegel's goal for the individual, defined as male, is only possible outside of the family. As I will
show, the fact that individuality and maleness continue to be linked is
a key component of anorexia.

The sacrifice continues. But if the sacrifice is self-sacrifice (and anorexia *is* a self-sacrifice), then all the better.[33] It's cleaner. No one to
blame but the victim. Therefore, Hegel is particularly fond of Antigone, who fits into his gender polarities with her unquestioned alliance to "blood ties" and the family, and the self-sacrifice she is ready
to perform for that family. For Hegel, Antigone is the feminine paradigm, which, in the form of the sister, has the highest intuitive awareness of the ethical. However, the sister does not attain consciousness
of the ethical, or of its objective existence, because she is affiliated
with the law of the family, and that law is an implicit, inner essence
"which is not exposed to the daylight of consciousness, but remains
an inner feeling and the divine element that is exempt from an existence in the real world" (*Phenomenology,* 274). Isolated in the private

sphere, "exempt from existence in the real world," the feminine exists in the realm of the unconscious, rather than that of consciousness.

The brother, by contrast, leaves the immediate, elemental, and therefore negative ethical life of the family in order to acquire and produce an ethical life that is conscious of itself and actual, but he needs the supplement of a wife. The difference of the sexes is a difference in ethical content. This gendered opposition of ethical content is an example of the movement of the Hegelian dialectic, a movement of two opposites toward unification, achieved through the husband's movement into the community where he attains his self-conscious being. The universal self-conscious spirit—man—becomes united with its opposite, unconscious spirit—woman—through the man's "individuality." Their immediate union converts the first two syllogisms, man and woman, conscious and unconscious, into the same syllogism, centered around consciousness, and unites the opposite movements into one process: "one from actuality down to unreality, the downward movement of human law, organized into independent members, to the danger and trial of death; and the other, the upward movement of the law of the nether world to the actuality of the light of day and to conscious existence. Of these movements, the former falls to man, the latter to woman" (278). Sexual difference is used to give gender to an oppositional hierarchical structure in which unreality, downward movement, and death fall on the side of the feminine, while upward movement and conscious existence fall on the side of the masculine.

Since for Hegel the body seems largely unworthy of analysis, sexual difference is attributed to the mind. In Hegel's *Philosophy of Right* the male mind is characterized by conceptual thought, self-subsistence, and volition, while the female mind is concrete, rather than abstract, characterized by its connection to emotion:

Thus one sex is mind in its self-diremption into explicit personal self-subsistence and the knowledge and volition of free universality, i.e., the self-consciousness of conceptual thought and the volition of the objective final end. The other sex is mind maintaining itself in unity as knowledge and volition of the substantive, but knowledge and volition in the form of concrete individuality and feeling. In relation to externality, the former is powerful and active, the latter passive and subjective. It follows that man has his actual substantive life in the state, in learning, and so forth, as well as in labour and struggle with the external world and with himself so that it is only out of his diremption that he fights his way to self-subsistent unity with himself. Woman, on the other hand, has her substantive destiny in the Family, and to be imbued with family piety is her ethical frame of mind.[34]

An idealist justification for traditional gender roles rests on the much-repeated split between male activity and female passivity, male "self-subsistence" and female dependence.

Hegel's account of the founding of civilization is similarly gender specific: "In the sagas of the founding of states, or at least of a social and orderly life, the introduction of permanent property is linked with the introduction of marriage. . . . the Family as a legal entity in relation to others must be represented by the husband as its head. Further, it is his prerogative to go out and work for its living, to attend to its needs, and to control and administer its capital" (116). Here the given categories are set and unchangeable for each individual. Hegel offers a dialectic that resolves opposites, but that they *are* opposites is an assumption related to the essential connection posited between women and the family/body, and between men and the mind/state. Since Hegel has said that legally the family must be represented by the husband, and that it is his place, as the "conscious" individual, to take part in the larger social order so as to provide for the family's "needs," it is clear that in his philosophy and social context the persons "recognized as persons in the eyes of the law capable of holding free property" are men and men only. This point is emphasized in *The Phenomenology of Spirit*: "the husband sent out by the spirit of the Family into the community in which he finds his self-conscious being" (276) is a "being" explicitly opposed to that of woman as "the unconscious spirit" (278).

There is a paradox here that resurfaces in anorexia. Women are constituted as an embodiment that consigns them to a position of "unreality" or nonbeing. Physical being becomes a form of emptiness. To repeat: "It is only as a citizen that [one] is actual and substantial—the individual, in so far as he is not a citizen but belongs to the family is only an unreal impotent shadow. . . . in truth the calm and universality of a self-conscious being do not belong to nature" (270). Since Hegel has asserted that women are not "self-conscious beings," and that they find their "ethical destiny" in the family, this consigns them perpetually to the status of "impotent shadows," to the status of nonbeing. The same paradox that allows embodiment to express nonbeing operates in the logic of anorexia, where, having internalized nonbeing as their metaphysical status, anorexics struggle to drag themselves into existence through the reduction or elimination of their flesh. Accepting the idealist logic linking masculinity with the mind, state, and self-conscious existence, and the femininity with the body, family, and unself-conscious being, anorexics attempt to become mind in order to exist—which often leads to their literal nonexistence.

In Hegel these designations of the nature and ethical destiny of woman are never subjected to the same dialectical method that other assertions are. There is no conflict or struggle for recognition between man and woman as there is between master and slave; the existing state of affairs, as Hegel reports it, is simply assumed. Confined eternally to the temporal, fragmented world of unconscious spirit affiliated with nature and the family, through their "nature," defined as bodily, women cannot participate in the workings of the state and culture. They therefore must accept a position that is culturally devalued, and subordinate themselves to the "higher" good of the state. Hegel's thought is a monument to female self-sacrifice on which the female body is erased, consumed, and subordinated to the "higher good." Hegel articulates a tradition that expresses itself, among other forms, in anorexia, which is the literalized expression of the cultural devaluation of women—female nonbeing—and which makes the anorexics' cultural status as "impotent shadows" an actuality. I cannot think of a better phrase to describe the anorexic, at sixty or seventy pounds, with sunken flesh and cavernous shadows under her eyes, unable to walk and simply fading away in the later stages of the disease, than "impotent shadow."

Plato and Hegel define men in opposition to women, but Freud initiates a crucial historical turn. In the more practical, "therapeutic" context of psychoanalysis, Freud makes it clear that the masculine is defined in opposition to the feminine, but the psychoanalytic model makes women believe they *define themselves* in opposition to men. An "anorexic" structure is operational in Freud's theory of sublimation and its connection to the body, where in its basic assumptions the psychoanalytic model replicates the polarity between the male spirit and the female body that exists in the philosophical models.[35] I will limit myself here to a discussion of the aspects that lead Freud to the conclusion in *Civilization and Its Discontents* that aim-directed love (the body and its passions) and the feminine are on the side of nature; and that sublimated or aim-inhibited love (the mind and its restraint) is on the side of the masculine and culture. Drawing on various essays in *Sexuality and the Psychology of Love,* I will summarize how Freud comes to this conclusion: in girls the castration complex precedes the Oedipus complex, and in boys the former initiates the dissolution of the latter. It is only the dissolution of the Oedipus complex and the resulting transference and sublimation of object love that "leads to the creation of the super-ego and thus initiates all the processes that culminate in enrolling the individual in civilized society."[36] The formation of the superego is grounded on the renunciation of loving Oedipal wishes. For the boy the superego is formed through at least a partial renunciation of his love for the mother. The castration complex, which leads to this renunciation, is "the discovery of the possibility of castration, as evidenced by the sight of the female genital" (198). This interpretation of the female genital as castrated happens only retroactively: "He begins by showing irresolution and lack of interest. . . . it is not until later, when some threat of castration has obtained a hold upon him, that the observation becomes important to him" (187). The paternal function or intervention associated with the father instigates this threat, which the boy then connects to the female genital. An effect of the castration complex is that in addition to renouncing mother love (and thereby the female body), there is "a measure of disparagement in his attitude towards women, whom he regards as having been castrated" (198).

A girl, however, "make[s her] judgment and [her] decision in a flash. She has seen it and knows that she is without it and wants to have it" (188), so the castration complex comes first. She "acknowledges the fact of her castration" (198), and this leads to three possible outcomes: that she renounce her sexuality; that she form a "masculinity complex"; or that she take her father as a love object and "thus [arrive] at the Oedipus complex in its feminine form" (199). For the girl the castration complex does not destroy but rather creates the feminine form of the Oedipus complex, whose dissolution and subsequent creation of the superego is a requirement for "enrolling the individual in civilized society" (198). She therefore lacks motive for the dissolution of the complex, and "only too often a woman never surmounts it at all" (199). In fact, it is part of her "proper femininity" to love the father. Since it is only through a "third, very circuitous path" that she arrives at this "ultimate normal feminine attitude in which she takes her father as love-object" (199), the difficulty of achieving this state leaves her little energy or motive for sublimation, since she is a "good girl" if she loves her father and family as a "devoted daughter." Much like the scenario seen in Hegel, a girl is encouraged to play this role, while the boy is encouraged to break from the family and establish an identity of his own.

Whichever path the girl takes, she is excluded from the public, from "civilization" and "culture." The first path, renunciation of sexuality, is said by Freud to require "all those energies which otherwise they would employ in cultural activity" (28). If she takes the second, she is an anomaly, not fully a "woman," because she wants to be a man and participate in culture. If she manages to follow the third, there is little motivation for her to give up father love, since it is culturally sanctioned. Whatever her "choice," the Oedipus complex doesn't dissolve, the superego doesn't form, and none of the object love/body is renounced and diverted toward a "higher" aim. She later transfers the father love onto a husband, thereby remaining on the side of the body and of love. The primary anorexic symptom is that the woman takes on a "male" position when she renounces her ties to both the body and love. The boy renounces body/love (becomes figuratively anorexic) and attains culture. The girl is stuck with the body, and it is this cultural configuration that the anorexic most tries to rewrite: "It is this difference in the inter-relation of the Oedipus and castration-complexes which gives its special stamp to the character of woman as a member of society" (199). "Women, as the true guardians of the sexual interests of the race, are endowed with the power of sublimation only in a limited degree" (32). For Freud, women, as bodies, can't sublimate. Since it is this capacity for sublimation that enables an individual to "transcend" love and family and move up to culture, we see in Freud a repetition of Hegel's designation of body/love as that which requires transcendence on the way to culture or State. These aspects of Freud's theory, like Hegel's, are predicated on an unquestioned connection between women and the body, which they can't seem to escape, even though that body is defined as lack: lack of consciousness for Hegel, and lack of a male genital for Freud. The plausibility of Freud's scenario depends on both the girl's and boy's interpretation of the penis as "superior" and of the female genitals as "castrated" or "lacking"—which can be formed only through an intense cultural mediation that transforms the female body into a cipher, a lack, an absence. The anorexic physically performs this transformation upon her own flesh in order—ironically—to prove she is not the lack, the cipher, the nothingness that, influenced by the tradition, she truly believes that she is. Without her body, she thinks, she will finally *be*. Exist. As she nudges herself toward nonexistence.

The political message derivable from these aspects of Plato, Descartes, Hegel, and Freud helps to situate the anorexic paradox. In their relentless process of designating the soul, the mind, subjectivity, and civilization as masculine, these "figures" have formed a tradition that some women, to whom the tradition is newly accessible, internalize in an attempt to enter the magic inner circle of culture and become something other than the bodies, sexualities, loves, and flesh with which this tradition equates them. Paradoxically, they do so in order to become the subjectivities denied them. Ironically, in the attempt to gain access to that subjectivity through male identification and an acceptance of male terms, women literally become the "impotent shadows" of Hegelian or Platonic discourse when, by internalizing that discourse, they become anorexic. As Naomi Wolf writes of the admission of women into the elite circles of higher education, "They admitted their minds, and let their bodies go. Young women learned that they could not live inside those gates and also inside their bodies. . . . the anorexic may begin her journey defiant, but from the point of view of a male-dominated society, she ends up as the perfect woman. She is weak, sexless, and voiceless, and can only with difficulty focus on a world beyond her plate. The woman has been killed off in her. She is almost not there" (*Beauty Myth*, 181, 197). The situation is further complicated by the struggle of anorexic women to incarnate the individuality of the "masculine mind" while simultaneously incarnating an ideal femininity represented by the thin body.

Granted institutional access not as women but as "minds," many women try to manipulate, to get rid of, the bodies that define them, to become disembodied, "not there." Clearly, women obsessed with the control and maintenance of their bodies, an obsession common to many, "can only with difficulty focus on a world beyond [their] plate[s]." Such women would be calm, quiet, tractable, and supportive of the status quo, that is, of a masculinist tradition as it currently operates. In *The Beauty Myth,* Wolf writes, "If anorexia is defined as a compulsive fear of and fixation upon food, perhaps most Western women can be called . . . mental anorexics. . . . Girls and young women are also starving because the women's movement changed educational institutions and the workplace enough to make them admit women, but not yet enough to change the maleness of power itself. . . . the worldview taught young women is male" (183, 210).[37] That worldview is very "white" as well.

The anorexic, physical and mental, is usually a male-identified woman who has accepted white male philosophical ideals and standards while simultaneously rejecting the traditional gender roles that go along with those standards or if she or he is a member of an ethnic minority, rejecting traditional cultures in order to assimilate to what is perceived as the norm. The white male-identified woman defines herself in terms of her achievements, which she thinks are independent of any particular group. Yet she defines herself according to standards and prizes she strives to fulfill and win, standards and prizes that function as rules telling her how she must change and what she must become. Paradoxically, part of the "achievement" that is required of her if she is to accord with the dominant culture is the physical appearance of an acceptable feminine beauty usually defined as white. A male-identified woman (even though she may look like the feminine ideal), defines herself as a cipher, a lack, a black hole or empty shell. She is continually struggling to fill this shell with both her attainment of ideal feminine beauty and her collection of masculine achievements, affirming daily that she is not good enough, that she must fight to overcome herself, to cancel herself out, to go beyond herself. This is anorexic thinking, and it applies to women and men who identify with dominant cultural ideals of masculinity and achievement. In *The Golden Cage,* Bruch reports that for many of her anorexic patients, the fathers treated the anorexics "intellectually as sons; [one] was particularly proud that [his daughters] all knew how to throw a ball 'correctly' (namely, like a boy). . . . It is significant that the fathers value their daughters for their intellectual brilliance and athletic achievements [and] rarely if ever do they pay attention to their appearance as they grow into womanhood, though they will criticize them for becoming plump" (26). Taking the cue from Daddy and the world defined as his tradition, the anorexic identifies with those aspects of herself that are termed "masculine" and therefore valued. She struggles against those aspects of herself designated "feminine" in a struggle that becomes articulated in bodily terms. Yet, in her emptiness, in her desire to please and to succeed at pleasing, she struggles to attain ideal physical femininity, even as she strives to cancel it out. Her thin body is her masculine achievement that, until her anorexic artistry goes too far, is the embodiment of cultural standards of female beauty.[38]

III. Consumer Culture. Nike.
The Relentless Logic of the Gym.

> *Don't you feel eyes moving over your body,*
> *Clarice? Don't your eyes seek out the things*
> *you want?*
>
> Hannibal Lecter, in *The Silence*
> *of the Lambs*

The tradition that values women only for their "masculine" attributes is not limited to the households of anorexic patients. As Irigaray writes in *je, tu, nous,* "Value is what matters. . . . whatever has it must be masculine" (70). As Hegel appears and begins to stroll (or perhaps jog with Hannibal?) down Madison Avenue, the tradition that values only the masculine is so common that Nike made use of it in a successful ad campaign launched in the summer of 1992, which I, a lapsed anorexic, keep on my bathroom wall. "Did you ever wish you were a boy?" the ad asks, in italicized white letters surrounded by a black block. "Did you? Did you for one moment or one breath or one heartbeat beating over all the years of your life, wish, even a little, that you could spend it as a boy? Honest. Really. Even if you got over it."[39] The ad cleverly makes use of the sense of female insufficiency internalized through the very male identification that makes women feel the need to achieve athletically and wear Nike shoes in the first place. In this way they prove, like Bruch's anorexics, that they are closer to boys than other women (and are therefore superior to other women): "Only a few [anorexics]," Bruch writes in *The Golden Cage,* "admit frankly that they would have preferred to be a boy. Some will talk about it when they start to express their disgust with the female body." An anorexic "feels that her slenderness makes her look more like a man, and she wants to be equal to men, in particular to prove that she has the same stamina" (73). Like Clarice, who in her FBI training grinds her way through a torturous obstacle course with gritted teeth and determined eye, passing signs nailed to a pine tree reading Hurt, Agony, Pain, Love-It, women may find the athletic arena the perfect place to prove their worth, and thereby their identity, by demonstrating their physical capabilities. The Nike ad makes use of this feminine preoccupation, historically determined, by trying to appear to affirm women as women, pointing out later in the ad that "you wake up. . . . and you learn to stop beating yourself over the head for things that weren't wrong in the first place." That women are women and not men is supposedly the premise for the Nike Women's Products line "in the first place"; however, what the ad can't take into consideration but makes use of is the confusing malleability of subject positions (a biological woman can occupy the subject position of a biological man and vice versa). This "choice" of position is mediated by a culture that acknowledges on the one hand that gender is gender (sexual difference is constructed, not innate), while it takes gender back with the other. As in this ad, our culture is willing to offer the idea that sexual difference is a construct if it will make us buy products but does not allow us to live accordingly. Instead, most people's daily lives are still largely constructed according to traditional gender roles. But in advertising, gender is offered as a choice that you buy, a fanciful construction, with no examination of the real limitations imposed on those choices and no questioning of how limitations are imposed. For even if you do "wake up," as the Nike ad puts it, and stop renouncing yourself through male identification, stop "beating yourself over the head for things that weren't wrong in the first place," you still need to struggle for the self-definition that Nike wants to help give you.

For what "are" you after all? It's quite easy to say "a set of competing heterogeneous discourses," but that doesn't quite provide a satisfactory answer to this grim daily struggle with embodiment. If you are still your body (cultural residue), but your body is okay (we're all "with it" and know that there's no longer any problems with being a woman, that such problems were all "back then"), why do you then have to work on that body incessantly, day after day, for hours and hours, wearing Nike shoes and Nike running tights and Nike bra tops and Nike warm-up jackets and Nike wristbands and headbands and Nike socks and Nike baseball hats? Why do you have to spend a significant portion of your daily life shaping, molding, sculpting that body, as well as a significant portion of your disposable or even your indisposable income on Nike products to enhance that body? In consumer culture the textual logic of linearity, clarity, and revisable, improvable form becomes a bodily logic. We are trained to shape our bodies as works of art that resemble minimalism rather than rococo ("Body by VH-1 on VH-1." "Body by Sports Connection." "Body by Soloflex."). The segment of the female population, including myself, that attempts to shape itself according to aesthetic principles is the target of this advertising campaign. The compulsive workouts that are so much a part of so many women's daily lives, and that define them, keep them constantly striving toward an unattainable physical perfection that is part of contemporary culture's definition of the strong, successful woman. This regime sells Nike products.[40]

It is no coincidence that this ad campaign, undoubtedly written by a woman, plays on that definition of strength and presents it as if it were internally defined, based on an internal sense of strength and self-acceptance, which is perhaps the most elusive and important goal for women today.[41] When Barbara Ehrenreich said in a talk on third-wave feminism that the stumbling block for feminism at this point in history is women's self-esteem, she hit upon the problematic central to anorexia, physical and mental.[42] This problematic sells not just workout apparel but also gym memberships, diet programs, liposuction, psychotherapy, low-fat cookbooks and ice cream and popcorn and soda—and thousands of accoutrements it seems to take to sustain a "successful" woman's sense of well-being. Such a subjectivity seems a precarious, ghostly construction, sharing some affinities with the character of Beloved, whom I evoked in the preface, who is never certain when "she would fly apart. . . . pieces of her would drop maybe one at a time, maybe all at once."[43] This is a fragmentary sense of well-being, eternally in need of reinforcement, of new products, of props to hold it together. Advertising rhetoric can promise its attainment through the purchase of the product, mainly because that sense of well-being is not something that's really granted in the first place. Nike, consumer culture, and the relentless logic of the gym are further mutations of the dominant cultural logic that connects anorexia, embodiment, violence, and female subjectivity.[44]

Many of us growing up in the United States, Latina and Caucasian, black and Asian, heterosexual and homosexual, rich and poor, have suffered from some form of physical anorexia and the poverty of self-definition connected with it. If we have "gotten over it" or never had it, we may still suffer from a form of "mental anorexia," the preoccupation that leads one to incessantly engage in mental monologues like this: "It's only 11:15 in the morning. You just ate at 7:00. You can't have a bagel until after 2:00, especially since you only ran three miles this morning and haven't been to the gym yet, and you spent all day yesterday systematically consuming a bag of low-fat nacho-flavored tortilla chips, which despite the fat content have undoubtedly added to your girth, bulk, and general sense of slovenliness. As a matter of fact, you shouldn't have anything at all, you don't deserve it, but that's not supposed to be a healthy attitude, so I won't say it." While mental anorexia like this is not as time consuming, intensively focused, and energy consuming as the real thing, it still makes a significant difference. Anorexia, mental and physical, is central to the self-definition of most women, particularly educated women attempting to gain access to the "white male power" that requires them to cancel out their bodies. If, as an inheritor of the canonical Western tradition, she internalizes a worldview that is male, a view spelled out clearly in Plato, Descartes, Hegel, and Freud, among others, a woman almost cannot do otherwise than develop a preoccupation with her body since that body has made her the negative other of culture. According to canonical cultural sources said to embody all that is valuable, her body is the base materiality that is deceptive and destructive to the empowered philosopher on a quest of cultural advancement. "I am not that body," she wants to insist unless she is confident enough to define herself according to standards different from those of a dominant cultural logic that now encompasses racial and class difference. This logic tells her she is that body; and because she is, she is lacking, insufficient, flawed, as well as fetishized, commodified, loved, and sexually desired—a devastating set of contradictions that virtually ensures that any real confidence a woman may possess is canceled out. She can only be someone, according to this logic, if she is not herself, if she identifies with the masculine while simultaneously maintaining the appearance of the feminine: "Raised to compete like men in rigid male-model institutions, [young women] must also maintain to the last detail an impeccable femininity" (Wolf, *Beauty Myth,* 211). This is the legacy of the generation of women born in the sixties and later. The legacy requires the mind/body split which characterizes not only Cartesian subjectivity but also the logic of eating disorders that affect (if you include those who worry about calories, fat, exercise, and eating) virtually every woman and increasingly large numbers of men. And these cultural standards do not discriminate in terms of race and class. The ads are relentlessly democratic: *anyone* can attain a great body if she or he works hard enough.

If the concluding text (which follows) of the Nike ad on pages 30–31 corresponded to an existing "reality," it would be something I could say, shout, scream, whisper, and not feel ashamed of: "And one day when you're out in the world running, feet flying dogs barking smiles grinning, you'll hear those immortal words calling, calling inside your head *Oh you run like a girl* and you will say shout scream whisper call back 'Yes. What exactly did you think I was?'" (*Vogue* [June 1992]). The feminine subject position would exist as a position one doesn't have to escape or transcend or suppress or annihilate through bodily manipulation or the purchase of products. There would be a respect for the female body, and thereby the self-respect that Ehrenreich named as essential to the "third wave" of feminism.

Because that respect does not exist, the anorexic logic continues to function. It operates in a recent body phenomenon that has drawn

widespread attention, and that is often thought to represent the opposite of anorexia and therefore the idea of hopeful progress for wom-
en's struggle with embodiment. Female bodybuilding, often read as
the obverse of anorexia, is a sport in which many anorexics participate
after their recoveries. Concerned with building up the body, rather
than eliminating it, and said to present an image of female power, the
female bodybuilder seems to offer a hopeful alternative to anorexia
and the anorexic logic. I use a brief analysis of a recent pictorial article
in *Flex* magazine to explore this possibility and to show that an apparent alternative is often consumed by the structure it most seeks to
subvert.

Taking the name from one of Madonna's concert tours, the magazine titles its central pictorial "Blonde Ambition." The title in itself
has come to signify a form of disruptive female power, a subversion
of the old norm of the stereotypically feminine blonde who exists only
to attract a man. The blonde's "ambition," as in Madonna's, is read as
the blonde taking matters into her own hands, displaying herself in a
way that "takes the power back." She is no longer defined by a man,
she is defining herself—powerfully. That the reference comes from
the phrase "blind ambition," which is, among other things, the title of
a best-selling book on the Watergate scandal, shows a short cultural
memory, since the slippage between "blonde" and "blind" isn't part
of the way this term culturally functions. What this construction of
female ambition may be "blind" to is the way in which her self-
construction still functions within the terms and context of the norm.

The "Blonde Ambition" pictorial features the female bodybuilder
Debbie Muggli, formerly a kindergarten teacher from Texas, who
placed third in the recent Ms. Olympia contest, the most prestigious
bodybuilding contest for women. In the pictorial, Muggli poses both
completely naked and wearing traditionally pornographic accessories
like lace gauntlets, black high heels, leather, and using such props as
Victorian sofas and stools. These poses are traditional in cheesecake,
but Muggli, with her pronounced muscularity, presents a different
body image from the nonmuscular feminine norm. She thinks she is
unsettling the old stereotypes and defies anyone to criticize her for
posing as she has. In a quotation that appears next to the pose with
her legs spread over the Victorian stool, she says, "I've worked ten

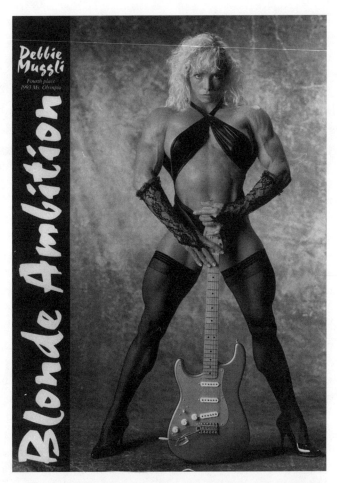

Debbie Muggli
Fourth place
1993 Ms. Olympia

Blonde Ambition

2. The bodybuilder Debbie Muggli posed as part of *Flex* magazine's pictorial series dedicated to showing women bodybuilders "offseason [when] they carry more bodyfat, presenting themselves in a much more naturally attractive condition. To exhibit this real, natural side of women bodybuilders, *Flex* has been presenting female competitors in softer condition. We hope this approach dispels the myth of female-bodybuilder masculinity." Femininity, then, is associated with higher body fat and, apparently, with lace, leather, and high heels accompanying the all too familiar phallic prop. The more things change . . .

years to create my physique, and I'm proud of my accomplishment: I'm a woman, I'm muscular, I'm feminine, and I'm sexy—it's liberating to feel this way and I have chosen to display that liberation."[45] She finds the combination of femininity, sexuality, and muscularity "liberating," presumably since that muscularity mimics the ideal for the male body in a way that undermines the old norm for the female body—an ideal not based on a power aesthetic.

Yet, if that muscularity is cloaked by the dominatrix leather, thigh-high stockings, elbow-length lace gloves, and six-inch black heels, to what extent can this be an image of "liberation"? The shot in question (see Fig. 2) has Muggli posed, head slightly down, mouth pursed, and eyes looking beyond the camera, with legs spread apart, standing holding the neck of a guitar at crotch level, so that it rests phallically between her black-stockinged legs. If one considers the context or horizon these images belong to—that of the woman defined by her sexuality, not defining it—how does this image "display liberation"? "Liberation" from what? As Foucault points out,

There may be a reason that makes it so gratifying for us to define the relationship between sex and power in terms of repression: something that one might call the speaker's benefit. If sex is repressed, that is, condemned to prohibition, non-existence, and silence, then the mere fact that one is speaking about it has the appearance of a deliberate transgression. A person who holds forth in such language places himself to a certain extent outside the reach of power; he upsets established law; he somehow anticipates the coming freedom.[46]

Muggli makes use of the "speaker's benefit" when she claims that the mere fact of displaying a female body with muscles is a "deliberate transgression," that she is "outside of the reach" of the "established law and power," simply because she has "worked ten years to create her physique." She "anticipates the freedom" of a self-created female form without paying any attention to the cultural ideals and ideologies that have contributed to the making of that form, that have determined the particular form her body takes. She sees herself as the sole author of her body, but what forces have contributed to the text of her flesh, the "ideal" she represents?

Her body is a testimony to the contradictory ideals of male identification and conventional femininity, and in this way it is very similar

to the anorexic body. Her body manages to hold up both norms without mixing them. Rather than deconstructing the opposition between
masculine and feminine, her body, as the bodies of other female
bodybuilders who combine conventional female attractiveness with
muscles, holds them both in place. She doesn't redefine desire but
replicates it, combining the conventional props of desirable femininity, signs of weakness, the veils that in the traditional construction are
supposed to cover "lack" in order to reveal it, with a body that in the
traditional masculine construction signifies not lack but strength. This
reduplication makes it seem as if she is putting on the masculine for
the purposes of seduction, since she is using her body in the conventionally seductive way, explicitly sexualizing it. Putting on the masculine is in fact seductive since it reveals that her attempt at strength, at
a masculinity untainted by the female sexuality that signifies weakness, is a failure, that her muscular body is a fraud, a prop, that renat-
uralizes the masculine as strength and presence and the feminine as
lack. Self-created weakness is seductive since it says, "Look, I will
perform for you and assure you of your own strength."

Muggli's pose is a direct performative of a "willing (and often eager) participation in cultural practices that objectify and sexualize
[women]," an instance of "individual self-surveillance and self-
correction to norms" that is performed in a fundamental misrecognition of power. What Muggli asserts and perhaps even genuinely feels
is "liberation" is a reduplication of norms that sexualize women, so
that the source, as in the perennial backlash myth of the femme fatale,
of her feelings of strength and self-determination is still her gendered
body: "I'm a woman, I'm muscular, I'm feminine, and I'm sexy." Why
can't her body simply stand as a body—"a work of art" as bodybuilders put it—without having to insist that it is still "sexy," still "feminine," and thereby still desirable? Ironically, a shot of Muggli completely naked seems more disruptive to expectations regarding the
female body and its purpose (see Fig. 3). Without the leather and
lace, the focus of the photo on the dense ropes of muscle lining her
back and legs, her body may be read in a context less saturated with
traditional assumptions. Still, this image is only one in a series that
insist on Muggli's accordance with normative femininity. A female
body that doesn't have some relation to male desire is simply too devi-

FLEX
Blonde Ambition

3. Debbie Muggli in the same *Flex* magazine pictorial—does this shot exemplify an alternative to the conventional femininity in the previous shot?

ant, too fundamentally out of sync with the networks of desire as they currently exist in the dominant culture, so Muggli feels "liberated" and that she "displays liberation" only if she has a body that is "sexy," still pleasing to males. Yet, if the network she plays to is still that of male desire, what, exactly, is she liberated from? Her assertion of liberation in the context of the same old scene helps to collude with and reinforce the very norms that sustain that scene. She willingly, actively, contributes to her own disempowerment through defining "power" in the same old way, as the ability to attract male desire. She doubly dehumanizes herself: first through "passing," through sculpting her body in such a way that it approximates the norm of the male body and accepts that body as the standard, and second, through self-correcting that body to conform to the norms of conventional femininity. Like anorexia, her resistance erases itself twice, a gender schizophrenia, a schizophrenic liberation that cancels itself out.[47]

Muggli's contradictory pose of self-erasure is compelling to me because it is a scenario I have acted and continue to act. The weight lifting I did with the track team grew into a lifelong habit of self-construction, so that I have at this point been a bodybuilder for sixteen years. The "ideal" body she claims to have created, and the power and "liberation" she feels as a result, are feelings I struggle with daily—ideological fetishes I participate in despite knowing better. As Slavoj Zizek writes, "Even if we do not take things seriously, even if we keep an ironical distance, *we are still doing them.*"[48] Despite my ironic distance from Muggli, my ability to deconstruct her assertions and poses, I am still doing what she is doing. Long after the passing of the disease itself, I am still a vital participant in the anorexic logic of a protest that cancels itself out: I live my life according to the norms I criticize. My life is still structured by the contradictory promise of male identification coupled with ideal femininity. I continue to identify with a structure that cancels me out, to construct myself in accordance with its terms. And yet. As Derrida suggests, there is always the remainder. The system never functions completely intact. The letter never arrives.[49]

IV. Philosophical Anorexics: The Flip Side

Indisputably, women's internalization of "anorexic philosophy" contributes to anorexia. While there is no direct causal relation between passages of Hegel and Plato and women on college campuses, in corporate America, or in Iowa kitchens, there is a striking similarity in the logics expressed in these philosophic texts and in texts written by anorexics. Bordo makes the distinction clear: "Anorexia is not a philosophical attitude; it is a debilitating affliction. Yet quite often a highly conscious and articulate scheme of images and associations— one could go so far as to call it a metaphysics—is presented by these women. . . . in the anorexic's 'metaphysics' elements are made explicit, historically grounded in Plato or Augustine, that run deep in our culture."[50] For women who have internalized the dictates of the philosophical tradition and accepted them as truths, whether the source is the philosophy itself or its numerous forms of enactment in popular culture, they will dedicate their lives, as Glück puts it, to hunger. They attempt to identify themselves with the masculine and exist, as Chernin writes, "from the neck up," engaged in a daily battle with food and the desire to become something else (white male), instead of writing or philosophizing, culturally producing, themselves (*Obsession*, 55). As Wolf argues in *The Beauty Myth*, "Dieting is the most potent political sedative in women's history. . . . women's bodies are not our own but society's, and . . . thinness is not a private aesthetic, but hunger a social concession exacted by the community" (187). Some women writers such as the contemporary American poet Glück and the Irish poet Eavan Boland, writers I term "philosophical anorexics," use literature as a way of articulating the anorexic logic by which hunger becomes a communal function and a central agency in the constitution of female subjectivity. Glück and Boland clearly articulate how the communal imperative affects women in general physically and emotionally, and how it affects women writers in particular, deflecting them from individual development and poetic production to an all-encompassing obsession with their bodies and food. As Ellen West, one of the most famous anorexic case histories (who is known, perhaps, because of her unusual degree of literary competence), writes, "I felt all inner development was ceasing, that all becoming and growing were being choked, because a single idea was filling my entire soul."[51] When one can only worry about calories, how much one has worked out, how much one eats, one runs on an endless treadmill that absorbs most of one's productive energy, indirectly assuring that aesthetics and culture will remain primarily a "masculine" province.

Contemporary women writers like Margaret Atwood write specifically about effects of the masculinization of aesthetics on women.[52] In her work, anorexia becomes the locus where cultural anxieties intersect in the cultural construction of the female body, and her prose enacts the struggle to imagine a different construction. Similarly, Glück writes about the living in a cultural context where the female flesh is rejected as unaesthetic and intrusive. "Art" is defined in opposition to the materiality the female body represents despite its fetishization as a subject for art. The ways in which actual women internalize this dialectic and use it to form and constitute their own bodies is something that Glück's poetry makes explicit, thereby producing an "alienation effect" to that process.[53] The 1980 poem "Dedication to

Hunger" begins with the focus on what Noelle Caskey sees as a "unity with the father against the mother and all that the mother represents," that is, the maternal body as circumscribed and projected by cultural codes that reduce women to body and reproductive capacity.[54]

In the opening image of "Dedication to Hunger," the identification of daughter with father is central. The mother watches this identification, rather than takes part in it, but because she has internalized the codes that encourage that identification, she takes pleasure in it. I quote the first section of the poem:

> 1. *From the Suburbs*
> They cross the yard
> and at the back door
> the mother sees with pleasure
> how alike they are, father and daughter—
> I know something of that time.
> The little girl purposefully
> swinging her arms, laughing
> her stark laugh:
>
> It should be kept secret, that sound.
> It means she's realized
> that he never touches her.
> She is a child; he could touch her
> if he wanted to.[55]

Here the mother's pleasure is derived from a likeness, a similitude between the father and daughter that negates the daughter's femininity, and by extension the mother in that it removes her from the equation—she is watching, not participating. The daughter is valuable—from the mother's point of view—only to the degree that she is not like the mother. The mother in Glück's poem is self-negating in that her pleasure is dependent upon her own cancellation, upon the daughter's apparent lack of feminine qualities associated with the mother.

"I know something of that time," the narrative voice breaks in, beginning an identification between the speaker and the young girl in the poem, who as the poem progresses becomes an anorexic in training: the identification with the father that leads girls to reject their

bodies as the agency of femininity, since their bodies destroy the identification when they are therefore seen as essentially different from
their fathers. The father "never touches her" because according to
cultural configuration she is different from him, feminine, and the
speaker has seen this. Her realization breaks any unambiguous identification with the father and makes it something unattainable and
therefore perpetually desired. The poem is about this moment of realization: that the feminine, figured as difference, is the basis for rejection. Through this realization the girl also begins to reject what is
most obviously feminine in herself: her body. Wanting to define herself as different from her mother so as to gain back the likeness with
her father, she rejects her mother as feminine and what in herself
resembles her mother.

This leads to the poem's second section, which presents the female
part of male/female relations as a position of powerlessness:

> 2. *Grandmother*
> "Often I would stand at the window—
> your grandfather
> was a young man then—
> waiting, in the early evening."
>
> That is what marriage is.
> I watch the tiny figure
> changing to a man
> as he moves toward her,
> the last light rings in his hair.
> I do not question
> their happiness. And he rushes in
> with his young man's hunger,
> so proud to have taught her that:
> his kiss would have been
> clearly tender—
>
> Of course, of course. Except
> it might as well have been
> his hand over her mouth. (30)

Rejection and powerlessness become linked in this second section.
Her grandmother's voice reports what the speaker of the poem sees
as her grandmother's victimization. The grandmother's voice reports

that "often I would stand at the window—/your grandfather/was a young man then—/waiting, in the early evening." The speaker interprets the grandmother's waiting as an essential passivity that she wants to avoid, for it encodes the grandmother's cancellation. "That is what marriage is," asserts the narrative voice. "And he rushes in/ with his young man's hunger,/so proud to have taught her that:/his kiss would have been/clearly tender." According to the speaker, the grandfather teaches the grandmother that marriage means waiting for him, suppressing herself in order to validate him. "His young man's hunger," his sexuality as demand, teaches her that, and when she internalizes this lesson, it makes him "tender." Tenderness or love is bought at the price of self-suppression: "Of course, of course," the speaker ironically states, "except it might as well have been his hand over her mouth." Here, from the speaker's perspective, the only way the grandmother can gain acceptance and love is through voluntary self-cancellation. The grandmother's husband "might as well have" put "his hand over her mouth," silencing her words and, by implication, preventing her from eating. The grandmother's self-suppression is the same kind of cancellation the mother exhibits in the pleasure she takes in the likeness between father and daughter, the same kind the little girl internalizes in her "stark laugh," and the same kind the speaker chooses in the self-cancellation through the flesh that is anorexia: a "dedication to hunger" or perpetual desire for a male body and position, which the father's initial rejection of her initiates.

That her rejection of the mother and the rejection of self is painful and not at all "natural" is something the third section of the poem comments on, invoking the bond between the maternal body and the children it bore:

3. *Eros*
To be male, always
to go to women
and be taken back
into the pierced flesh:

I suppose
memory is stirred.
And the girl child
who wills herself

into her father's arms
likewise loved him
second. Nor is she told
what need to express.
There is a look one sees,
the mouth somehow desperate—

Because the bond
cannot be proven. (31)

Through heterosexuality, the male is "taken back" into the flesh he had separated from. The girl child gravitates toward the father only through an act of will, coming to identify with him as she does in the first section only after cultural mediation. But the telos of that act of will and how it manifests itself physically is made explicit in the fourth section:

4. *The Deviation*
It begins quietly
in certain female children:
the fear of death, taking as its form
dedication to hunger,
because a woman's body
is a grave; it will accept
anything. I remember
lying in bed at night
touching the soft, digressive breasts,
touching, at fifteen,
the interfering flesh
that I would sacrifice
until the limbs were free
of blossom and subterfuge: I felt
what I feel now, aligning these words—
it is the same need to perfect,
of which death is the mere byproduct. (32)

Here the speaker identifies the cultural narrative of female flesh as decay and death as deadly to women. Certain female children dedicate themselves to hunger, that is, to starving away their flesh, in an attempt to thwart the death with which the cultural narrative has equated them. In that narrative "a woman's body/*is* a grave." Yet, the speaker brings into focus the status of that story as a story, rather than a "truth," in the connection that she makes between this narrative, her attempts to write, and her anorexic impulses. Here the anorexia is a remedy that removes the flesh that is perceived as the cause of the implicit criticism that the young girl experienced in the first section of the poem when her father would not touch her. Her body, which made her untouchable in the first place, also makes her untouchable now but in different terms. Her anorexic body can't be rejected, because it is now perfect, stripped of its femininity.

Anorexics perceive themselves as beyond reproach, because they think they have defeated that aspect of themselves that equates them with the grave ("a woman's body/*is* a grave"), but in becoming anorexic, they align themselves with death. The speaker in Glück's poem experiences her body as "interfering flesh" that she "would sacrifice/until the limbs were free/of blossom and subterfuge," of "soft, digressive" breasts that would falsely identify her with the passivity of her waiting grandmother. She sacrifices the "blossom," the feminine that she experiences as "subterfuge," as something that deceives and conceals her "true" masculine self by its flesh. This is an ironic reversal of the common interpretation of anorexics, who are seen as attempting to escape and evade their "true" adult sexuality as women. But through this irony, which marks her attempt to align herself with the father, what she really does is to align herself with her mother and grandmother in a position of powerlessness. She participates in a fetishistic structure in that her denial of her body that results in a more "masculine" body becomes a fetish intended to cover what she perceives as lack, her female body. She makes herself indeterminately gendered. The anorexic body functions as a disavowal of gender or as a postponement of a choice between masculine and feminine. It gives her the illusionary horizon of an ungendered space, which destroys her, and which, because of cultural mediation, can only postpone the inevitable "fall" into the female body. Rather than using anorexia as a strategy of protest, she leaves the definition of female body as lack firmly in place. Contrary to interpretations of the disease like Sandra M. Gilbert's that describe anorexia as a parodic strategy that protests the social order, anorexia cannot function as a form of self-assertion but rather as a fetishistic structure that leaves

women believing the cultural narrative of female as lack.[56] Glück's
poem enacts the alignment of three generations of women—grandmother, mother, and daughter—in an alignment of its words that articulates a complicated awareness of their parallel processes of self-
cancellation.

Most significant, the speaker experiences the purgation of her flesh
as an artistic process equivalent to the artistic creation of poetry: "I
felt/what I feel now, aligning these words—/it is the same need to
perfect." "Perfection" is defined as the successful elimination of female flesh. The speaker of this poem has internalized this logic, but
in making it her subject she brings it to the level of consciousness.
She begins to rewrite the narrative about how we conceive of bodies.
In Glück's work the definition of anorexia as "heroic" is ironized in
such a way that we can see the destructive paradox such a definition
necessitates.

The last section of the poem shows how art is a process necessarily
based on the renunciation of the feminine as flesh, making that
awareness part of a conscious, painful deliberation:

> 5. *Sacred Objects*
> Today in the field I saw
> the hard, active buds of the dogwood
> and wanted, as we say, to capture them,
> to make them eternal. That is the premise
> of renunciation: the child,
> having no self to speak of,
> comes to life in denial—
>
> I stood apart in that achievement,
> in that power to expose
> the underlying body, like a god
> for whose deed
> there is no parallel in the natural world. (33)

Here the speaker's achievement of a "self" is the denial of self, which
both sets her apart and constitutes her identity. Renunciation enables
her both to align words and to stand apart as different, as something
other than the female body that if stripped away leaves the more authentic, male "underlying body." It removes her from the mortal, material, feminine realm of nature, making her "like a god/for whose

deed/there is no parallel in the natural world." This achievement gives the speaker a new identification, makes her godlike because she has transcended the natural world. The denial of feminine flesh makes her godlike both in her difference from other female corpses invoking death and decay and in her ostensible participation in the "eternal." The transcendence of flesh is related to the poetic transcendence: "Today in the field I saw/the hard, active buds of the dogwood/and wanted, as we say, to capture them,/to make them eternal." Making the buds eternal through poetic language invokes the topos of transcending the material dimension of flux and change, but it does so explicitly in reference to gender and how gender codes create a narrative of female flesh that the anorexic then responds to in her self-creation. "The hard, active buds of the dogwood" are contrasted to the passivity and softness of the feminine flesh she experiences as "soft, digressive breasts," as "blossom and subterfuge." The poetic impulse to make eternal is similar to the anorexic impulse to constitute oneself through the renunciation of female flesh, thereby evading the "fear of death, taking as its form/dedication to hunger." "Dedication to hunger" constitutes both poetry and evasion of the woman's body that by an anorexic cultural logic "*is* a grave."

The fierce control of Glück's poetry, the suppressed rage in the narrative voice, enacts on a formal level the anorexic's self-suppression, even as she makes that suppression her subject. By connecting masculinity, activity, and aesthetics on the one hand and femininity, passivity, and bodily flesh on the other, Glück calls attention to a narrative we all have too readily accepted. The fierce detachment of the narrative voice is the expression of an equally fierce pain, which comes from what the logic of renunciation has encouraged us to will into our flesh, what it has encouraged us to shape our bodies into. In accepting the cultural narrative that makes bodily renunciation heroic and masculine, we try to make ourselves more powerful, "godlike," in a way that destroys us. Glück's poem admits and shows that we still constitute ourselves as gods or heroes through masculinization along the thin side of the thin/fat divide. In doing so, however, the poem evokes a different consciousness about the way we tell stories about ourselves, the way we create ourselves through gendered patterns of language.

The poet Eavan Boland connects anorexia, masculinity and femininity, and the Western philosophical and religious, rather than literary, tradition in her poem "Anorexic":

> Flesh is heretic.
> My body is a witch.
> I am burning it.
>
> Yes I am torching
> her curves and paps and wiles.
> They scorch in my self-denials.
>
> How she meshed my head
> in the half-truths
> of her fevers
>
> till I renounced
> milk and honey
> and the taste of lunch.
>
> I vomited
> her hungers.
> Now the bitch is burning.
>
> I am starved and curveless.
> I am skin and bone.
> She has learned her lesson.
>
> Thin as a rib
> I turn in sleep.
> My dreams probe
>
> a claustrophobia
> a sensuous enclosure.
> How warm it was and wide
>
> once by a warm drum,
> once by the song of his breath
> and in his sleeping side.
>
> Only a little more,
> only a few more days
> sinless, foodless,
>
> I will slip
> back into him again
> as if I had never been away.

> Caged so
> I will grow
> angular and holy
>
> past pain,
> keeping his heart
> such company
>
> as will make forget
> in a small space
> the fall
>
> into forked dark,
> into python needs
> heaving to hips and breasts
> and lips and heat
> and sweat and fat and greed.[57]

In Boland's poem the anorexic narrative is spelled out from a distinctively female subject position—the black hole, to which history, symbology, and her own efforts have consigned her. Enacting the internalization of the logic expressed in the witchcraft trials in Puritan New England, the anorexic differs from those "witches" in that she burns her own body, consumes her own flesh, by refusing to take anything in. Boland's poem creates a voice, a female subject position involved in the process of canceling herself out, which clearly articulates the logic that the historian Carol F. Karlsen describes in her work on the place of gender and ideology in the Puritan "witch" scandal. In Puritan ideology, based in the European tradition of Institoris and Sprenger's well-known treatise *Malleus Maleficarum*, "Women were by nature more evil than men: in their wickedness, they imitated the first woman, Eve. Created intellectually, morally, and physically weaker than men, the argument continued, women were subject to deeper affections and passions, harbored more uncontrollable appetites, and were more susceptible to deception."[58] Through a process that seems like ventriloquism, the voices of this European tradition speak in Boland's poem. They speak in the voices of actual anorexics, like another patient from Bruch: "My soul seemed to grow as my body waned; I felt like one of those early Christian saints who starved themselves in the desert sun. I felt invulnerable, clean and hard as the bones etched into my silhouette."[59]

And yet it is not entirely ventriloquism. Self-starvation is a process anorexics have decided for themselves, a subject position they have *chosen,* paradoxically, as a means of self-definition. The starved body becomes their identity, their identity *is* the process of self-cancellation. This is not something willed upon them by culture— everyone around them becomes united in an attempt to facilitate a "cure." Still, there is something strange in these torturous twists. If anorexia is a choice, *why* do so many women choose it? But if it is the result of a convergence of historical forces, of a certain form of Christian logic, of philosophic logic, of psychoanalytic logic, of rhetorical logic, if it is the subject position offered to women as redemptive to "cure" or to supplement their "lack" as nonmale, then why don't all women have anorexia? These are questions an analysis of Boland's text can begin to answer.

For anorexics the body is experienced as entirely distinct, as "other"; the body is not the self. The body is gendered female, while the mind that attempts to control it is gendered male.[60] Bruch writes in *The Golden Cage* that

> many [anorexics] experience themselves and their bodies as separate entities, and it is the mind's task to control the unruly and despised body. Others speak of feeling divided, as being a split person or two people. . . . when they define this separate aspect, this different person seems always to be a male. . . . They had felt throughout their lives that being a female was an unjust disadvantage, and they dreamed of doing well in areas considered more respected and worthwhile because they were "masculine." Their overslim appearance, their remarkable athletic performances, with perseverance to the point of exhaustion, give them the proud conviction of being as good [as men]. (58–59)

"Flesh is heretic," says Boland's anorexic speaker. "My body is a witch./I am burning it." Speaking a synthesis of attitudes expressed in Plato, Institoris and Sprenger, Hegel, Descartes, and Freud, she splits herself off from her body, labels it "heretical," a "witch," and "burns" it. To combine flesh and heresy collapses the literal and the figurative in the way characteristic of anorexic logic. "Heresy" is defined as "an opinion of doctrine contrary to church dogma; dissent or deviation from a dominant theory, opinion, or practice; an opinion, doctrine, or practice contrary to the truth or to generally accepted beliefs or standards."[61] When the speaker says, "Flesh is heretic," she describes her body as a deviation from "truth," from "church dogma," from the "dominant theories" of subjectivity and being. Her body asserts an alternative subjectivity "contrary to generally accepted beliefs and standards" that she herself works to annihilate. Her body is not a "natural" object; it is a set of discourses, of dogmas and their contraries. It is a competing set of definitions, in which she cancels the second alternative, the embodied female subject, in order to reinforce the traditional dualist masculine subject.

In the embodiment that the poem's speaker struggles to overcome, she identifies her body with a "witch" upon whom she is imposing her own version of "burning" at the stake. The heretical burning body is witchlike in its dissent from the dominant disembodied tradition, just as "witches" dissented from the dominant religious tradition that consigned them to the social position of a man's "helpmeet." As Karlsen writes in *The Devil in the Shape of a Woman,* "Puritans defined discontent as thinking oneself above one's place in the social order," and they defined "witches" as those who were dissatisfied with the status quo: "It was [women accused of witchcraft's] perceived dissatisfaction with the religious system—and by extension with the religiously defined social system—that linked them to their sister witches. . . . By treating female dissent as evidence of witchcraft as well as heresy, the authorities may have effectively silenced Puritan women's opposition [to the religious system]" (127, 125, 197). Paradoxically, the anorexic is both dissenter and prosecutor, the accused and the judge. In her unconscious protest against an ancient logic that defines her by her body, this protest is nonetheless at war with an identification with that logic, an internalization and acceptance of that logic's standards: Yes, I am an evil body. Yes, I am a witch. Because I am this, I will destroy myself, this part of myself. I will become something else. I will become male, or at least not-female. Prelapsarian identity is for me a space without sexual difference, a space where there are no demarcations between masculine and feminine, between his world and mine. Ellen West, a famous anorexic case study, wrote that "I feel myself quite passively the stage on which two hostile forces are mangling each other."[62] With West's self-conception, characteristic of most anorexics, she cannot experience herself as anything but "passive," as a stage on which "two forces," detached from her own will, "mangle each other." Those "forces" are the struggle between an identification with the Western tradition and a rejection of it. Her anorexic obsession with her body is the convergence of those forces. As Chernin writes, "Obsession is, in fact, a drama, in which that inner being one has hoped to dominate and control keeps struggling to return" (*Obsession,* 190). That "inner being" Chernin identifies with emotion, passion, creative potential: "Thus, from Ellen West we learn how a young woman invariably rejects, along with the female body, the passionate, 'feminine' side of her nature, from which her creative development would arise" (186). Anorexic obsession takes the place of creativity, of thought, of activity, of the "world beyond her plate."

In Boland's poem, the speaker's anorexia is the act of "torching," through the venerable religious tradition of "self-denial," the body which is, presumably, self-indulgent: "her curves and paps and wiles." The speaker splits off from her body, designating that body first "it" and then "she" and "her," so that the gender of this flesh is clear. For the speaker, "curves" are equated with "wiles," which are defined either as "a trick of a stratagem intended to ensnare or deceive . . . to lure by or as if by a magic spell," or as "to pass or spend pleasurably." Furthermore, "pap" is defined as "nipple," "a soft food for infants or invalids," "political patronage," or "something lacking solid value or substance."[63] The "curves" are the female flesh traditionally thought to lure men from their important, culture-/state-based sublimated activities and into the fleshly self-indulgence of sexual gratification and love. The female body is the "lure" into pleasure, and the speaker, through "self-denial" (the "self" defined as hungering body), "torches" and "scorches" that flesh in a violence that reflects and internalization of the larger cultural attitude of violence toward that flesh. Like Plato and the biblical tradition she later explicitly draws upon, the speaker identifies this hungering female flesh as a distraction from truth, for "she meshed my head/in the half-truths/of her fevers/till I renounced/milk and honey/and the taste of lunch." Her "fevers," her bodily desires, are a distraction from truth and can only be conquered by a renunciation of "milk and honey," which in the biblical tradition signify the plenty and prosperity of God, who smiles down upon you and provides if you are "good." Defined as the other of "good," the speaker denies herself this plenty, the reward from which she knows she is by definition excluded. The self-inflicted violence toward her desires, femininity, and flesh continues, through violence, toward hungers succumbed to: "I vomited/her hungers./Now the bitch is burning." The hungers are vomited; the burning continues; "she," the body, has been properly punished: "I am starved and curveless./I am skin and bone./She has learned her lesson."

At this point in the poem the violence stops, and the tone shifts to a tenderness bound up with masculine identification. The speaker is an Eve who has accepted the male definition of herself as inherently evil, desiring, fleshly, and thereby responsible for the Fall and death of the human race. This punitive Eve longs to redeem herself through the loss of sexual difference and of the body that has caused all the problems in the first place. In a reverse parody of the psychoanalytic account of male self-differentiation from, and womb-longing for, his mother, here Eve wants to rejoin Adam, to literally become him again, to fit back into the rib from which she has ostensibly come, a fit accomplished by the "burning" of her body that she performs in the earlier stanzas of the poem. "Thin as a rib," Eve says, evoking the second and more widely taught creation myth in Genesis: "I turn in sleep./My dreams probe/a claustrophobia/a sensuous enclosure./ How warm it was and wide/once by a warm drum,/once by the song of his breath/and in his sleeping side." Like the psychoanalytic myth of the child's longing for the warm womb, here the "sensuous enclosure" is Adam, since he has mythologically given birth to Eve. Her desire is a regression to this undifferentiated state where she is literally part of him and thereby male. Sinless, fleshless, beyond need, she will forget her own hungers, her own designation as fleshly evil: "Caged so/I will grow/angular and holy/past pain,/keeping his heart/such company/as will make me forget/in a small space/the fall/into forked dark,/into python needs/heaving to hips and breasts/ and lips and heat/and sweat and fat and greed." The renunciation of her flesh allows her to "forget" herself, to become male, to become Adam, apparently a subject position that is beyond "python needs," since it does not partake of, or at least is not defined by, "hips and breasts and lips and heat and sweat and fat and greed." She attains this subject position only through self-starvation and the resulting disappearance of the body: "Only a little more,/only a few more days/ sinless, foodless,/I will slip/back into him again/as if I had never been away." The lack of food leads to the lack of body, which leads to the lack of sin, which leads to a male subject position, or least to that prelapsarian state of gender identity before sexual difference—before the inevitable split and rejection when "us" is not necessarily different from "them," when the boys will still play with us at recess.[64]

Boland's poem remarkably details the anorexic logic. At the same time, it gives that logic a specific historical and cultural context, connecting the current manifestations of male identification in women that help define anorexia, the Puritan witch scandals and the subject positions relegated to women therein, and the biblical tradition of the Fall, so important in structuring gender and power configurations throughout Western culture. It brings together religious, philosophical, and historical strands that help form a reading of the disease, its logic, its passions, and the cultural conditions that have helped produce it, as well as a reading of those who suffer from it. Boland's poem decodes and enacts the very set of presuppositions that can be traced to the literary ideals of the early twentieth century. Identifying these ideals locates another missing element in the emerging picture of the cultural determinants of anorexia.

These literary ideals are the focus of the pages that follow. I situate myself differently from the little work that has been done on the relation between literature and anorexia, although the goals of my work might be the same. A common interpretation of anorexia offered by feminist literary critics like Sandra M. Gilbert who "want urgently to examine what we might call the feminist implications of anorexia" is that it reflects a strategy through which "women . . . have consciously used literal hunger as a means of protesting the metaphorical starvation in their lives" ("Hunger Pains," 11), starvation for meaningful life choices.[65] These critics see a parallel between the anorexic and the woman writer: "Denied all other means of self-creation, both the starved woman poet and the starving anorexic transform self-denial into self-assertion, a hunger/pain into a hunger/strike" (Gilbert, "Hunger Pains," 12). "Starved poets" include Emily Dickinson, Christina Rosetti, and the Brontës, and these critics examine their texts for anorexic behavior among characters, which they interpret as a protest against the patriarchal order. They draw an analogy between the political activities of suffragists like the Pankhursts, who went on hunger strikes as a means of obtaining the vote, and the behavior of anorexics.[66] While this interpretive model raises anorexia as an important issue for feminist literary study, it is problematic in that it gives artistic status to a "strategy of resistance" that is only self-destructive, and that ultimately affirms the very order it protests.

Furthermore, this model is too gender specific in that it cannot account for a common occurrence in many modernist texts by male authors—anorexic male figures like Kafka's Gregor Samsa, Conrad's Marlow, or Faulkner's Joe Christmas. Nor can it account for the curiously "anorexic" strategies of revision in modernist literary manifestoes, such as imagist poetics, that mandate the radical reduction of textual bodies. As recent theorists have repeatedly insisted, anorexia needs to be examined in relation to the gendered context that produces it.[67] For white male modernism a dominant aesthetic was anorexic. Theories of creativity relied on an ideology that posited the necessity to renounce "the feminine" as flesh, a "necessity" that functioned as a "higher truth" that the artist alone apprehends. In contrast to the Gilbert thesis, these writers used the disease to refute the very female self-expression referred to above. In short, female disease was transformed into male textual practice, but both disease and textual practice had a grounding in specific cultural and historical contexts.

Bordo has named these contexts "psychopathologies" and argues that they express some of the most vexed points of tension in our culture. Eating disorders, she writes, "reflect and call our attention to some of the central ills of our culture—from our historical heritage of disdain for the body, to our modern fear of loss of control over our futures, to the disquieting meaning of contemporary beauty ideals in an era of female presence and power" ("Anorexia Nervosa," 88). The way the various forms of anorexia—mental, physical, and textual—work to cancel out "female presence and power" will be the focus of the pages that follow. I will attempt to track some of the ways in which an anorexic, male-identified logic is still characteristic of our basic processes of reading and writing in institutions of higher education. Thus, along with many others, I begin to recover the female bodies, the murdered subjects that tradition has so relentlessly skinned, dismembered, and generally done violence to in its imposition of a white, upwardly mobile, masculine worldview that explicitly defines itself in opposition to the emotional, the personal, the bodily, the feminine.[68]

As a version, then, of Clarice in *The Silence of the Lambs*, as a member of the Feminist Bureau of Investigation, I have a kind of mission to complete. Speaking of the serial killer and his victim, Clarice says, "If he sees Catherine as a person and not just an object, it's harder to tear her up." Her mission is to keep women and herself from being torn up; mine is to help keep them and myself from tearing ourselves up. But also like Clarice, whose career as a federal investigator is emotionally motivated by an identification with her policeman father, I have my own identifications and engagements with the tradition I analyze. In a relation like Clarice's to Catherine, I am bound up in the same problematic structure as Hillary, the desperate thirteen-year-old in the gym. During the film's agonizing showdown, when Clarice shouts to Catherine, "You're safe," at precisely the moment she herself is in the most danger, Clarice shows her vulnerability to a tradition of male violence in which one is never "safe," and in which one can function as only the most tenuous form of "savior." Even as I attempt to make Hillary and others like her "safe," bound up in the very structures I analyze, as a lived female body in the cultural matrix, I reveal my own vulnerabilities.

By positioning some of the sources of the hatred of the female body that becomes a hatred of the self, I hope to help dismantle the macabre sisterhood of self-hatred that exists on a daily basis between myself and thirteen-year-olds, twenty-two-year-olds, and thirty-nine-year-olds in the women's locker room in the gym, each of us tensely huddled over her own body as we change clothes, silent in shame, sucking our stomachs in, each hoping that the other women will not "see" the bulges "disfiguring" our bodies. I hope to work toward a strategy in which the literal and the body need no longer function as the vilified others of discourse.[69] If, in the cultural narratives that constitute the gendered body, there could be a reconfiguration of the hierarchical relationship between the ideal, figurative body and the biological, literal body, this reconfiguration would affect the problem of subjectivity as well. Such a reconfiguration might help inoculate us against the first strain of anorexic logic, which I encountered in university athletics parading past football players toward the scales. But the second might prove tougher—a kind of Beijing flu. It infects that group of women (and some men as well) who sit in self-imposed silence in the margins of the classroom, or who freeze in frustration and self-abasement in front of computer screens. These women and men feel inadequate to the task of mastering discourse, of "rising" to the occasion of academic debate that is articulated in terms of conquest, domination, or simple one-upsmanship. In order to bring them from the "shadows" of academic discourse into embodiment, we need to change the paradigm that dictates education in general—the ways of reading, writing, and thinking about ideas—so that women and men who are uncomfortable articulating themselves according to male models can really feel they have entered the academy as more than masculine imitations, more than Hegel's "impotent shadows."

I will argue that the persistence of high modernist literature and literary ideals is central to the contemporary quest to reconfigure learning. If we are to change the ways we imagine literature, ideas, the bodies of people in classrooms as well as bodies represented in texts, we need to reexamine modernism and some of its less-discussed assumptions. I hope to show an affinity between "anorexic thinking" and "modernist thinking," and that anorexic logic that produces both. If we are to reclaim the body and recode the systems of logic, the abstract registers we work within, in ways that are integrative rather than exclusionary, we need a pedagogy that has a place for the nonlinear as well as the linear, the literal as well as the figurative, the personal and emotional as well as the logical and the abstract, and the feminine as well as the masculine. We need a pedagogy that *values* both modes of discourse and that allows persons of both sexes to articulate both in peaceful conversation.[70] Currently, we remain either locked in the "body" and its registers, "the empirical," or locked in abstract logic, the "theoretical." Good modernists in this particular sense, we have not practically deconstructed the opposition between the empirical and the theoretical. In the academy there remains a violent scar, always in danger of retearing, bifurcating into "girl books" and "boy books," "the canon" and "black books," "women's and minority's issues" and "issues," the practical and the theoretical. As Bordo emphasizes in "The Feminist as Other," "theoretical" issues are often considered the "real thing," while gender, race, or class issues are considered extra, special, something else, very like the medical school models of the body that designate parts specific to the female body as extra.[71] There is still an insufficiently questioned relationship of hierarchy and subordination between these registers, a hierarchy that has real effects on real bodies sitting in classrooms every day, as well as on bodies outside of the classroom. It is still a war zone, and there are still political prisoners.

Chapter Two

From Female Disease to Textual Ideal, or What's Modernism Got to Do with It

He liked to imagine himself the abbot of a highly exclusive monastery, whereto only fair young monks of brilliant talent and soft manners were admitted. . . . He disliked and mistrusted everything female; it gave him goose flesh.

Isak Dinesen,
"The Deluge at Norderney"

It is part of the novelist's convention not to mention soup and salmon and ducklings, as if soup and salmon and ducklings were of no importance whatsoever, as if nobody ever smoked a cigar or drank a glass of wine. . . . The human frame being what it is, heart, body and brain all mixed together, and not contained in separate compartments . . . one cannot think well, love well, sleep well, if one has not dined well.

Virginia Woolf,
A Room of One's Own

In the previous chapter I traced some of the cultural contexts of anorexia. In texts as seemingly diverse as continental philosophy, Freudian psychoanalysis, and contemporary consumer culture, an underlying logic emerges based on the philosophical and psychoanalytic designation of the feminine as emptiness or lack. This essential emptiness or openness, radical indeterminacy, functions paradoxically to determine the female body as a synechdoche for women. The female body is constructed as a sign of the feminine as "too much," an emptiness voraciously hungering. The female body, its physical presence, is connected with openness, immanence, emptiness, nothingness. This dual cultural sense, the feminine as both "too much" and a sign of nothingness, contributes to the anorexic structure. A further paradox emerges when the cultural context offers some women the subject position of the closed, determined individual presence associated with masculinity, but simultaneously demands the traditional femininity defined as individuality's opposite. Yes, a few women can get advanced degrees, serve on the boards of corporations and on the Supreme Court, but they are still expected to maintain bodily standards of feminine attractiveness that define them as objects radically open, plastic, subject to the intervention and expectations of others.

As the logic that emerges from philosophy, religion, and popular culture is crucial to the production of anorexia, the poetry of Louise Glück helped me situate a perhaps even more fundamental determinant: the connection between a dominant strain of high modernist aesthetics and the disease itself. Glück experienced the same "urge to perfect," whether the text was her body or her poetry. The convergence of these impulses points to the essential connection between standards applied to "good art" and the mind-set of the anorexic. In both the high modernist artist and the anorexic there is a rejection and will to eliminate the feminine, a will to transcendence, and to shape the "base material" into a "higher," masculine form. Glück provides a starting point toward a rereading of a dominant strain of high modernist aesthetics that follows the anorexic logic.

It is, I argue, crucial to reread modernism when we are trying to understand anorexia, because it is in modernism we find the kind of truth claim that may be even more influential than the dominant media images and beauty ideals for women that are so often said to "cause" the disease. As I will show, the claim to construct an elite community that stands apart from the common crowd was a continual effort in some of the most influential modernist writing, a claim that dovetails neatly with increasingly hysterical preoccupations with individualism in late capitalism. The individualism of the modernist artist or artist figure sets a paradigm for the anorexic, who wants beyond all things to be different, to stand out as superior. The claim to superiority and truth within modernism most often involves the renunciation of the feminine, just as the anorexic excises the outward sign of her femininity in her quest for distinction. This mind-set, I argue, is not pathological. Rather it is the literalization, the furthest logical extension, of a dominant cultural preoccupation with an individuality presented in the guise of the neutral but intrinsically defined as male. Some origins of contemporary popular culture—advertising, in particular—can be traced to ideas about individualism, distinction, and their gender, which we find most clearly expressed in modernist literature. Like Glück did, like I did, girls hungering with all their being for an individuality promised but never delivered can internalize modernism's "truth" as an absolute, a way out of the paradox of gender. A woman or girl can momentarily forget that she has a female body. Comforting herself with a "truth" seen by only the enlightened few—of which she is of course a member—she can forget all the cultural designations that determine and devalue that body. Only, as the Dinesen epigraph describes, the price of membership to the enlightened few is the willful self-destruction of anything culturally constructed as feminine. In the Dinesen story "The Deluge at Norderney," a young girl contemplates cutting off her breasts with a sword; in anorexia those breasts are burned by the body itself. Literary modernism presents the set of assumptions tracked in the first chapter as indisputable ontological "truths" to which only the privileged, enlightened, masculine subject has access. Anorexia stands as the internalization of these "truths"—what the anorexic thinks will gain her membership to the club. Any analysis of our culture today that includes eating disorders like anorexia as part of its inquiry needs to look to modernist literature to understand the mystic writing pad, the palimpsest that underlies those disorders.

A few critics have begun to do so. In "Anorexia and Modernism, or How I Learned to Diet in All Directions," Mark Anderson juxtaposes two fields of inquiry previously discussed only in isolation, if at all: the autophagous quality of a certain group of modernist texts, largely canonical and male authored, that are characterized by an anorexic logic; and the emergence of anorexia as a historically identifiable medical discourse, a "disease" that gave its practitioners, generally female, the label of "patient." Anderson notes that a gender switch has taken place in which anorexics and figures of anorexia in canonical male modernist texts are almost exclusively male, while contemporary cases of anorexia involve women. He argues that the figure of male anorexics in modernist texts "embody an ambiguity of gender that would either deny sexual difference or fuse male and female identities in a complex androgynous form. . . . the modernist produces an 'anti-body' which withdraws from the traditional arena of male privilege, authority, and responsibility" (37).[1]

In making this statement Anderson highlights the absence of a third term that is necessary to outline the parameters of the question at hand: the historical context within which canonical male moderns like Franz Kafka, T. S. Eliot, Ezra Pound, and William Carlos Williams, representative figures in whom the problem was central, were working. For the denial of the body in their texts does not take the form of "androgyny" or the "denial of sexual difference." Instead, these canonical modernist texts that demonstrate the "anorexic" tendency reinforce, not question, "the traditional arena of male privilege, authority, and responsibility." Rather than problematizing traditional notions of gender, the negation of the body in literary modernism seems, quite explicitly, a negation of the feminine, a reinscription and privileging of masculine prerogative in a realm of human activity that in the nineteenth century had become progressively "feminized," that of literary production. From Nathaniel Hawthorne's infamous railing against the "damned mobs of scribbling women" to the characteristically modernist rejection of Victorian sentimentality, "effeminate" prosody, and stylistic and emotional "excess," the modern was, among other things, an attempt to "purge" the "feminine" from what can only be termed a masculinist literary ideal. As Jean-Michel Rabate writes, "The enemy is for Pound the soft mass, the bloated flesh"—a fleshiness indissolubly associated in modernism with matter as "female chaos."[2] Of course, this is a much-discussed issue,[3] but what has not been specified is the regularity with which that "purgation" is repeatedly expressed in male modernist texts through figures of anorexia: the male creative principle defined in opposition to feminine flesh, a creativity made possible by an expurgation of the flesh as female.

Anorexia has been interpreted in widely divergent ways, from a paradigm of liberal democracy to a fear of orality to a parody of femininity. Still it remains an unreadable text, a system of signs that refuses to signify. Its meaning is "secret" and refuses to give itself up. And yet there is a clear trajectory between the anorexic body as an individual or cultural ideal and the commonplace ideals of modernist texts: clean form, the emergence of art through the formal technique of cutting, and the isolation of the artist from the mass consciousness of the modern world, Baudelaire's "man of the crowd" intact and elevated in his solitude and difference from that undifferentiated "crowd." The following chapters trace that trajectory through modernist poetry and prose, documenting a path that traverses a poetics of gender as complicated as it is uncertain. Through the act of tracing, I hope to make some sense of the agonized relation to the body in literary modernism and, specifically, of the ambivalent, even hostile relation to that body as feminine and as maternal. From Eliot's "shred of platinum" as a figure for the imagination to Kafka's "hunger artist," there emerges a path of gender identifications that shares a clear affinity with the anorexic body and the logic that produces it. An examination of anorexia enables an identification of the impact of gender on concepts central to literary modernism: authority, language, the speaking subject.

I believe that both cultural and literary analyses are deepened in a framework that can make connections between them. To make those connections, I examine figures of anorexia in some of the most famous canonical aesthetic treatises, poetry, and prose of the modernist period, in conjunction with two specific historical phenomena: the emergence of anorexia as a "disease" and the suffragette practice of hunger strikes that was an instrumental step toward women's gaining the vote. In my discussion of anorexia I define the term broadly, not just in reference to literal anorexia but primarily in terms of a metaphysics, or metaphorics, of eating that informs the actual "disease": anorexia is not so much a question of organic eating as it is a metaphysics of eating. It has confounded doctors precisely because its causes are psychosomatic, rather than purely somatic—thus the French term *anorexie mentale*.[4] I apply the term to patterns of renunciation that include all "physical," bodily dimensions of life, including sexuality and basic modes of human interaction, which is consistent with actual behaviors associated with the disease. In its broadest sense, the term *anorexia* refers to any elimination of what is considered stereotypically "feminine" and a preference for "the masculine." In literal, or physical, anorexia this choice manifests itself in a preference for the male body over the female. There is a dialectical relationship between literal anorexia and anorexic literature. Literal anorexia shares tropological and ideological similarities with some modernist literature and has important implications for the configuration of gender in that literature; anorexic literature provides a clear example of a dominant cultural logic that also finds expression in the disease.

As a consequence of bringing literature, disease, and history into collision, I would like to explore why there is such a prevalent anorexic logic in modernist texts; why that logic is expressed in male figures when historically anorexics were almost always female; and what these questions can reveal about a logic that underlies much of what has been termed the most significant literary development of the early twentieth century. By carefully studying what I call the anorexic logic of canonical modernist texts, I hope to illuminate the ways in which early twentieth-century gender dynamics inform and structure what has been until recently hailed as *the* literary modernism, even though there were many alternative forms. The isolation of this logic should say something about why this particular strain of literary modernism came to precede others that seem to resist it, and how that logic influenced our thinking about issues so crucial to literary study as the question of artistic authority and the necessary conditions for literary production.

A brief investigation of these historical dimensions of anorexia is necessary to foreground its particular manifestation as a trope in literary modernism. For, as Joan Jacobs Brumberg, the leading historian of anorexia, writes in *Fasting Girls,* "Today's anorectic is one of a long line of women and girls throughout history who have used control of appetite, food, and the body as a focus of their symbolic language" (2). I wish to investigate early twentieth-century uses of this cultural phenomenon in literature as a way of further exploring the gender dynamics of that period and how anorexic dynamics affected and were appropriated by literary production and representation. To read closely the underlying anorexic logic of literary modernism, I must pay attention to its primary contributing factors. These include the soul/body, male/female oppositions that have gone through different permutations throughout history until arriving at configurations particular to the period. The dominant cultural stereotype that associates nonwhite peoples with the body and materiality is a factor as well.

I. Inside Every Fat Body There's a
Thin Body Struggling to Get Out:
More Historical Contexts

Historically, anorexia as a "disease" was named as such in the 1870s, although the phenomenon of female self-starvation extends at least to the medieval period and probably earlier.[5] Historians such as Caroline Walker Bynum have shown how the lives of women in the thirteenth through fifteenth centuries were marked by long periods of fasting, and how the renunciation of food was used symbolically to indicate a higher form of spirituality and commitment to religious ideals.[6] Characterized by "the reign of the expert" anxious to name, categorize, and control "women's disorders," the Victorian period was logically the time in which anorexia became classified as a disease.[7] As Helena Michie writes in *The Flesh Made Word,* in the Victorian era "Delicate appetites are linked not only with femininity, but with virginity."[8] In a culture that relegated its spiritual function to woman but divided women into perhaps the most rigid historical manifestation of the virgin/whore dichotomy, consumption of food and its bodily representation in amount of flesh became the outward embodiment of a sexually hungering nature. The "pure" woman was as fleshless as possible, exhibiting a revulsion toward food. According to Michie, Victorian attitudes toward women and eating bear a marked "equation of starvation and feminine spirituality" (17). The exhibition of Sarah Bartmann, a black woman, between 1805 and 1810 as the "Hottentot Venus" was a graphic and demeaning demonstration of the cultural logic that further associated fleshy bodies with racial darkness and sexuality, a demonstration meant to differentiate between sexualized black women and desexualized white ones. A white, thin body was the outer sign of a spiritual nature; a dark, fat body, of its opposite, bringing together sexist constructions rendered even more brutal by their racism.[9]

This symbolization, as well as a preoccupation with food and its renunciation, was necessarily race and gender specific. It was formed in relation to an ancient Western cultural ideology perhaps most clearly expressed in Aristotle's *De Anima* and "On the Generation of Animals": "the body cannot be soul; the body is the subject or matter, not what is attributed to it. . . . the soul is the cause or source of the living body. . . . the source or origin of movement, it is the end, it is the essence of the whole living body."[10] We then see that the duality of soul and body is explicitly gendered: "the male contributes the principles of movement and the female the material" (678). The "principle of movement," previously correlated with the soul, is in Aristotle's biologically deterministic system a male principle, and the material, bodily dimension is female. This trope, the body as female, recurs throughout the centuries. Even though anorexia emerges much later, this trope is important to any discussion of anorexia, whether the trope is found in classical antiquity, medieval monasteries, or early twentieth-century literature.

The body/spirit duality and its gender implications have been much discussed. What is particular to this duality in the case of anorexia is that the anorexic logic does not reflect a separation between body and spirit, and a desire to transcend the first; rather, it is a fight between two bodies, male and female, where one remains as the common standard for the body and the other should disappear altogether. Becky W. Thompson's work shows how the standard body is white and middle class, as well as heterosexual. In *Conversation with Anorexics*, Hilde Bruch records the voices of anorexic women who do not wish to escape a gender-neutral body but rather a female body: "I want to avoid curves—I always avoided looking like a woman. . . . I do not want to have the kind of body females have. From childhood on I had a negative association, felt it was not nice to look like a woman," says Annette, one of Bruch's anorexic patients.[11] "I want to stay slender," she explains, "because I look more like a man. I push myself to do as much as any man can do" (125). "Looking like a man" is associated with competency and action, as if a thin body would enable a female to "do as much as any man," with the implication that otherwise this would be impossible. Femaleness is associated with fatness and passivity. The language of Ida, another patient, indicates the cultural definition that equates femininity and softness; and softness, with body fat: "I accepted only recently that being soft and feminine could be attractive. I always felt it was disgusting. I wondered how anybody found it attractive to be voluptuous" (137). Femininity is interchangeable with softness; softness is represented by bodily fat; and all of these things—femininity, softness, and fat—are "disgusting." The reason for the symbology of this anorexic's language is no mystery. Anorexia is a reaction to pervasive cultural symbols related to femininity, and it tries to create its own symbols, a male body that "can do as much as any man can do," that signifies competence, rather than dependence. But in the creation of this "new" symbol and body, the anorexic ironically upholds the very definitions she fights against, accepting the pejorative definition of femininity. As Richard Gordon writes, "[U]nder the persistent influence of gender bias and negative stereotypes, female curvaceousness is associated with a lack of intelligence and competence (i.e., the 'dumb blonde'). But . . . the roundness of the body, particularly any implications of fatness, is also closely linked with notions of fertility and reproductive capacity."[12] The anorexic fights the reduction of herself to this symbology of incompetence and dependence, the synecdoche that makes the body and reproductive capacity of "woman" stand for the whole identity of individual women, and that defines reproduction as dependence. When race and sexual orientation are considered as well, some bodies are doubly, or even triply, stigmatized.

Through the language of the body, using the body as language or symbol, the anorexic enacts, on the most literal and concrete plane, the same purge of femaleness that characterized the canonical modernist definition of literature. This purge was a central part of the genesis of this literature, the male "body" of its theoretical precepts. As in an argument about Wallace Stevens's creative process where Frank Lentricchia states that "if you're male you must police yourself for traces of femininity," the anorexic polices herself for just these signs. Finding them all too abundant, she sets out on a course that will purge these signs from her body, a starvation that she thinks will make her more "male."[13] This "policing" and purge in literary modernism is masked as the elimination of a gender-neutral body, the suppression of "physical nature" in order to write. Or this suppression is masked as transformation from physical to textual materiality, a commonplace modernist ideal. Anorexics and a particular strain of modernist writing pursue the same goal, which is characterized by a symbology of the body structured by a shared cultural logic: that which defines the female as extraneous, dependent, and chaotic, in need of control by reduction.

An important theory of the body and sexual difference in modernism that achieves this goal depends upon anorexia as a trope. In this trope the female body is consumed in order to give birth to the male body as text. This is specifically modernist because the privileged term here is not the *spirit* but the *male body* as *created through words*—the "hard body" of the imagist poem, the "extinction of personality," the insistence on purification, dissection, cutting to arrive at the work of art. The female body is eliminated to create the textual body as art. Art as such is opposed to the "fat" that is the material dimension. Art is generated from fat, is whittled and formed from fat. Art emerges from excess, like the sculpture that emerges once the sculptor has chiseled away the superfluous stone: Inside every fat body there's a thin body struggling to get out. One of the consequences of a logic that designates stereotypically feminine characteristics as fat, as extra, as something it is desirable to reduce, is that the persons who fit those characteristics are themselves seen as reducible, expendable material to be consumed and burned off just as food is consumed and utilized for energy. In this sense, then, it seems particularly important to identify the gender dynamics of this logic. Yet, much discussion of anorexia identifies it as a negation of "the body," gender neutral despite the empirical "truth" that anorexics are and have been primarily female. For example, Anderson asserts that the negation of the body in modernism also means the negation of gender: "both [modernism and anorexia] involve a crisis of gender that calls into question the very categories of male and female" ("Anorexia and Modernism," 37). This argument makes sense and has been accepted as standard, because of characteristics particular to the form of modernism I discuss. In this strain the representative subjects are male characters with male bodies created by male authors who seem to struggle against "the body." Thus, an assertion that the actual subject of erasure or incorporation is the female body seems logically problematic.

Yet, under closer examination, the logic is clear. In male modernist texts an apparently all-encompassing rejection of bodily materiality that cuts across any designation of gender can be shown to reflect an urge to privilege one kind of sexuality and one kind of body. The privilege occurs through a reversal, with a difference, of the Victorian tradition in which men are "animalistic" in their bodily desires and in their need for gratification, while women lack sexual desire and desire for food, and hate meat. The difference is that the terms are not only reversed in modernist texts, so that women become carnivores and men anorexics, but there is also the attempt to replace the physical body with the textual sign. The textual body *is* the body, not a sign for something else. "The point of *Imagisme*," says Pound, "is that it does not use images *as ornaments*. The image is itself the speech. . . . the image is not an idea."[14] In this sense, then, the image of the body is the body, not an idea about it, and a nonornamental body is a body without extras, without softness, without superfluous curves. It is by definition a male body.

Unlike the modernist ideal, in the Victorian era the body was a sign of something else. Because especially the white female role required the cultivation of the spirituality men supposedly lacked as a result of their participation in the competitive, often brutal world of work, a "disembodied" woman's relationship to food became the locus of attention. As Brumberg explains in *Fasting Girls*, "The woman who put soul over body was the ideal of Victorian femininity. . . . one of the most convincing demonstrations of a spiritual orientation was a thin body—that is, a physique that symbolized rejection of all carnal appetites. To be hungry, in any sense, was a social faux pas. Denial became a form of moral certitude and refusal of attractive foods a means for advancing in the moral hierarchy" (182). This designation of gender in its relation to appetite and food becomes increasingly reversed in the modernist texts I examine. The male takes over the anorexic position. The woman is placed in the traditional position of consumer/ enchantress/temptress and is figured in modernist texts as the non-anorexic femme fatale. The stereotypes are switched. The male becomes the anorexic, the figure of resistance. The female becomes the impediment to or distraction from resistance. This is a secularized reference to the Fall. For some modernist writers, most extravagantly

Kafka, that resistance is a necessary precondition for artistic genesis and makes the production of art possible.[15]

II. The Metaphysics of the Flame: *Fasting Girls, Kafka's* Letters to Felice, *and "A Hunger Artist"*

Nowhere is the necessity of the anorexic position for literary creation seen more clearly than in Kafka, who argued that to create, he had to "diet in all directions." A devotion to art became an activity that necessarily excluded all others. It was all consuming. His dedication necessitated a clear break from the world as a source of nourishment and food, and made that nourishment purely textual. As he writes in a much-quoted diary entry of January 3, 1912, "[W]hen it became clear in my organism that writing was the most productive direction for my being to take, everything rushed in that direction and left empty all those abilities which were directed toward the joys of sex, eating, drinking, philosophical reflection and above all music. I dieted in all these directions."[16] Kafka's text does not reject only the body in order to institute the primacy of spirit but also breaks completely from the social context. He expresses the need to cut out and separate himself from anything like a personal, empirical existence as the necessary condition for the production of texts. Existence, gendered feminine, is, in effect, eliminated as "fat," the female body supplanted by the male textual body.

Critics have often discussed Kafka's sense of separation from the world: "Kafka's works shut themselves off so emphatically from the empirical realities of life, as well as from everything 'in the air' around him, precisely because they originated in a hermetically sealed space, in 'solitary confinement.'"[17] This "confinement" extends to Kafka's manuscripts, which were often confined to tiny notebooks; in the case of "First Sorrow," to a single page. The reduction of written space parallels the reduction of form. Kafka's texts become increasingly abbreviated and self-referential, autophagous. Textual reduction also parallels the reduction of content in both a radical rejection of the author as "personality" and the intensely personal. Kafka's writing chamber became the world, setting the stage for the title character in "A Hunger Artist," a figure whose world is reduced to the process of reduction itself. This text, oblique and resistant to interpretation, like all Kafka's literary works, demonstrates through a historical parallel the anorexic logic I claim is central to literary modernism and its designation of gender.

For the designation of gender is central to this text as well as others. Although women appear only once, as props to the impresario's staging of the end of the hunger artist's fast, there is a historical referent for the story that has not, to my knowledge, been discussed in reference to Kafka. This referent raises the gender question all the more fervently, because it seems absent from the text. For the hunger artist's status as public spectacle directly parallels a historical phenomenon in the nineteenth century, widely discussed in the medical and popular press, that of "fasting girls." As Brumberg reports in her book of the same title, "[T]he term 'fasting girl' was used by Victorians on both sides of the Atlantic to describe cases of prolonged abstinence where there was uncertainty about the etiology of the fast and ambiguity about the intention of the faster" (61).[18] And these cases, which were fairly frequent, always involved women "hunger artists." Brumberg argues that a conflict between the designations *anorexia mirabilis* (the idea that abstention from food signifies the independence of spirit from the flesh and is made possible by and evidence of divine miracles) and *anorexia nervosa* (a disease of the "nerves," related in medical discourse to hysteria and said to originate in women particularly independent and stubborn) was staged in the "debate over fasting girls" that raged between the public and popular press and the medical men of the day. Brumberg reports that "despite medical skepticism . . . fasting girls attracted the attention of the British reading public in the last decades of the century . . . all of whom received attention in the London and regional newspapers as well as in the medical journals of the day . . . because public fascination with these cases seemed not to ebb, British medicine was aggressive in its efforts to instruct the public in the proper medical interpretation of the behavior." (73).

The girls' fasts provoked mass public pilgrimages to their houses where round-the-clock watches were instituted to verify the truth of their claims. One of the most famous, Sarah Jacob, "the Welsh Fasting

Girl," began to fast at the age of twelve in 1867. She claimed to eat nothing until her death, from starvation, in 1869. What began as anxiety for her parents became a public spectacle in which hundreds of people came to visit her bedside, bringing gifts and money and creating an economic boom for the local railway. Seeking to discredit her as a hysteric typical of girls her age, the medical men proposed a round-the-clock watch that ended after nine days when she died. Although it was determined she had somehow been receiving tiny amounts of food during the two-year fast, public interest in other fasting girls remained. In 1893, an agent from P. T. Barnum tried to recruit the Brooklyn fasting girl Molly Fancher for exhibition at his circus. As late as 1910, fasting girls received attention in the popular press, but attention declined thereafter. Brumberg attributes this decline to the triumph of medical discourse, in which "the ambiguous fasting girls [were] mov[ed] . . . from the realm of piety to disease, that is, from anorexia mirabilis to anorexia nervosa . . . an indicator of *mentalities* in transition" (98–99).

Since there was common public knowledge of the fasting girls at the time, and since the situation in "A Hunger Artist" so closely parallels theirs, it is likely that Kafka had heard of them. His story opens with the line "During these last decades the interest in professional fasting has markedly diminished."[19] This "diminish[ment] of interest in professional fasting" had its basis in an historical transformation: from women as spiritual icons to women as hysteric patients. "Everywhere," Kafka's narrator declares, "as if by secret agreement, a positive revulsion from professional fasting was in evidence" (195). Brumberg reports that during the late nineteenth century "fasting girls and other displays of pietistic virtuosity [became] sharply disdained. . . . during those hundred years food refusal was transformed from a legitimate act of personal piety into a symptom of a disease" (*Fasting Girls,* 98). Historically, then, the hunger artist was a fasting girl. The parallels are too close for us to think otherwise. Compare, for instance, Kafka's description of a hunger artist as spectacle to Brumberg's description of a fasting girl:

We live in a different world now. At one time the whole town took a lively interest in the hunger artist; from day to day of his fast the excitement mounted; everybody wanted to see him at least once a day; there were people who bought season tickets for the last few days and sat from morning till night in front of his small barred cage; even in the nighttime there were visiting hours, when the whole effect was heightened by torch flares. ("Hunger Artist," 188).

> Throughout 1869 and 1870 the emaciated girl was visited in her bed by hundreds of strangers, who brought her gifts and money. . . . One visitor described village men and boys, waiting on the railroad platform to receive the pilgrims, wearing large caps bearing strips of paper that said "To the Fasting Girl." Another described the wasted Sarah in bed: "She had a victorine about her neck, and a wreath about her hair." Her bed, strewn with ribbons, flowers, and religious books, was also adorned with a small crucifix. . . . ritualism with overtones of Catholic practice was combined with a degree of commercial showmanship. (*Fasting Girls,* 65)

Like the hunger artist who sometimes would stretch "an arm through the bars so that one might feel how thin it was" (Kafka, "Hunger Artist," 188–89), "some visitors came only to touch the girl, to feel her hands or face" (Brumberg, *Fasting Girls,* 65). The staging of the spectacle is virtually the same in both cases. Brumberg describes, "Two local men who worked shifts from 8 A.M. to 8 P.M." (65), which parallels Kafka's "relays of permanent watchers selected by the public, usually butchers, strangely enough, and it was their task to watch the hunger artist day and night, three of them at a time, in case he should have some secret recourse to nourishment" ("Hunger Artist," 189). Both accounts depict a carefully crafted commercial spectacle, orchestrated by the impresario in Kafka's story and the girl's parents in Brumberg's description. In both cases the underlying question is not whether the fasters were "authentic," or whether they were exploiting a gullible public or being exploited, but rather why they chose this particular form, bodily suppression and appetite control, as their means of expression. This choice receives a different figuration in both cases.

Again, to return to Mark Anderson, "a clarification of the issue of gender is needed" ("Anorexia and Modernism," 35). By what logic did the figure of the hunger artist become male? And what was the importance of this figure to modern literature and the theories of value that grew up around it? Older readings of Kafka's story tend to interpret the hunger artist as a figure for the artist in the modern world, ignored by a banal or fickle public. More recently, the hunger artist is seen to create a "performance of self-effacement," in which the very activity from which he derives his identity, fasting, also eliminates him entirely.[20] The later interpretation reads the hunger artist ironically, especially since, by his own admission, he is not really an artist at all: "you shouldn't admire [my fasting] . . . because I have to fast, I can't help it" (Kafka, "Hunger Artist," 200). As Anderson writes, "According to German classical tradition, the aesthetic realm is defined as lying outside the domain of need or necessity. An artist produces or performs as an expression of personal freedom. The hunger artist's 'I can't help it' . . . erases his identity as an artist, and because he has no other identity, it erases him" ("Unsigned Letters," 246). In most recent interpretation the figure of the hunger artist is ironic, self-canceling, not a figure for the artist in the modern world.

And yet there is a way of reconciling these interpretive impulses. Although fasting as necessity is nonartistic, fasting as a necessary stage on the way to art is artistic. Even though the artist who cancels himself out is ironic, self-cancellation is characteristic of the figure of the artist, of whom the anorexic logic of modernism requires "a continual extinction of personality." Ironic detachment is an integral part of the anorexic logic of modernism. That irony functions to uphold, rather than to challenge, anorexia as an ideal for the artist. As Slavoj Zizek writes, "Cynical reason with all its ironic detachment, leaves untouched the fundamental level of ideological fantasy, the level on which ideology structures the social reality itself."[21] Without the recognition that the necessity to renounce the feminine as flesh is ideological fantasy rather than a "higher truth" the artist apprehends whilethe common person does not, the "social reality" will continue to be structured by that idea of "truth," and the ideal of the male anorexic will be reinforced. Although the figure of the self-canceling artist may be ironic, this kind of irony distances in order to disguise the importance of this figure to the idea of "art" in the modernist period. This idea was so pervasive that it created a mythos that lingers in creative writing programs to this day. This mythos explicitly excludes women from the realm of authorship. It institutes a "poetics of impersonality" that stifled traditional women's subjects and writing for years. It also reinstituted a female stereotype that refers to a much older cultural tradition.

Anorexia in Kafka is the necessary precondition for production, yet Kafka is careful never to describe it in gendered terms and questions the validity of that production. Anorexia is more a function of his philosophy of writing than of the writing itself. The logic is most clearly articulated in his letters, which emphasize that writing is a process that, in order to occur, requires an anorexic reduction of the writer's material world. The shrinking material world is literally replaced by a literary one. Kafka's quest to "become literature" represents a particularly marked confusion of the literal and figurative. Kafka makes his life figurative and his writing literal. As he strives to eliminate his own life, which is supposed to be material and literal, his writing, which is supposed to be figurative, is literal in its demonstration of how cultural exclusion operates.[22] His alienated characters, treated like cockroaches, literally become cockroaches, just as the anorexic, reduced to her body by cultural stereotypes about women, literally reduces herself to that body. Kafka and the anorexic share a similar method.

As Erich Heller notes in his introductory essay to Kafka's *Letters to Felice,* Kafka's articulated desire that his works be burned after his death indicates a further desire that "after they had been burned, [they] would rise again from the ashes, purified, in unheard-of beauty and perfection . . . the never satisfied claim he made upon art, his art[,] was that it should cleanse the . . . world . . . by means of the absolute perfection of its language."[23] Such perfection, never attainable, is nonetheless the goal of the artist who has a "magnificent, inborn capacity for asceticism." As Kafka writes to Felice on August 14, 1913, "I . . . am made of literature, I am nothing else, and cannot be anything else."[24] This insistence on literature as more than a raison d'etre, as what he is actually "made of," refers to more than asceticism. Here asceticism, the voluntary discipline of the body, becomes anorexia, something one cannot help.

Kafka "cannot be" anything other than an anorexic, because that is the means by which one can become "made of literature," rather than simply producing it. It is the incorporation or absorption of the writer into his text, a "becoming word" made possible by his status as an anorexic, and by Felice's status as a nonanorexic who embodies the world Kafka defines himself against: "my worries about you and me are the worries of life, are part of the fabric of life, and for this reason would ultimately be compatible with my work at the office, but writing and office cannot be reconciled, since writing has its center of gravity in depth, whereas the office is on the surface of life" (279). Office, Felice, and the "fabric of life" are "on the surface." Only writing has "its center of gravity in depth," and to reach that depth Kafka must become word, become writing, leaving the corporeal female body as world behind. This is modernist literary anorexia: the anorexic body as the position from which one may become text, with the author incorporated into that text through burning away his physical materiality and giving birth to a text that has consumed him. Self-consumption has cleared the way for the production of "purified" art.

An example is the hunger artist, who cancels himself out in order that he may be replaced by the panther, which "seemed not even to miss his freedom; his noble body, furnished almost to the bursting point with all that it needed, seemed to carry freedom around with it too; somewhere in his jaws it seemed to lurk; and the joy of life streamed with such ardent passion from his throat that for the onlookers it was not easy to stand the shock of it" (Kafka, "Hunger Artist," 201). The hunger artist's self-cancellation has cleared the way for this figure, a necessary stage of diminution, in order to arrive at greater richness and fullness, which for Kafka is only possible—and even then, this possibility is highly qualified—in the realm of art. For him art is only possible through struggle against the body and world gendered as feminine: "The world—F[elice] is its representative—and my ego are tearing my body apart in a conflict that there is no resolving" (*Letters to Felice*, xiii). This "conflict" is repeatedly figured as an attraction to and repulsion from the world as equated with and embodied in women, the "world's representatives." "I am held back," Kafka candidly tells Felice, from the kind of "worldly" relationship she desires, "by what is almost a command from heaven; an apprehension that cannot be appeased . . . it is my dread of the union with even the most beloved woman, above all with her" (288–89). Such "union" is impossible because literature and the world are necessarily opposed, and to participate in the latter would destroy the former: "I have a definite feeling that through marriage, *through the union, through the dissolution* of the nothingness I am, I shall perish" (289). In accordance with the anorexic logic, Kafka must *be* nothingness in order to survive and produce the literature that is his life.

"My whole being is directed toward literature," Kafka writes to Felice's father, in what becomes a kind of musical refrain in his letters. "I have followed this direction unswervingly until my 30th year, and the moment I abandon it I cease to live. Everything I am, and am not, is a result of this. I am taciturn, unsociable, morose, selfish, a hypochondriac, and actually in poor health. Fundamentally I deplore none of this: it is the earthly reflection of a higher necessity. . . . I lack all sense of family life" (313). "A sense of family life" is "lower"; a dedication to literature, "higher." His inability to function as a social being is a sign of this "higher calling," as are his physical shortcomings, his "poor health." A strong body is a sign of being fully grounded in a material way within the world; a weak, thin body is a sign of the higher calling. Kafka appropriates the Victorian logic that women's "higher spiritual natures" are figured in the thinness of their bodies for the artist, so that his spare frame and illness are "an earthly reflection of a higher necessity." He doesn't "feed"; worry feeds upon his body, brought on by the desire not to feed upon the world: "God knows from what source these perpetual, steadily revolving worries feed! I cannot get the better of them. . . . the desire to renounce the greatest human happiness for the sake of writing keeps cutting every muscle in my body. I am unable to free myself. Everything is obscured by the apprehensions I feel at the idea of not renouncing" (315). "Every muscle in [his] body" is "cut" by the desire to renounce. The desire to cut has the effect of cutting, and he is "unable to free [him]self" from this desire. "For the sake of writing" he must suffer the cut. He must sever his ties from the usual forms of human nourishment and from the actual frame of his own body.

This anorexic logic, the cutting or burning away of the material body as the necessary precursor for the transmutation of matter into higher forms, was described by Jacques Derrida as "the metaphysics of the flame" in his reading of Novalis's *Fragments*.[25] Derrida described two contradictory opponents within this logic in terms of a metaphysics of eating: an infinitude that is the idea of a "pure taste," an originary taste of innocence that is beyond death, and a finitude that partakes of death and is therefore limited and dependent, as opposed to absolute. These ideas exist side by side, battling it out. In its infiniteness this pure taste would be the work of art, within this logic an idea both possible and impossible. Pure art is the form the artist incessantly strives to get back to, despite an awareness that the ideal of pure art is the wound, the lack, the absence, the fissure that can't be healed, that cannot be attained as an originary moment of pure taste such as one might have had before the apple was bitten and the idea of finitude introduced. In his letters to Felice, Kafka overtly struggles with these two combatants and finds himself divided by them, his very being defined by that division. "As you know," he tries to explain in a letter,

there are two combatants at war within me. . . . I strive to know the entire human and animal community, to recognize their fundamental preferences, desires, and moral ideals, to reduce them to simple rules, and as quickly as possible to adopt these rules so as to be pleasing to everyone, indeed (here comes the inconsistency) to become so pleasing that in the end I might openly act out my inherent baseness before the eyes of the world without forfeiting its love—the only sinner not to be roasted. . . . of the two who are at war within me, or rather whose war I consist of—excepting one small tormented remnant—the one is good, the other evil. . . . the loss of blood was too great. The blood shed by the good one (the one that now seems good to us) in order to win you, serves the evil one. . . . for secretly I don't believe this illness to be tuberculosis, at least not primarily tuberculosis, but rather a sign of my general bankruptcy. (*Letters to Felice*, 544–45)

As "the only sinner not to be roasted," Kafka would escape roasting through the production of rules "pleasing to everyone," creating texts that show "the human and animal community" their "fundamental preferences, desires, and moral ideals." The production of texts would ensure that the community won't discard him in his "baseness," which he defines as his rejection of the human and animal community in order to write. Despite the fact that writing would thus justify his existence, in his will Kafka asked his friend Max Brod to eradicate the mark or product of his "sin." He asked that "all diaries, manuscripts, letters . . . be burn[ed] unread" upon his death.[26] He wished to burn the very thing that would save him from burning. In this particular context, what was good was the Kafka attached to the world, the gentleman who had courted Felice, "the good one, the one that now seems good to us," the one who had shed blood in order to win her. The gentleman was the combatant connected to the world, to human attachments and the physical and emotional nourishment that those attachments provide. This combatant was fundamentally opposed to, locked in mortal combat with, the writing subject who must be detached from the world in order to write, who must be anorexic. "What is stopping me," he says, "can hardly be said to be facts; it is fear, an insurmountable fear, fear of achieving happiness, a desire and a command to torment myself for some higher purpose. . . . But then again there is that tyranny which my very existence imposes upon you; this contradiction tears me apart. . . . that terrible humming top inside me will start spinning again." (*Letters to Felice*, 314). Kafka "consist[s] of" the war between these forces, and his tuberculosis is the inevitable sign of his worldly "bankruptcy" and need to write. The contradiction between his duties as a man of the community and the isolation he thinks writing requires "tears him," sets off the "terrible humming top." Kafka must be tormented to create; he must have unfulfilled desires. He voluntarily denies himself worldly happiness, renounces it, just as the anorexic renounces food, as well as other forms of "happiness." My point is not that Kafka was an anorexic, but rather that the frame of mind central to the anorexic logic is also central to canonical modernist ideas about literary creativity.[27]

Yet literature is sometimes "evil" for Kafka, since it renders him incapable of living an ordinary life in the world. As he tells Felice:

as soon as we lived together I would become a dangerous lunatic fit to be burned alive. The havoc I would create! Would have to create! And if I didn't create it I would be more lost than ever, for it would be against my nature, and whoever happened to be with me would be lost. You have no idea, Felice, what havoc literature creates inside certain heads. It is like monkeys leaping about in treetops, instead of staying firmly on the ground. (*Letters to Felice*, 288).

"Leaping about in treetops instead of staying firmly on the ground," Kafka as writer is severed from that ground that Felice represents. In this peculiar narrative of ascension, reaching the trees and following one's "nature" is dependent upon *not* living together, not forming a bond in the material sense that would distract from the literary ideal. Kafka condemns this aspect of his nature, calling it "evil" and himself a "lunatic." Nonetheless, he feels it as a pressing necessity, continually articulating it by using the metaphor of the flame: "I would become a dangerous lunatic fit to be burned alive."

What Derrida termed "the metaphysics of the flame" is clearly operational here and is a preoccupation throughout Kafka. He would be "fit to be burned alive" if he did live in the world, but his existence as a writer always partakes in the process of burning. In Derrida's reading, the fire is the attempt to burn off all sense of the finite, of the material that decays, as well as the failed attempts to reach the originary purity not possible in daily life. The attempt is to burn off the other failures to get back to the absolute until one gets it right. That Kafka saw his literature as a "failure" accounts for his desire for its destruction through burning upon his death. But in this logic of fire and ashes, body and text, the problem of anorexia claims its own position: because it is finite, the female body, as representative of all that is bodily, needs to disappear into the infinite text, has to be cut in a certain way to be "born again" more purely as text. The logic is circular, cyclic, and recyclic: burning, purgation, purification, vision, transformation, art. As art, literature is another failed attempt to kill certain parts. Literature tries to destroy what is seen as excess, unnecessary, *le reste,* the remainder. Much like the logic set out in the Platonic ladder, literature participates in a destruction that is seen as a means of attaining the absolute. Each failure provides the need for the remainder to be burned again. Here, in the anorexic impulses of literary modernism demonstrated by Kafka, that remainder is the body envisioned as consuming, material, dependent, feminine. The body is a synecdoche for the domestic and worldly spaces of the family and community, connections Kafka feels he must renounce in order to write.

But this death of the remainder is only possible literarily speaking: the body, figured as female, is only "killed" or purged through language. Its destruction is only possible tropologically. The trope of the spiritual rebirth in literature is made possible by getting rid of the dependent, the finite. Its obverse is the idea of the infinite that is a symbolic structure made to seem organic through the trope, a totality that therefore carries away the residue of the finite. The body as female, as fat, is purified, eliminated by taking it into the flame. The transformative totalization of the remains is the process posited as a means of getting to the symbolic nature of the "pure" work of art, which is "organic" in its creation through language. The flame situates the genesis of literary modernism, for artistic creation is based on principles of selection that designate what is to burn. There is no way to avoid some principle of exclusion. According to that principle, however, what is labeled extra, fat, garbage, need not always be the same. But within the anorexic logic it is.

The principle of selection figured as burning gathers together different strands, ideas, or impulses. The artistic imagination or creative process figured as flame binds what is separated *and* disassociates what is bound, deconstructs to constitute, decomposes different perspectives to create a single perspective, kills off, designates as expendable what is seen as dependent and secondary to generate new life. The birth is in the process of continual burning away or cutting. This makes it a spiritual, rather than a material, production, and the double movement of binding and separating mirrors the opposition between infinite and finite that acts as the catalyst for the flame. An apocalyptic desire produces a flame that consumes everything until it has become something better, disembodied in the form of light.

For Kafka the fissures in "the metaphysics of the flame" are always sadistically beckoning. His "small tormented remnant" in the struggle between literature and daily life is the ever-present awareness that it is impossible to burn off "the fat," not just because it fuels the flame, but because there is no affirmation, no simple return to anything prior. He wishes to burn the totality of his texts that are endlessly striving for the space of pure art but are continually falling away from that space. He wants to burn what strives to occupy the space that has been torturing him. He sees that dying through words isn't simply a process of purification. Something is lost, whatever could not fly with him as he "leap[ed] about in treetops instead of staying firmly on the ground." That loss tortures him as much as his texts, which are the reminder of that loss, the embodiment of loss in words. A loss of worldly weight, of ground, of physical corporeality figured as feminine is continually desired in the anorexic logic of literary modernism, and some, like Kafka, are continually haunted by that loss.[28]

The further, and perhaps most significant, consequence of this anorexic logic is the effect that it has on the representation of women within modernist texts. In Kafka, as well as in Eliot, Pound, and Williams, one of the necessary logical consequences of the logic of "burning" and "purification" is the stereotype of women that emerges, monolithic and seemingly unquestionable, which makes "purification" necessary: "woman" as ground, body, sex, flesh. This stratification is clearly reflected at the end of "The Metamorphosis" when upon Gregor's death, his sister exclaims, "Just see how thin he was. It's such a long time since he's eaten anything. The food came out again just as it went in." The narrator concurs, stating "Indeed, Gregor's body was completely flat and dry." The male occupies the anorexic position, while the position of embodied sexual potential and life in the world and community belongs to his sister. "While they were . . . conversing," the narrator reports,

> it struck both Mr. and Mrs. Samsa, almost at the same moment, as they became aware of their daughter's increasing vivacity, that in spite of all the sorrow of recent times . . . she had bloomed into a pretty girl with a good figure. They . . . [came] to the conclusion that it would soon be time to find a good husband for her. And it was like a confirmation of their new dreams and excellent intentions that at the end of their journey their daughter sprang to her feet first and stretched her young body.[29]

His sister, Grete, as body, as sexual potential, is placed in obvious contrast to the anorexic Gregor. She is reduced to that function, that position. Her body becomes a synecdoche for Grete. Gregor, as anorexic, brought only "sorrow" to his worldly family, but Grete, as body, brings "new dreams" of a "good husband" and continued material (re)production.

In a brilliant analysis of Kafka's characterizations of women, Reiner Stach makes connections between Kafka's female characters and Otto Weininger's enormously influential *Sex and Character* (1903), which conceptualized and concretized the old female stereotypes of the natural body, primal mother, and femme fatale into intellectual theory. According to Stach, there is a "profound similarity between Weining-

er's theoretical description and Kafka's aesthetic projection of femininity." Significantly, he finds that Weininger's theory is based on the
assumption that the feminine should be annihilated, that "the essence
of woman, the substratum of the feminine, must be obliterated"
(150–51, 156).[30] Weininger's theory corresponds to what I have been
analyzing as the anorexic logic, as exhibited in the theoretical and the-
matic desire to cut or burn the fat or flesh that is feminine.

The desire to purge the feminine involves the necessary projection
of the attributes of voraciousness and encompassing corporeality onto
women in Kafka's text. A good example is the figure of Brunelda in
Amerika, who, so fat as to be nearly immobile, is nonetheless voraciously sensual: "Although she's so fat, she's very delicate. . . . 'I'm
burning, [she says] I must take off my clothes.'"[31] His women characters, in their reduction to body/sex/hunger, lose all individuation and
function merely as implacable forces, as stereotypes that are the reverse of the anorexic Victorian heroines. As Stach writes, "The tendency of Kafka's abstract characterization corresponds to a precise
ideological premise that puts the coded female body into an empty
ego. Her body is her essence" ("Kafka's Egoless Woman," 161). In
relationship to the anorexic logic, with its ideological priorities in
terms of the elimination of the body as female, the textual priorities
are the creation of women as "monstrous" bodies with little individuation or volition outside of the corporeal. While this process works itself out differently in different writers and is of course not the case in
all writers, it is nonetheless a dominant tendency that encodes the
logic in differing ways. An examination of Eliot, Pound, and Williams,
as representatives of canonical, modern Anglo-American poetry, who
initially seem to approach the question very differently than Kafka,
will help to unravel several of this logic's permutations.

III. "The Female Is a Chaos": Male Anorexia in Eliot and Pound

Valerie Eliot's unexpurgated facsimile and transcript version of *The
Waste Land* reveals what seems to be a deep disgust with male sexuality and the male body in "The Fire Sermon," a great deal of which
was cut by Pound. Significantly, Pound describes himself as a midwife

figure in the birth of the poem, claiming in a letter written to Eliot
that he had delivered by Caesarean section:

> These are the poems of Eliot
> By the Uranian Muse begot;
> A man their Mother was,
> A Muse their Sire.
>
> How did the printed Infancies result
> from Nuptials thus doubly difficult?
>
> If you must needs enquire
> Know diligent Reader
> That on each Occasion
> Ezra performed the Caesarean Operation.
>
> . . . .
>
> He writes of A.B.C.'s
> And flaxseed poultices,
> Observing fate's hard decrees
>   Sans satisfaction;
> Breeding of animals,
> Humans and cannibals,
> But above all else of smells
>   Without attraction.[32]

While Pound claims that he "writes of . . . Breeding of animals,/Hu-
mans and cannibals,/But above all else of smells/Without attraction,"
which he certainly does in *The Cantos*, this is the kind of writing he
cut out of Eliot's text in order to "deliver" it. In the uncut version, the
poem struggling to be born, the peculiar gender switch designated
here by the muse as sire and a man as mother is replicated in the logic
of Eliot's finished poem. Much of what Pound cuts to facilitate the
birth of the poem is the logic of the gender switch in its relation to
anorexia. Most of what refers to the body physically, rather than metaphorically, is cut, leaving ambiguously suggestive figures of physicality
such as the lines that ultimately open "The Fire Sermon" section of
the poem (the forty-second line of this section becomes the first):

> Admonished by the sun's inclining ray,
> And swift approaches of the thievish day,
> The white-armed Fresca blinks, and yawns, and gapes.

These lines are replaced by:

> The river's tent is broken: the last fingers of leaf
> Clutch and sink into the wet bank.[33]

In the latter lines we can best see Eliot's mythopoeia of "poetic materiality" and Pound's facilitation of it, a poetics that claimed to provide an alternative to the modern experience of alienation—an embodied alienation. Eliot's "poetic objects" are the mythical and literary "bodies" that he scatters throughout his own poetic body. The devastated corpse of his "waste land" has become disjoined from its mythic poetic body and has dwindled into brute material sexual and cultural production. His "poetic materiality" can be seen at work in this part of "The Fire Sermon," where the female body is displaced or purged into a poetic body that redeems it. The title itself, from Buddhism, indicates purgation or the transformation of the passions of the body toward a "higher" life that has "escaped" the banality of feminine flesh. The section's title, "The Fire Sermon," invokes the logic of the flame analyzed in Kafka, the purgation effected through burning as necessary to literary genesis. The parallel between escaping the banality of the poetic "I" and escaping the (female) body is clearly made in this section of *The Waste Land. After* Pound's cuts, and the elimination of the passages that referred to literal materiality, the poem opens with sexual imagery already displaced. To move from the body of "woman" to the body of the river is already the kind of aesthetic containment set out in imagist ideology: the poetic re-creation of nature by a poetic nature, the representation of a broken hymen as a river's broken tent. This image recalls a female body but doesn't embody it. Rather, it gives body to, personifies, something that is bodiless. To sexualize the river creates a "better" poetic sexuality in Eliot's terms. The woman's body is denaturalized and therefore made more meaningful and "authentic" through its sublimation through poetry and projection onto the Thames. This river, as a poetic river, will eventually reunite the waste-land world with its tradition, therefore becoming "genuinely," because poetically, productive. The river, then, can be seen as one of Eliot's "poetic objects" that disjoins the signifier (river) from the signified (body of woman), so that the immaterial becomes the productive force, the constitution or rehabilitation of the material. Language, the poeticization of the woman's body through the image of the river, becomes the primary mode of production, re-creating her body as value. The body's valuelessness is redeemed through a poetics of replacement or displacement.

At this point, I will quote primarily those lines from the unexpurgated version of *The Waste Land* that were cut from the textual body in order for "the poems of Eliot" to be delivered by Caesarean section from "the man [who] their Mother was." What is cut, what is discarded as fat, is precisely that material that reveals the anorexic logic of literary modernism. In the switch from "the Uranian Muse" as feminine to the gendering of that muse as the "Sire," a peculiar logic is created that allows for the circumvention of the feminine, that allows for "a man their Mother was." Eliot is enabled to occupy that position through Pound's procedure of cutting—he cannot become "Mother" until he has been reduced, the body of the poem cut open and much of it discarded as the inassimilable "guts, the strings of my eyes and the indigestible/portions/which the leopards reject" (*Ash Wednesday*).[34]

Part of what cannot be digested by Pound is Eliot's earlier version of the "young man carbuncular," his hair "thick with grease, and thick with scurf" (*Waste Land*, 33), who "munches with the same persistent stare,/He knows his way with women and that's that!" (33). In this characterization, Eliot seems to comment on and condemn the rigid, mechanized "modern" body, one of little spontaneity and vigor, made repugnant by the displaced desires and doldrums of the time, produced by an increasingly industrialized, mechanical culture. In such a setting, sexuality becomes mechanical consumption, much as the empty ritual of eating. "Munch[ing] with the same persistent stare" that he, "one of the low on whom assurance sits/As a silk hat on a Bradford millionaire," employs in his daily rounds "from flat to flat" (33), the young man carbuncular is indicted as much for his class aspirations and presumptions as for his body. But this body is the sign of his lower-class status, the indisputable marker of his animal, bodily origins that make him unfit for the class position he aspires to. His body betrays his valuelessness, his lack of cultural worth. His mechanical attitude toward culinary and sexual consumption is the mark of his impostor status, the betrayer of pretensions that reveal him as the "scurf" that he really is, the class pretender who doesn't follow the proper rules and regulations of courtship, but who rather "knows his way with women and that's that!" In his obtuse lack of culture and preoccupation with bodily satisfaction derived from sexual consumption, he "assaults at once . . . /His vanity requires no response,/And makes a welcome of indifference" (35). Here his lack of bodily restraint is a sign that he lacks culture, for by the last decade of the nineteenth century and by the early twentieth, the visible sign of culture was bodily restraint. A thin body and abstemiousness from physical function placed distance between the leisured classes, who did not have to physically labor, and the working class, who did. A thin, even frail body became the sign of prosperity. This replaced the traditional view that a rotund, well-fed body signified wealth and means.[35] Here the young man carbuncular betrays his true class origins through his lack of anorexic behavior, the lack of restraint that Tiresias has "fore-suffered . . . /enacted on this same divan or bed, . . . I who have sat by Thebes beneath the wall/And walked among the lowest of the dead" (35).

The perceived lack of restraint "enacted on this same divan or bed" directly refers to Oedipus and the lack of restraint he exhibited at Thebes. This becomes the motif Tiresias foresuffers, since he sees that lack of restraint repeated throughout history. Eliot's reference is to an earlier trope for figuring woman and her desires than that of the Victorian anorexic. In the earlier tradition, exemplified by the Neo-platonic marriage of the woman-as-body trope with the Christian body-as-sin, the urge to bodily sexuality is expected of a woman. Eliot is distressed because in the degraded modern world the gender roles have been reversed. The idea of the desiring female is necessary to maintain the definition of woman as defined by her procreative function, and in the poem the typist exhibits anorexic behavior or lack of desire. Simultaneously, the cultured male, who should by definition be properly abstemious because of his "higher" relation to the spirit than body, is acting out his desires.[36]

As we will see, the typist is indicted in Eliot's earlier version of *The Waste Land* precisely because she *is* anorexic, while the young man carbuncular is indicted because he *isn't*. Instead, he has "his way," then "bestows one final patronizing kiss, . . . and at the corner where the stable is,/Delays only to urinate, and spit" (33–35). He has performed each bodily function in quick succession: eating, a sexual act, and urination, with spitting thrown in as another figure of bodily excess. Eliot explicitly labels these bodily acts as a fall from the cultured state of humanity into animality. In an image of the stable the young man carbuncular brands himself as one of the animals by urinating in the open before passing on. This section of the poem reveals the anorexic logic underlying so many canonical modernist texts: an elaborate system of signs in which the body and bodily activity are defined as female and in opposition to culture, and in which the symbol or signification of culture itself is anorexia, a restraint from these activities whether figured as abstention from food, sex, excretion, or sleep. In this earlier characterization of the young man carbuncular, we find that anorexia is the ideal modernist state. In the anorexic mind-set reflected in the poem, the poet seems to desire complete transcendence of the physical, so that, as in the disease itself, each degraded bodily function goes into remission.

Yet, the figure of the typist renders this interpretation problematic. For it isn't just a longing for the transcendence of *the* body that structures Eliot's poem. Instead, there is a longing for a genderless space that would be genderless precisely because one gender, the "deviation" and the gender equated with the body, would have been eliminated. Only the gender that has always functioned as the standard or norm, that gender equated with the spirit through its freedom from reproduction and lack of physical limitations and ties, would remain. The definition of the male body is the definition of the body, whereas the female body is extra, more body. Like the anatomy models still studied in medical school in which the male body is presented as the body, and all the different apparatus that women have are treated as extras and their study relegated to obstetrics and gynecology, the underlying logic of modernist texts figures the body as by definition male, and the female body as more body than that, with "more" interpreted negatively. Eliot's urge to "trim the fat" from bodies, textual and otherwise, is a desire to cut out and discard this extra, to reject the feminine as body to affirm the masculine body.

It is possible to arrive at this conclusion through a series of steps that begin with a description of food and eating rituals within the typist's home:

> The typist home at teatime, who begins
> To clear away her broken breakfast, lights
> Her stove, and lays out squalid food in tins,
> Prepares the toast and sets the room to rights. (33)

The strange adjective "broken" to describe "breakfast" establishes the reason for the speaker's indictment of the typist. The problem, the sign of decay, is not that she consumes, but that she doesn't consume enough. If the breakfast is "broken," it can only be partially consumed, as if toyed with but not eaten. It is not just dishes that she clears here, since it is the breakfast, not the dishes, that is "broken." The phrase "broken breakfast" is particularly marked, since *breakfast* literally means "to break a fast." In the figure of the "broken breakfast," semantically the break of the break of the fast means that she is still fasting, that she hasn't eaten. Furthermore, the "squalid food" she does prepare is not primarily for her but for the young man carbuncular, or at least the poem refers to his eating, not to hers. His eating and sexuality are the basis for the speaker's indictment, while hers seems based in the lack of such activities: "A bright kimono wraps her as she sprawls/In nerveless torpor on the window seat" (33). One definition of *torpor*, "stagnation of function," is particularly applicable here. She has refused to embrace her function as desiring body, properly consuming and reproductively active, as the proper womanly position. Her lack of sexual desire disturbs the speaker:

> The meal is ended, she is bored and tired;
> [He e]ndeavors to engage her in caresses,
> Which still are unreproved, if undesired. (33)

She may consume, or have sex, but she doesn't desire to; she is indifferent, even "glad it's over" (35).

The speaker, who plays on the stereotype of sexual activity as "folly" in a woman, actually has a very different definition of *folly* here. This meaning is revealed in the transcript, not in the final version of the poem:

> When lovely woman stoops to folly and
> She Then moves about her room again, alone,
> She smoothes her hair with automatic hand,
> And puts a record on the gramophone. (35)

The correction that appears in the second line is the replacement of "she"

> When lovely woman stoops to folly and
> Then She moves about her room again, alone,
> She smoothes her hair with automatic hand,
> And puts a record on the gramophone. (35)

with "then," which puts a completely different emphasis on "folly," the more conventional one. But when the lines read

> When lovely woman stoops to folly and
> She moves about her room again, alone,
> She smoothes her hair . . .

the "folly" does not seem the act of sex, the referent when the word is "then," instead of "she"; rather, "folly" is the act of moving about her room alone and indifferently putting a record on the gramophone. Her lack of concern with the process, her lack of desire, is her "folly." The unusual line break at "and" places emphasis on "folly" and makes it possible to read even the corrected version in this manner. The "and" implies and emphasizes a continuation, not a break, in the thought that has been developed, the idea of her lack of desire. This continues the same emphasis and further develops her indictment for *not* desiring and therefore violating that earlier cultural logic of the voracious female body that Eliot wishes to "restore" to the fallen modern world.

Other female characters in the poem also fail to conform to expectations of insatiable desire:

> Fresca! in other time or place had been
> A meek and lowly weeping Magdalene;
> More sinned against than sinning. (41)

"Lowly" because of her position as prostitute, a Magdalene, Fresca
was in her proper position "in another time or place." In the present,
however, she has become something else that disturbs Eliot's fixed
definition of femininity, which is:

> For varying forms, one definition's right:
> Unreal emotions, and real appetite. (41)

"Real appetite" is the proper definition of woman; and one sign of
degradation in the modern period is that she has become something
else, an anorexic who has gone beyond her body: "Women grown intellectual grow dull,/And lose the mother wit of natural trull" (41).
For Eliot, what is "natural" and the only "wit" that woman can have
lies in the maintenance of her function as "trull," or prostitute. Without this, she grows "dull." For Eliot, a woman *should* maintain her
bodily appetites, as Fresca does in the opening of the unexpurgated
version of "The Fire Sermon":

> The white-armed Fresca blinks, and yawns, and gapes,
> Aroused from the dreams of love and pleasant rapes.
> Electric summons of the busy bell
> Brings brisk Amanda to destroy the spell;
> With coarsened hand, and hard plebeian tread,
>
> . . . .
>
> Depositing thereby a polished tray
> Of soothing chocolate, or stimulating tea. (39)

Here Fresca is the sexually voracious female, ready even for rape and
served by a "plebeian." This sexual voraciousness is figured through
the "soothing chocolate" and the "stimulating tea" that she will consume along with other eatables that she devours as she reads, for she
devours words as well, "Their scribbled contents at a glance devour[ed]" (39). Only here, through eating, can Fresca occupy the
"properly" female position according to Eliot, which does not "[d]is-
guise the good old hearty female stench" (39), and which does not
pretend to the intellectualism that is the male's province. Fresca as
the nonanorexic is his feminine ideal, for a female anorexic disturbs
the cultural logic Eliot is anxious to reinstate.

Significantly, Fresca as nonanorexic, as a "wom[a]n grown intellectual grow[n] dull" has stepped into the position of the author, "bap-

tized in a soapy sea/Of Symonds—Walter Pater—Vernon Lee"
(41)—all of whom are "too emotional" and "unrestrained" according
to high modernist tenets. Thus baptized, Fresca can only produce
worthless poetry: "When restless nights distract her brain from sleep/
She may as well write poetry, as count sheep" (41). Because she isn't
an authentic anorexic who cuts her body out, she can produce only
literary garbage that is the sign of the times' degradation:

> Fresca's arrived (the Muses Nine declare)
> To be a sort of can-can salonniere
> But at my back from time to time I hear
> The rattle of the bones, and chuckle spread from ear to ear. (41)

The "bones," a figure of death, can also be read as the "rattle" of authentic art or the laughter of those who produce it, mocking the feeble attempts of the woman author. Because she isn't capable of producing a text as flame, a purified text, she can only exist as a "can-can
salonniere" despite the beguiling of her "flattering friends" (41) who
would tell her otherwise. In Eliot, the logic of anorexia is not about
the elimination of "the body" but rather the projection of all "undesir-
able" qualities onto the nonanorexic female body to maintain the male
body as the figure for the anorexic artist. Anorexia is criticized in the
guise of woman but is set up as a necessary ideal for men. Eliot twists
the phenomenon of female anorexia, which in the medical discourse
of the nineteenth century is described as an unnatural disease while
it was simultaneously part of the beauty ideals for women. He twists
a contemporary phenomenon to fit an older cultural logic that infers
that anorexia is appropriate to males, and that is reinscribed in literary
modernism as a necessary condition for the production of "high" literature, a phallic discourse that gives birth to itself.

The specific gender codes of this logic could be subjected to interrogation in the way of Lacan's "Signification of the Phallus." There
the phallic function is symbolically, rather than materially, based and
as a floating signifier can function only as a place marker or position
without a necessary anatomical reference. Women can "have" the
phallus too. Yet, in the anorexic logic of literary modernism, any attempt to transcend "the body" is an attempt to transcend that body as
female, casting out or burning through a femininity and arriving at a

"purer" masculinity that then makes creativity possible. Anorexia as a disease has long been diagnosed as a refusal of gender, where female secondary sex characteristics are sent into remission, leaving the illusion of maleness. Literary modernism attempts to institute a choice between two bodies through insistently placing "woman," or "the feminine," in the position of the nonanorexic while designating the male as anorexic. The hard/thin/clear/male phallically productive body—the essential, anorexic body—becomes the intermediary that marks the transition to the "higher" form of phallic creativity after it has effectively "cut away" and cast off the soft/fat/murky/female phallically threatening body—the ornamental, nonanorexic body.

In *Language, Sexuality, and Ideology in Ezra Pound's "Cantos,"* Rabate provides this equation in reference to Pound's thinking about artistic genesis. According to Rabate, Pound's presentation of this logic is more straightforward than Eliot's twist: "The striking feature is that phallic assertion needs the 'cutting' quality of thought, which dissociates, dissects the 'clots' which become clogs. . . . For Pound . . . castration opens the way to phallic drives" (219). "Castration," in this sense, is not a feminizing but a masculinizing operation, just as when the anorexic "castrates" herself by eliminating secondary sex characteristics, making her more "masculine." "In the domain of poetry," Maud Ellmann writes, "[Pound] inveighs against padding and adornment because they coagulate the poem's moving energies."[37] A poem must be hard and lean in order to "move," be active, rather than bloated and passive. When Pound became disillusioned with the "feminization" of imagism, he named it "Amygism" and switched to vorticism, declaring that "Vorticism is art before it has spread itself into flaccidity." In the words of Gaudier-Brzeska, whom Pound quotes, it is an art characterized by "manly firmness of composition" (*Gaudier-Brzeska,* 88, 37). "'Amygism,'" says Ellmann, "had become too feminine, too flabby and subjective for his taste" (*Poetics of Impersonality,* 167). The "thought" that "cuts through" the "soft mass," the "flaccidity" that "spreads" and so is not art, clears the way for "phallic assertion," for "manly firmness of composition." This is the position of the (male) anorexic, who eliminates the female padding on the way to phallic creativity. For Pound and Eliot, the feminine needs to be cut, cut up, burned away, to arrive at art. They affirm a return to an originary purity, some time or place that was "better" because more masculine and clear, less chaotic, where the poet had more control—in a vitally religious world; or in the Grail or Fisher King legends for Eliot; and in the troubadours and Chinese ideogram for Pound. Through cutting, like the "Caesarean Operation" that delivered *The Waste Land,* art emerges from the muck, the "fat"; the originary realm of "pure taste" can be approximated if the poet is good enough.

Female chaos is figured by a spreading body; male control, by a lean one—are these categories rigidly fixed in their designation of gender?[38] In a February 1919 letter to Marianne Moore, Pound writes

> [t]he female is a chaos,
> the male
> is a fixed point of stupidity, but only the female
> can content itself with prolonged conversation
> with but one sole other creature of its own sex and
> of its own unavoidable specie
> the male
> is more expansive
> and demands other and varied contacts;
> hence its combativeness . . .
> You, my dear correspondent,
> are a stabilized female,
> I am a male who has attained the chaotic fluidities.[39]

In the ironic "fixed point of stupidity," Pound seems to deride the conventionally masculine as much as the conventionally feminine and to designate a switch in positions to himself, "a man who has attained the chaotic fluidities," and to Marianne Moore, the "stabilized female," that seems to destabilize conventional boundaries. After all, fluidity is for Pound a positive quality, one necessary for circulation and production, so in this sense the feminine is not necessarily a negative. In other senses, though, the male is characterized by greater expansiveness "hence its combativeness," is stereotypical, and a "chaos" that keeps only to itself and its species is logically contradictory. Most important, however, fluidity in Pound also refers primarily to the spermatozoa as fluid. This fluidity is found in his reference to the brain as a clot of genital fluid in his postscript to his translation of Remy de Gourmont's *Natural Philosophy of Love,* where he argues that "[t]hought is a chemical process, the most interesting of all transfusions in liquid solution. The mind is an upspurt of sperm."[40] From the idea that money and (male) sexuality are both fluid when properly functioning—when they're not "clogged"—the fluidity Pound attributes to the "female chaos" becomes here also a property of the male. For the sperm to flow, it must be dissected by the cutting quality of thought, the "chemical process" that cuts away the clogs. As Rabate writes, "[F]or Pound . . . castration opens the way to phallic drives, and similarly money becomes positive when it is fluid, when circulation is swift and easy; a liquidized money loses its bad smell, it detaches itself sufficiently from the anal gift in which it found its origin. . . . The creation of forms is achieved when [sperm] goes back to . . . matter, or 'female chaos'" (219).

It is only through cutting that form can be detached from the material in which it found its origin. Sperm is the phallic shaping principle (echoes of Aristotle). The male imagination depends upon "female chaos" to achieve embodiment, but it gives that formless matter form. Just as Pound claims to deliver *The Waste Land* by Caesarean section, the phallic drives of creativity are made possible only by the anorexic position, the position of castration. This position is one of castration, because its subject has renounced the materiality of the body, cutting it off and throwing it away. This then leads to the transformation of the body into text by a logic very like Abelard's declaration that his castration freed him from bodily desires and therefore enabled him to live a much more "productive" life, writing instead of loving.[41]

The anorexic artist, free of bodily desire, is the position of autocastration in the moderns, which seems to eliminate maleness on the literal level but reaffirms it on the figurative level of literary production, or what Freud referred to in a more general way as the "work of civilization":

Women soon come into opposition to civilization and display their retarding and restraining influence. . . . Women represent the interests of the family and of sexual life. The work of civilization has become increasingly the work of men, it confronts them with ever more difficult tasks and compels them to carry out instinctual sublimations of which women are little capable. Since a man does not have unlimited quantities of psychical energy at his disposal, he has to accomplish his tasks by making an expedient distribution of his libido. What he employs for cultural aims he to a great extent withdraws from women and sexual life.[42]

This passage, although it contradicts others in Freud, clearly demonstrates what I call the anorexic logic of literary modernism.[43] To the extent that the work of civilization entails an "expedient distribution of the libido" whose expediency necessitates "withdraw[al] from women and sexual life," the passage demonstrates the logic that places the male in the anorexic, renunciatory position and the female in the material world that is opposed to the work of civilization that the poet would further.

Pound demonstrates this position thematically as well as theoretically in "Canto 39," in the explicit equation of women, sexuality (dependence and reproductive capacity), and fat. *The Cantos,* whose body is comprised of the bodies of other documents cut and pasted together, attempts to extract only the essential: those sections of documents' bodies that make a "true" history. The many voices in *The Cantos* invoke the transformation of the personal into the universal, the emotional into the objective. As Ellmann writes in *The Poetics of Impersonality,* "[L]ike Eliot, Pound presumes that poetry begins in the expression of emotion, though writing is a crucible which burns its privacy away" (139). "Canto 39"—mainly pulled from the Circe chapter of the *Odyssey* but containing fragments from the works of Dante, Catullus, and Virgil, and from a Middle-English lyric—includes explicit reference to this transformative burning. Its body is composed of references to fertility goddesses, eating, wanton sexualities, and, most important, a purifying flame. The theme of excess runs throughout the poem. It is figured in terms of bodily spreading that provides the symbolic underpinning for Circe's threatening sexuality and propensity for "bringing out the worst" piglike nature in men, turning men into beasts, spirits into bodies, thereby feminizing them. Odysseus reverses and contains this threat, and the poem ends in the transformation of flesh into light, of feminine into masculine. Elpenor, the ironic poet figure from "Canto 1," returns to describe the scene:

> Fat panther lay by me
> Girls talked there of fucking, beasts talked there of eating,
> All heavy with sleep, fucked girls and fat leopards.[44]

Figures of bestial sexuality are equated with fatness, followed by the mixture of human and beast in the reference to Pasiphae, Circe's twin, the mother of the Minotaur, and are interspersed with the invocation of fertility and spring: "Belly beautiful . . . new spring singing" (Terrell, *Companion to the "Cantos,"* 162). The story of Odysseus's taming of Circe through his resistance to her poisoned food and his sexual conquest of her is ornamented with references to various fertility goddesses. Among them are Hathor, an Egyptian goddess who combines woman and cow and is "bound in [a] box," so that "never will the delight part from [her]"; and Flora, a Roman goddess whose attributes are similar to Hathor's (Pound, *Cantos,* 194–95). In particular, the figure of Hathor invokes the connections between female reproductivity, fat, and passive flesh through the common perception of cows as "stupid meat" and the feminine as defined by excessive corporeality and reproductive function. This figure is contained not only by a box but also in the end of the poem through a fleshly transformation in which an unidentified speaker is "[b]eaten from flesh into light," a transformation made possible because the speaker "[h]ath swallowed the fire-ball" (196). This is followed by the lines

> His rod hath made god in my belly
> So the bride speaks
> So the bride sings.
>
> . . . .
> I have eaten the flame. (196)

These lines replace the earlier corpulent sensuality with the purification of the flame that produces "god" in the belly. To achieve a "higher" form of production, one must "eat flame" that will burn away bodily materiality, transforming it, incorporating it into a kind of poetic production on the level of gods, rather than men. The feminine impregnated with fire can be incorporated into the poetic process but only if the flame will consume the feminine as flesh and eliminate the excess figured by the "fucked girls and fat leopards" with which the poem begins.

The same logic is formally rearticulated throughout Eliot and Pound's respective literary bodies. Eliot's "extinction of personality," set out in the 1919 essay "Tradition and the Individual Talent," demonstrates the kind of anorexic logic that is ubiquitous in this particular form of modernism. The form was so pronounced that William Carlos Williams labeled this tendency "puritanical," claiming it as evidence of "literary sterility."[45] In "Tradition and the Individual Talent," "[T]he progress of an artist is a continual self-sacrifice, a continual extinction of personality. . . . the mind of the poet is the *shred* [emphasis added] of platinum. . . . the more perfect the artist, the more completely separate in him will be the man who suffers and the mind which creates; the more perfectly will the mind *digest* [emphasis added] and transmute the passions which are its material."[46] Artistic "progress" is measured in terms of self-sacrifice, not just its elimination, but the extinction of personality, the degree to which the "I" disappears altogether into the text that should consume him.[47] The poet is reduced to his mind, and that mind is reduced to a "shred." This eliminates the "suffering man," so as to allow proper digestion of the material passions that, following the logic of the Eucharist, are transmuted into a higher form. The materiality of the poet's experience will be digested and thereby controlled by the mind. The mind is a neutral and objective "shred," properly thin, that will have the good sense to cut out the excess "fat" of the personal, thereby remaining a "shred." Through the ideology of self-sacrifice, an idea also common to the anorexic experience, the poet is to make his personality extinct by means of digestion or consumption, autophagy.[48] "Passions" form the "material" made extinct through this consumption, just as in the anorexic experience the passions and even any relations with others are suppressed. The "objective" elimination of the poetic "I" is accomplished through the transmutation, or digestion, of the material world of experience, of the "man who suffers." Thus, that world and its personal dimensions are in fact reduced to a minimum and the materiality of the poetic image becomes materiality as such.

The tenets Eliot sets out in "Tradition and the Individual Talent" came to represent a dominant mode of thinking about writing in the period. His principles derive from the aesthetic movement that most clearly demonstrates the anorexic tendency and its system of gender coding. Imagism was a movement specifically defined in opposition to the soft sensuality exemplified by the work of the Pre-Raphaelite brotherhood; and it emphasized clarity, hardness, and precision.[49]

The rhetoric of imagism is, according to Natan Zach, "perhaps best viewed as a doctrine of *hardness,* the commonest, widest-ranging concept in the movement's vocabulary," a "hardness" that marks the movement's ideology of gender.[50] On a purely formal level this hardness is related to the imagist streamlining or condensation of language into the efficient image that stands as a metaphor for poetry itself, a poetry of condensation. On a philosophical or ideological level, imagism is a doctrine of asceticism or renunciation that can be seen as a secular purgation. It enacts a rejection of the world's materiality that is figured by the materiality of the female body, especially its sexual and reproductive capacities, which are symbolized by softness, by fat. It can further be seen as a dislocation or separation of "feminine" emotions from "masculine" artistic products. The raw material of "feminine" emotion and experience is reduced, clarified, condensed, purged. It is made over and replaced by the poetic image—masculinized.

In "Imagism and Vorticism," Natan Zach details the way in which this poetic "hardness" was achieved:

(1) through being concise and paring away all ornamental frills; (2) when, in remaining close to everyday speech, it conveys some of the harshness of quotidian reality; (3) when it tends towards concrete objectivity, thus avoiding sentimental effusions; (4) because, in rendering what purports to be an accurate account of its subject, it approximates the scientist's "hard" methods, his hard observation of detailed fact; (5) when it "dares to go to the dust-bin for its subjects" . . . ; (6) when it avoids symmetrical, isochronic metres, which are branded soft, monotonous and soporific, and instead traces in its rhythms the "rough" (i.e.[,] irregular) contours of "things." (238)

The gender implications of this passage are clear. To achieve high art, the poet must avoid "ornamental frills," "sentimental effusions," and "soft metres," while he should embrace the "hard" methods of science and "rough" rhythms. *Frills, effusion, softness,* and *ornamentality* are words that belong to the stereotypical vocabulary of femininity, while *roughness* and *hardness* belong to that of masculinity. The dissolution or removal of the "I," the psychosexual subjectivized ego, in or from the poem is a removal of the feminine. This achievement of the desired hardness is described by Eliot when he writes of the "extinction of personality" and the necessity of the "good" poet's "escape" from personality and emotions ("Tradition," 11). To follow the logic of the imagist precepts that Zach outlines, the excessive female "body" of emotions as expressed in verse must be "pared," its "ornamental frills" or "sentimental effusions" eliminated, thereby remaining closer to the "harshness of quotidian reality" as expressed in "everyday speech." Poetry, instead of being opposed to science, should approximate science in its "concrete objectivity." This objectivity is only made possible by the elimination of the poetic "I." The true poet is henceforth only words. He is only the corpus or body of his work, having stripped his body of feminine characteristics or "effusions." This emphasis on hardness, paring down, and reducing the poetic body can be read as a corollary for the paradoxical reduction or elimination of the female body within imagist poetics. It is a separation from the "brute materiality" of worldly existence and emphasizes the spiritualized or mythic dimensions of that experience.

The elimination of materiality is paradoxical in that it is precisely this kind of materiality, focused on the body with its need for food and shelter, that perhaps best expresses the "harshness of quotidian reality" set out in Zach's second tenet. The imagists, however, instituted a technics of the image to replace any natural body or world. The image is presented, rather than represented. The objective elimination of the poetic "I" also necessitates the reduction of the material world gendered as feminine. This evokes the long-used trope of "nature" as the female body, but what is new in the moderns is that here, the feminine is explicitly defined as fat. Fatness is female and femaleness is fat. In this symbology Eliot's "perfect artist" meets Kafka's "hunger artist" to form an anorexic brotherhood that has dominated canonical literary modernism and shaped our ideas about what high literature is.

The high modernist insistence on the reduction of the female, of fat, also reduces the social and political dimensions that the moderns claimed to "make new" in their critical reaction to culture. This is a central paradox: a denial of the very thing that is the object of critique. As a result of this paradox, a common contemporary reading of modernism indicts the moderns for their ahistoricism, apoliticism, and elite aestheticism. The anorexic is also resisting the cultural context, but precisely because her resistance is directed toward herself rather

than the sociopolitical dimensions of her world, her strategy supports
the object of her resistance and thus can only double back on her and
ultimately work to uphold the status quo. In *Fasting Girls*, Brumberg
reacts to what she sees as a tendency within feminist literary criticism
to idealize the anorexic, "[A]s a feminist, I believe that the anorectic
deserves our sympathy but not necessarily our veneration" (35).[51] Perhaps the same can be said of the canonical moderns.

IV. He Who Embraces the Flesh:
Anorexia and Gender in Williams

The sexual and textual anorexia in Eliot, Pound, and Kafka undergoes
a different permutation in William Carlos Williams. Williams argued
that the tendencies I have been analyzing in Pound and Eliot make
them definitively *American*, a nationality these poets, with their rejection of America as a place that lacks culture, found repugnant. What,
in their view, makes Eliot and Pound truly artistic and cultured, is for
Williams part of the Puritan legacy that prohibits vital intercourse
with the female body and therefore precludes true poets: "never a
woman, never a poet."[52] In his "Letter to an Australian Editor," Williams discusses what Sandra M. Gilbert and Susan Gubar later refer
to as "literary paternity": "Minds beget minds, there's no use denying
that. Newton begat Einstein just as Newton himself was got androgy-
nously out of Archimedes."[53] In his attitude toward literary history,
Williams is skeptical of the tendency to avoid what he calls the "sup-
plying female." For Williams, the anorexic avoidance of the feminine
creates a tradition in which male writers give birth to themselves
through literary "forefathers" whom they select to symbolically "father" their texts. Williams thinks this circumvents the feminine function of motherhood and produces writing "father to father. No mother
necessary."[54] "No mother," as Bryce Conrad writes in *Refiguring
America*, "tends to produce 'literary sterility,'" a reduction in the
power of the male imagination to give birth to new forms—the very
thing the modern struggled most to do in the Poundian urge to "make
it new" (106). This relationship to the male literary tradition is seen in
"Tradition and the Individual Talent," as well as in Pound's persistent

rejection of the American in favor of the European. This tradition relies on metaphors of the male body, like Pound's theory of creativity as an "upspurt of sperm" and his conception of the brain as a "clot of genital fluid." For Williams this exclusive privilege given to the male body is problematic. As Conrad points out in *Refiguring America,* Pound continually attempted to stand as Williams's literary father, and Williams resisted: "he had indeed rebelled against this symbolic father [Pound], developing a theory of literary creativity that replaced a sterile and didactic father with a fecund and iconoclastic mother" (107). For Williams it is only through "fertilizing contact" with the female body that a poet is engendered.

The need for the female is caused by the sterile Puritan legacy that denied her sexuality and labeled her body "evil": "The characteristic of American life is that it holds off from embraces . . . while the spirit, with tongue hanging out, bites at its bars—its object just out of reach" (Williams, *American Grain,* 175). In what seems a striking departure from literary anorexia, this is a desiring, not a transcendent, spirit. It is the physical materiality that is transcendent and "holds off" while the spirit hungers "with [its] tongue hanging out." The spirit, not the body, hungers. For Williams this hunger derives from the inheritance of starvation brought about by the Puritan anorexic ethos and denial of the body, particularly the female body.

In seeming opposition to Eliot and Pound, for Williams the hunger created by the Puritans creates the poetic desire to do something non-anorexic. In the preface to *In the American Grain,* Williams writes of the desire to "separate out from the original records some flavor of an actual peculiarity the character denoting shape which the unique force has given. . . . it has been my wish to draw from every source one thing, the strange phosphorus of the life, nameless under an old misappellation."[55] Williams's urge to "draw from every source one thing" is the logical counterpart of the desire to "rename the things seen." It has its telos in the discovery of the true character hidden by a misnaming that has made that character "nameless." His insistence on "no ideas but in things" also affirms the necessity of poetry. There are for Williams no authentic things except poetic things: "the poet thinks with his poem, in that lies his thought, and that in itself is the profundity."[56] It is only through "thinking with the poem" that the true character comes out of hiding, that the "strange phosphorus of life" can be named.

In contrast to the inauthentic legacy that the Puritans and puritanical poets offered, their denial of that "strange phosphorus of life," Williams finds a new "source" in the figure of the Jesuit minister Père Rasles, who was not afraid to "touch." Instead of the Puritans in their "hypocrisy, bigotry, encroachment, fraud, violence, and bloodshed," there was "Père Rasles, a spirit, rich, blossoming, generous, able to give and to receive, full of taste, a nose, a tongue, a laugh, enduring, self-forgetful in beneficence—a new spirit in the New World. All that will be new in America will be anti-Puritan. It will be of another root. . . . Contrary to the English, Rasles recognized the New World. It stands out in all he says. It is a living flame compared to their dead ash" (*American Grain*, 120). Although he claims that Rasles and his method comes from "another root," for Williams, as well as Kafka, Eliot, and Pound, "living flame" is important as a trope for the cultural products that shape history. But here the flame derives from sexual consummation, rather than purgation; from burning up, consuming, incorporating, rather than eliminating altogether. Rasles is "another root" because unlike the Puritans, who leave nothing but "dead ash," who "sterilize, draw back, fear, dry up, and rot," he is a disseminating figure who will "create, hybridize, cross-pollenize" (121) through his adoption of the Native American language and acceptance of their customs, his blending of their culture with his. Such a "marrying" of different strands characterizes Williams's own poetic method in *Paterson*, which incorporates personal letters, newspaper clippings, and prose passages—all under the aegis of poetry. His narrative is incorporated into "an image large enough to embody the whole knowable world," which includes "the whites of their eyes, [the] very smells" of his subjects (*Paterson*, iii).

"That," Williams says, "is the poet's business. Not to talk in vague categories but to write particularly, as a physician works, upon a patient, upon the thing before him, in the particular to discover the universal." This statement contains both the idea of the narrative coiled within the image, a universal cultural text within the individual, and the trope of poet as physician, who has the ability to diagnose and treat his patient. "The patient" is the previous (inadequate) mythological roots of culture. Williams's characteristic method is to diagnose the problem and then offer some kind of alternative as a restorative "cure."

The parallel to the Père Rasles passages and the enactment of his restorative tropes—the restoration of life to the corpse of American culture—can be seen in the fire sequences in "The Library" section of *Paterson*. For if Père Rasles is "a living flame, another root," this "living flame" is demonstrated in *Paterson* when

> An old bottle, mauled by the fire
> gets a new glaze, the glass warped
> to a new distinction, reclaiming the
> undefined. . . .
>
> . . . . . .
>
> the flame that wrapped the glass
> deflowered, reflowered there by
> the flame. (118)

Through language the flame deflowers and reflowers, destroys and creates simultaneously, disassociates and binds in order to create a singular perspective that incorporates everything. The fire that mauls, providing a new glaze, is associated with the poetic imagination in Williams. The fire is parallel to the roar of the Falls in "The Delineaments of the Giants," the

> water pouring still
> from the edge of the rocks, filling
> his ears with its sound, hard to interpret. (*Paterson*, 17)

The phrase "hard to interpret" marks Williams's sense of the insufficiency of poetic language, its inability to bridge or leap—"the word . . . drained of its meaning" (17)—in the moment of articulation. Once the roar of fire or water is fixed, its plentitude of meaning disappears. Meaning is always potential, never fulfilled. Similarly, Rasles, for all his disseminating power, is killed by his enemies "at the foot of his rude cross which he had erected in the center of his village— seeking to draw the fire of the enemy upon himself" (*American Grain*, 127). He dies once he has erected a signifier of his belief, just as Sam Patch bungles his leap as soon as he has found the words that will give that leap meaning. For Williams, then, although the "strange phosphorus of life" is accessible only through a destructive act, the "keeping/a secret joy in the flame which we dare/not acknowledge," once that joy is acknowledged and "the fire become[s] the person" (*Paterson*, 121–22) or the imagination becomes the poet, this necessitates a burden of signification that is often too much. The poet fails to embody the "strange phosphorus" of history because that history is unpredictable and exceeds him. History is also a force comparable to the roar of the fire or the Falls. As much as Williams would like to provide a diagnosis and remedy, to discover the particular in the universal and "keep [the poem] whole," the search for alternative mythologies of history has to take unpredictability into account and can never claim a final authority.

If the poet fails in his ritual of embodiment, in Williams the failure is at least partially attributable to women who are sexual anorexics in both the symbolic and physical sense: "Women—givers (but they have been, as reservoirs, empty) perhaps they are being filled now. Hard to deal with in business, more conservative, closer to earth—the only earth. They are our cattle, cattle of the spirit—not yet come in" (*American Grain*, 181). Women's denial makes men anorexics and therefore not poets, "their shriek of starvation" for contact displaced onto the disembodied image of the movie screen. "The cattle of the spirit" who would supply fertility are too "conservative" despite the fact that they are "closer to earth." Williams has it both ways here: women are and are not anorexics, or they are anorexics because the Puritan tradition has taught them to deny their true earth-bound natures that give a poet vitality. Despite his differing relationship to the trope of woman as body, which the literal anorexic seeks to escape, Williams remains firmly in the logic that creates the cutting impulse in Eliot and Pound. The difference is that Williams wishes to incorporate the flesh, not differentiate himself from it.

Williams's gender ideologies in relation to the flesh and the question of literary production also pose a question about the poet as male. For Williams the poet figure cannot be female. The closest precedent for such a figure is a sex-starved spinster, an anorexic who was poetic due to her "starvation": "Emily Dickinson, starving of passion in her father's garden . . . starving" (179). By this he suggests that Dickinson approached poetry, precisely because she didn't make the usual transfer from father to husband and was thus forced to become poetically, rather than biologically, productive. The negative equation that Williams makes between women and poets is related to another historically based equation that subtly connects the female with "the mob" and feminizes the mass culture that modern poetry and art ostensibly define themselves against. Placed in opposition to the autonomous, discrete, self-present male subject, the female is interchangeable with others, a mob, an undifferentiated body:

> A man like a city and a woman like a flower
> —who are in love. Two women. Three women.
> Innumerable women, each like a flower.
>
> But
>
> only one man—like a city. (*Paterson*, 7)

The poet-figure, the city, is a presence unto himself, a metaphor clearly demarcated and differentiated. Women are an undifferentiated mass, an endless metonymy of flowers. This places Williams within a specific historical situation marked by a particular politics of gender as a politics of the mob. As Andreas Huyssen writes,

When the nineteenth and early twentieth centuries conjured up the threat of the masses "rattling at the gate," . . . and lamented the concomitant decline of culture and civilization (which mass culture was invariably accused of causing), there was yet another hidden subject. In the age of nascent socialism *and* the first major women's movement in Europe, the masses knocking at the gate were also women, knocking at the gate of a male dominated culture. It is indeed striking to observe how the political, psychological, and aesthetic discourse around the turn of the century consistently and obsessively genders mass culture and the masses as feminine, while high culture, whether traditional or modern, clearly remains the privileged realm of male activities.[57]

Just such a politics of the mob is clearly at work in *Paterson,* although to give Williams credit, he is less certain about any absolute separation from this mob than is Eliot or Pound. An instance of separation occurs in a prose passage in which Doc Paterson speaks. Paterson writes that he "was more concerned, much more concerned with detaching the label from a discarded mayonnaise jar, the glass jar in which some patient had brought a specimen for examination, than to examine and treat the twenty and more infants taking their turn from the outer office, their mothers tormented and jabbering" (*Patterson*, 33). The doctor, the discrete figure who is to treat the "twenty and more infants" accompanied by "jabbering" mothers, is also the poet figure who is to treat the clamoring world that surrounds him. Here, unlike Rasles whom Williams praises because of his willingness to live with "his beloved savages . . . TOUCHING them every day" (*American Grain*, 120), Doc Paterson would rather wash the mayonnaise jar than touch the yammering babies that are, along with their mothers, representative of the undifferentiated mass the poet-doctor must diagnose and treat.

Women, "millions" of them, as interchangeable flowers, do not produce the imaginative fire that separates the poet-doctor from them. Instead, they are the object of the transformative flame, which can turn their physical materiality into art, text, poem. Just as Eliot displaces the body of the woman onto the body of the river, transforming the physical into the textual body in "The Fire Sermon," Williams turns female bodies into interchangeable flowers both here and in the early "Queen Anne's Lace": "Her body is not so white as/anemone petals . . . It is a field of the wild carrot taking the field by force."[58] Only in language, safely made into flowers, can a female body take anything "by force." Women as material bodies wait for the flame to act upon their materiality:

> You lethargic, waiting upon me, waiting for
> the fire and I
> attendant upon you, shaken by your beauty
> Shaken by your beauty
> Shaken. (*Paterson*, 125)

Although momentarily "shaken" and incapable of action, the poet-doctor, always "attendant," is also "the fire" the woman-patient awaits to make her either biologically productive through "giving her a child" or poetically productive by turning her, along with the other "flowers," into a "beautiful thing." "Woman" is

> a furnace, a cavity aching
> toward fission; a hollow,
> a woman waiting to be filled. (176)

She is also the "quiet group of singers" suddenly turned into "an infuriated mob" that can be directed by "the bravery of the Dean" (46). The Dean acts as a strong mediatory figure who can help give the mob form or at least break it into discrete entities to quiet its hysterical activity.

Because its members are undifferentiated, like the flowers that are all women, the mob also lacks imagination, unique outline, distinction:

> At the
> sanitary lunch hour packed woman to
> woman (or man to woman, what's the difference?)
> the flesh of their faces gone
> to fat or gristle, without recognizable
> outline, fixed in rigors, adipose or sclerosis
> expressionless, facing one another, a mould
> for all faces (canned fish). (166)

Here Williams demonstrates the specificity of his connection to the anorexic impulse: the mob is figured as "fat." Fat obscures outlines, differences, demarcations. It blurs boundaries and distorts clear lines. Within the mob as "fat," part of what is frightening is that characteristics like sexual difference collapse, "woman to woman (or man to woman, what's the difference?)"; and in that collapse, the mob repeats the interchangeability of women. "Packed" like "canned fish," the mob loses its "recognizable outline," or, to invoke Huyssen again, "[T]he fear of the masses in this age of declining liberalism is always also a fear of woman, a fear of nature out of control, a fear of the unconscious, of sexuality, of the loss of identity and stable ego boundaries in the mass" ("Mass Culture as Woman," 196). Without "stable ego boundaries," "one man" can no longer be the "city" (poet-culture) that defines itself in opposition to the "innumerable women, each like a flower" (nature, more explicitly, poetic flower-nature).

Retaining this need for distinction, Williams is sympathetic toward women and "the people" only from a distance. Although his poetry gives them voice in a way that Eliot and Pound only satirize, that voice is ultimately contained, directed, and "filled" by that of Williams, the poet-doctor who can provide treatment and fill the lacks and gaps in the mob's collective imagination. This, in turn, gives him a place in the history and tradition he wishes to remake. Although Williams engages with the woman-mob as an impetus for poetic genesis, he avoids specific alignment or identification with it because to do so would be to lose his identity as a poet. He would become, in effect, "fat." Williams's work is both different from and characteristic of the high modern anorexic poetic politics. In his relation to the mob, Williams, who started out nonanorexically as one who embraces the female flesh as a topos for literary productivity, becomes anorexic in the tradition of Eliot and Pound, one of resistance to the dominant culture as embodied by the mob.

Chapter Three

"Should Be Out of It"

Starving the Feminine in Joseph Conrad

> Conrad can never say what it is he wants to say, all his
> things end in a kind of hunger, a suggestion of something
> he can't say or do or think. So his books always look bigger
> than they are. He's as much a giant of the subjective as
> Kipling is of the objective.
>
> T. E. Lawrence

As a feminist critic, I've often been asked why I read Joseph Conrad.
What could a writer infamous for his characterizations of women (or
lack of them), a writer praised for concentrating on a "masculine
world where . . . little is left of the distracting, enigmatic world of
women," have to offer a feminist reader?[1] If that feminist is also someone who has internalized the anorexic logic, is male identified and
more comfortable in a "masculine world," Conrad's early work offers
an escape from gender through its reification of anorexic beliefs. For
an anorexic, Conrad is a comforting friend, a soul mate. If an anorexic
logic informs the subtext of theories of literary production and gender
configuration in Kafka, Eliot, Pound, and Williams, in Conrad this
logic verges on the obsessive. While an anorexic style does not characterize his finished products, in his letters and in his method of composition Conrad shows similar preoccupations with the body and literary
genesis. In his early work the anorexic logic functions to determine
relations between textual subjects and their experiences of their bodies. Characters, such as Marlow in *Heart of Darkness*, create themselves at least partially from the pressure of the anorexic logic. They
are made and remade by it—it is part of the "life of their own" that

Conrad attributes to those characters. When Conrad speaks of Marlow as a separate person, "[T]he man Marlow and I came together in the casual manner of those health-resort acquaintances which sometimes ripen into friendships," he alludes to the way in which Marlow's subjectivity is constituted before us through his own agency.[2] Conrad's work is concerned with the process of self-constitution through the internalization of cultural codes about the body, the anorexic logic of policing oneself, and how that policing is given narrative authority. In their self-creation through the anorexic logic, Conrad's early subjects present an aestheticized version of the anorexic's self-creation. Conrad's characters are aesthetic projections of an anorexic subjectivity that helps to shape the narrative authority that demarcates and creates the boundaries that form the text.

The most significant difference between Conrad and the writers examined in the second chapter is that instead of eliminating the personal as an ideal for the production of art, Conrad incorporates it. As Ian Watt writes of *The Nigger of the "Narcissus,"* "[T]he creative method . . . is characteristically personal without being directly autobiographical. . . . since T. E. Hulme and the Imagists we have demanded . . . hardness of outline, exactness of diction. . . . Conrad uses every device of sound and sense for the very opposite purpose."[3] Indeed, instead of the characteristic "hardness," Conrad often uses a method of narration most readily exemplified in the famous passage from *Heart of Darkness* where the first narrator explains to Marlow that "the meaning of an episode was not inside like a kernel but outside, enveloping the tale which brought it out only as a glow brings out a haze."[4] J. Hillis Miller calls this method "parabolic narration," a form in which Conrad's expressed goal to "make [the reader] see" is actually predicated upon its impossibility or failure.[5] That Conrad is sensitive to this failure marks him as a different kind of "anorexic" from those in the second chapter. Using sometimes overwritten, repetitive, or obscure language, he seems one of those modern writers whose method is characterized by too much language and the failure of clear definition. A contemporary review of Conrad's second novel, *An Outcast of the Islands,* sounds a good deal like the frame narrator's description of Marlow: "Mr. Conrad is wordy: his story is not so much told as seen intermittently through a haze of sentences. His style is like a river-mist."[6] None of Conrad's narrators can ever quite get it right, a failure that generates the necessity for more language and more stories, not less.

If Conrad's writing is not structurally anorexic, then how is anorexia important to a discussion of it? In his work the anorexic logic explicitly designates narrative authority. It manifests itself on one level in the description of characters, whose fatness or thinness seems to brand them as either despicable or heroic, obtuse or enlightened. Winnie, Verloc, and Michaelis—indeed, nearly every character in *The Secret Agent*—are described with a narrative horror of their corpulence, while characters in albeit precarious positions of enlightenment like Kurtz and Marlow are characteristically thin. As in Kafka, along with thinness comes a detachment from the ordinary world of human affairs, an abstention from the usual modes of human intercourse, particularly sexual modes. Fatness and lack of imagination verging on stupidity are repeatedly equated, as with Captain MacWhirr's "thick figure" that belays the fact that "it was, in truth, as impossible for him to take a flight of fancy as it would be for a watchmaker to put together a chronometer with nothing except a two-pound hammer and a whip-saw in the way of tools."[7]

In Conrad, thickness of body equals thickness of mind. The narrator, a doctor, in "Amy Foster" describes Yankoo Goorall in a way that makes the equation explicit: "One would think the earth is under a curse, since of all her children these that cling to her the closest are uncouth in body and as leaden of gait as if their very hearts were loaded with chains. But here on this same road you might have seen amongst these heavy men a being lithe, supple, and long-limbed, straight like a pine, with something striving upwards in his appearance as though the heart within him had been buoyant"(*"Typhoon" and Other Tales*, 326). In a logic that seems distinctly Platonic, in this passage to "cling" to the earth is to have no imagination, physically figured in the "uncouth" bodies of the "heavy men" with "leaden" gaits. Lack of imagination is signaled by material bulk, spreading flesh, fatness. In beings who are "lithe, supple, and long-limbed, straight like a pine," there is no corporeality to weigh down the heart and mind but "something striving upwards" that indicates a buoyant heart, a greater soul. Fatness indicates dullness and limitation; thinness, a

sharpening of the senses and a desire to strive beyond the merely corporeal.

In Conrad, unlike the writers treated earlier, fat is not necessarily
equated with the feminine on the level of character. Rather, the feminine is philosophically constituted as that which should be "kept out."
Males and females are fat in Conrad, and those characterizations are
his most ambivalent and sometimes very negative, like the "flabby stupidity" of the "robust anarchist" Ossipon in *The Secret Agent*.[8] Fatness
is the sign of some fatal flaw, or lack, or form of corruption and inefficiency, as with the metaphor of the "flabby devil" to describe the imperialist project in *Heart of Darkness*. On this symbolical level fat becomes gendered. Although there may be men who are fat, and who
possess the moral qualities associated with fatness, the early Conrad
explicitly opposes fatness and its attendant qualities to his ideal masculine universe.

This ideal, like those of many of his contemporaries, is linked with
a rejection and mistrust of materiality, a prevalent attitude that reflected the changing economic circumstance of the period. Materiality, in the form of goods and bodies, had become opposed to intellectual and spiritual values and thereby degraded. As Conrad writes to
his friend R. B. Cunningham Grahame, with whom he exchanged
many deeply distressed letters, "You with your ideals of sincerity,
courage and truth are strangely out of place in this epoch of material
preoccupations."[9] Conrad voices a preoccupation characteristic of his
historical period, in which industrialization, mass production, and the
advent of the department store had permanently changed the cultural
horizon. Materiality was seen as expanding dangerously, as voraciously devouring the hearts, wills, and ambitions of those who had
"sincerity, courage and truth." Expansion of the body reflected "material preoccupations," and women—who were conventionally associated with the material, rather than the spiritual—therefore became
in this period even more threatening. When the women's movement
of the twentieth century's second decade publicly advocated birth
control and discussed female sexuality for the first time, the Victorian
"angel in the house" took on frightening bodily dimensions.[10]

Historians like Roberta Pollack Seid explain the development responsible for attitudes such as Conrad's: "between 1880 and 1920 life

in America and western Europe was revolutionized, propelling society into the modern age. Industrialization, mechanization, and mass production produced the systems, the perceptions, the mentality, and the artifacts of the present: the bicycle, the streetcar, the automobile, the airplane, and the phonograph, moving pictures, and the telephone."[11] These innovations produced what seemed like an overwhelming availability of material goods, a reduction in the need for physical labor, and an increase in leisure. But along with these new conveniences came an anxiety about the deterioration of intellectual and spiritual values that were forgotten in the seemingly vast onslaught of material progress. Suddenly, there were goods to acquire, and time that might have formerly been spent in intellectual improvement was devoted to their acquisition. Furthermore, technological innovations that eliminated the need for physical labor contributed to an anxiety that the body would become useless, turned from a productive machine into an inert, spreading blob without form or function.[12] All these factors led to an anxiety about the flesh and materiality in general that appeared in modernist texts like Conrad's early work. This anxiety further exacerbated the opposition between masculine and feminine that had, with the possible exception of the Victorian period, gendered materiality as feminine. Materiality, progress, and all the values associated with them were nearly the opposite of the intense skepticism that Conrad espoused as "the tonic of minds, the tonic of life, the agent of truth—the way of art and salvation."[13] In this view, a skepticism toward the body would refine, cut, and purify it in the same way that intellectual skepticism cuts through its objects.

As in the writing examined in the second chapter, Conrad's early work sacrifices materiality and femininity (as figured in the body) for the discipline of artistic form. Through self-discipline conceived as the sacrifice of those qualities, artistic form is realized. For Conrad, in accordance with the Nietzschean tradition, art is purchased at the cost of personal agony: "Suffering is an attribute, almost a condition of greatness, of devotion, of an altogether self-forgetful sacrifice to that remorseless fidelity to the truth of his own sensations, at whatever cost of pain and contumely, which for me is the whole Credo of the artist."[14] Self-forgetfulness means to Conrad subordinating personal emotion to the "truth of . . . sensations." Comfort in personal life is sacrificed for art. In his biography *Joseph Conrad,* Jeffrey Meyers reports, before finishing *The Nigger of the "Narcissus,"* "[Conrad] said that he could not eat, suffered from nightmares and terrified his wife" (171). Often complaining about the "torment" of writing and therefore not eating or sleeping, as well as suffering from a variety of illnesses mostly nervous in nature, like Kafka, Conrad sees himself as exchanging bodily comfort for art.[15] In his letters he constantly complains about "my wretched health" and describes how art brings this on: "I am haunted, mercilessly haunted, by the *necessity* of style. And that story I can't write weaves itself into all I see, into all I speak, into all I think. . . . I am distinctly conscious of the contents of my head. My story is there in a fluid—in an evading shape."[16] Writing, the need to produce form, was for Conrad an ongoing physical torment, something he "wrenched out" of the "fluid" and chaos of his mind. His health was a necessary sacrifice. Since fluidity is conventionally associated with femininity, predictably Conrad envisions his unformed stories as "evading shape[s]" flowing through his brain.[17] Like the trope of the elusive, enigmatic woman, the material of his stories, initially fluid and chaotic, produces in Conrad a sense of "the *necessity* of style" to give them solid form. The privilege given to style and form as a higher necessity than the physical has obvious gender connotations. Aristotle wrote about semen as the tool that shapes the fetus, "in the male of those animals which emits semen, Nature uses the semen as a tool just as tools are used in the products of any art. . . . such is the way in which these males contribute to generation."[18] At least since then, style and form, gendered masculine, have been seen to shape and create art from base matter, gendered feminine. Conrad was no exception.

If Conrad's relationship to the feminine was problematic in his work, his relationship to actual women was even worse. In the estimation of most critics Conrad's literary and actual affiliations with women were notorious. In his own life he had little interaction with them. With the exceptions of his wife, Jessie, the journalist Jane Anderson, and the writer Marguerite Poradowski, who probably served as the model for Marlow's aunt in *Heart of Darkness,* Conrad appears to have had few women acquaintances or friends.[19] There is a theory that Conrad was hostile to women because his mother had died when he was seven, creating intense feelings of abandonment; and his relationship to his wife seems to have been an extremely conventional one.[20] Soon after his marriage, Conrad writes in a letter to Edward Garnett that "I have ordered her to get everything ready for work there in a week's time. Her efforts are superhuman. I sit still and grumble." Jessie herself describes what happened: "He had written the most minute instructions. I was to be ready dressed for the evening and taking my ease in the drawing-room three days after the arrival of the furniture; the new maid was to be instructed to answer his ring and show him into the room; the meal was to appear; he was to be shown to his study." When Jessie, excited by his arrival, answers the door herself, she is criticized for not following instructions to the letter: "Unable to restrain myself, I dashed to the door to receive him. . . . He received me coldly, and began to reproach me with concentrated bitterness. . . . There followed some really painful criticisms, sweeping condemnations, indeed, of all or nearly all I had done."[21] Clearly, Conrad had an English gentleman's conception of household decorum. In the book Jessie published after his death, she fully accepts her role as a conventional homemaker and mother figure, and seems to sense that this is the only way in which Conrad needs her: "I remember him once telling me that . . . he perceived very soon [after the wedding] that the young girl, now his wife, could not only take care of herself but also knew how to take care of him; and then he understood the blessedness of the married state."[22] If indeed Conrad relied on his wife as much as he seemed to, this reliance shows his dependence upon what he marginalized. Although their relationship as it is articulated in the letters does seem to have been based on a genuine affection, it seems that this affection was dependent upon Jessie's unquestioning acceptance of a role as caretaker and unpaid domestic servant. In the Conrad household the unquestioned ideology of separate spheres structured their daily relations. Watt writes, a little wistfully, in *Conrad in the Nineteenth Century* that "the marital record of the great modern writers falls sadly short of any ringing endorsement of the new models of sexual fulfillment and human freedom which they and their century proposed" (71). The best that can be said for Conrad is that, unlike some of the others, at least he didn't "get up any pretty fictions about it."[23]

Jessie Conrad was often attacked by her husband's friends, and a good deal of their ammunition seems to derive from the fact that she was fat. At five feet two inches she weighed more than two hundred pounds toward the end of her life. Although she looks slim in pictures taken during the period when Conrad was courting her, the birth of two children and an accident that damaged her knees seriously restricted her mobility and led to considerable weight gain. The period's prejudice against fat, comparable to our own, is reflected in the comments of Conrad's friends. Lady Ottoline Morrell reported that "[Jessie] seemed a nice and good-looking fat creature, an excellent cook . . . and was indeed a good and reposeful mattress for this hypersensitive, nerve-wrecked man, who did not ask from his wife high intelligence, only an assuagement of life's vibrations." Although the picture of Conrad offered here is not complimentary either, it is clear that Jessie as a "fat creature" is linked to the idea of Jessie as a "good and reposeful mattress." The implicit suggestion in Morrell's comment is that fat women can only be mattresses, and that they are not intelligent but only good to cushion and assuage. Virginia Woolf's assessment of Jessie as Conrad's "lump of a wife" is more explicit: fat women have no form or shape, and are therefore decidedly unaesthetic. H. G. Wells's description of Jessie as "a Flemish thing from the mud flats" makes a connection between obesity and the lower classes, which was emerging at the time, as well as the connection between the fat body and the formlessness of mud.[24] Conrad never mentions an aversion to his wife's weight, but the recurrence of fat as a negative motif in his texts suggests that he could not have felt positively about it. As he seems to have felt affectionately toward her as a capable but not very intelligent domestic caretaker, it is quite possible that in such a capacity her weight would not have been a cause for complaint. It perhaps served as a pretext for the distance and lack of intimacy shown in their rigid role playing.

If Conrad was not exemplary in his actual relationships with women, his literary characterizations of them have long been under attack. As Watt writes in *Conrad in the Nineteenth Century,*

Conrad's works deal much less than those of most novelists with women, love, sex, and marriage; most of his critics have felt that where Conrad attempted these subjects he failed; and several have connected this with his own unresolved sexual conflicts. . . . His works tend to reflect the nautical mythology which divides women into two wholly separate categories—the idealised asexual mother figures, and the venal sexual aggressors. (69)

It is true that in the early work, women occur infrequently and are given problematic roles such as Aissa's as the agency of male destruction in *An Outcast of the Islands,* or as competitors in the melodramatic love triangle between Nostromo, Giselle, and Linda. On certain levels it is clear in the early work that anything with a feminine connotation must be "kept out," as in Marlow's infamous injunction that women "should be out of it," or as in Conrad's critical advice on his friend Norman Douglas's manuscript: "What is that woman doing in here? Take her out!"[25] Ruth L. Nadelhaft has recently argued that "through . . . women characters . . . Conrad chose to express some of his most penetrating scepticism and criticism about the social and political order of Western Europe . . . from the beginning of his career," but she is alone in this estimation. Most feminist critics see Conrad, through his representations of women, as affirming imperialist ideologies he otherwise critiques.[26] Furthermore, a long critical tradition that has privileged Conrad's early work and praised it for its purgation of femininity has led us to mostly read the early writing and ignore the later work that does not participate in this purge. Thomas Moser's reading, which largely established the "achievement and decline" theory of Conrad's work, speculates about "why Conrad, rather than subordinating women and love in the full-length novels, did not *cut them out altogether and produce only perfect works* [emphasis added] like *The Nigger of the 'Narcissus'* and 'The Secret Sharer'"[27] Moser's idea of perfection, then, seems characteristically anorexic: perfection in artistic terms is achieved through "cut[ting women] out altogether."

I. Text over Flesh: Heart of Darkness
and the Fat Man

Go, ... and when you have found the land
where there is happiness and where there are
no women, send me its latitude and longitude;
and I will join you there.

George Bernard Shaw,
Heartbreak House

The definitive structural characteristic of anorexic thinking seems its
protest against or criticism of a social structure that participates in
and reinforces the very construction it resists. The anorexic takes a
complicated network of social meanings and codes about her body as
female and internalizes them, believes them, misrecognizes them as
truth. As we have seen, because those codes are, as Noelle Caskey
writes, part of "the cultural and biological interrelationship of fat and
femininity,"[28] the body that is rejected as fat is also rejected as female.
Women biologically have a higher percentage of body fat than men,
which is necessary to maintain secondary sex characteristics. Due to
this seemingly inevitable biological fact, fat becomes coded as one of
the primary definitions of femaleness.[29] In itself, the biology of a
higher fat percentage has no significance. But as it is represented,
encoded, and understood in sources that range from health maga-
zines to advertisements for diet soda, weight loss programs, or Coors
beer, fat is an utterly repellant substance responsible for everything
from lowered self-esteem to loss of love and sexual attractiveness to
physical well-being.[30] As Wolf writes, fat is portrayed as "expendable
female filth, virtually cancerous matter, an inert or treacherous infil-
tration into the body of nauseating bulk waste."[31] This representation
helps to form the views of countless women and girls who, like some
of my students, define *abstemious* as "being able to refrain from
eating in order to lose weight." The way misrecognition is central to
the narrative of *Heart of Darkness* is structurally very similar to the
misrecognition seen in anorexics, who accept the pejorative definitions of fat and femininity as truth. These are definitions the text also
seems to accept.

Of the early works, *Heart of Darkness* is one of the most explicit in its use of body weight as a sign system. Even though Marlow exclaims that "it seems to me I am trying to tell you a dream—making a vain attempt" (30), showing that *Heart of Darkness* is concerned with the failure of signs, one system not questioned in the text is the imagery of fatness and thinness.[32] The connection between fat and everything threatening to the masculine order marks one place in which the narratorial perspectives of Marlow and the frame narrator converge. Marlow's narrative undercuts the frame narrator's naive praise of the imperialist project as "bearing the sword, and often the torch, messengers of the might within the land, bearers of a spark from the sacred fire" (8). Yet, his position as enlightened storyteller who "felt so sure they could not possibly know the things I knew" (70) corresponds to the frame narrator's description of Marlow as having "sunken cheeks . . . a straight back, an ascetic aspect, and with his arms dropped, the palms of hands outwards, [he] resembled an idol" (7). Marlow in effect becomes the bearer of his own torch, one that claims to illuminate and expose the hypocrisy of the first. The description of Marlow as an ascetic idol indicates that his words are authoritative. A long historical tradition equates ascetics and philosophical or religious sages, and Marlow is one of those figures whose outward thinness represents his intellectual sharpness.[33]

Marlow's narrative is a complicated interweaving of anorexic tropes that operate on several levels. In the way his anorexic logic is articulated, fat signifies a host of negatives. First, there is an equation between inefficiency and fat, between the imperialist project as barbaric and the fat bodies of its perpetrators. This equation is set up through a series of minor characters, the first of whom is encountered in the Company offices. A contrast is made between the secretary and the "great man," which marks the start of a pattern: "A door opened, a white-haired secretarial head, but wearing a compassionate expression, appeared, and a skinny forefinger beckoned me into the sanctuary" (14). The secretary is the one "compassionate" person Marlow comes across in this setting, and the seemingly innocuous detail of the "skinny forefinger" foreshadows this affiliation of skinniness and compassion in characters encountered later. In contrast to the compassionate secretary, "[F]rom behind [a heavy writing desk] came out an impression of pale plumpness in a frock-coat. The great man him-

self" (14). An "impression of pale plumpness" becomes Marlow's code
for everything that is inefficient, morally suspect, and even viciously
corrupt. The heavy writing desk mirrors the heaviness of the man behind it and, to a greater degree, the sluggishness and inefficiency of a
bureaucratic process that takes itself much too seriously, mistaking its
weight for importance.

This pattern is repeated so often in the text that it is impossible not
to see it as a preoccupation of Conrad's. Most often, those with whom
Marlow sympathizes are thin, and those with whom he does not are
fat. Early in the narrative, when he gets his first passage up the river,
Marlow's concern with inefficiency and immorality is shared by the
Swedish steamer captain. In his comments to Marlow he duplicates
what Marlow has just said: "'Fine lot these government chaps—are
they not?' he went on speaking English with great precision and considerable bitterness. 'It is funny what some people will do for a few
francs a month'" (18). Significantly, this captain whose perspective is
so close to Marlow's is described as "a young man, lean, fair, and morose" (18). The adjective "lean" comes to be nearly interchangeable
with "good" through repeated association, while "fat" is associated
with everything negative. Of the friend Marlow makes at the Central
Station, the man he dances with on the deck of his defunct steamer,
he says: "This was the foreman—a boiler-maker by trade—a good
worker. He was a lank bony yellow-faced man with big intense eyes"
(31). For Marlow, in his dedication to efficiency, "good worker" is the
highest compliment he can pay, and this approval is linked with the
foreman's "lank" boniness. In contrast, the Manager's uncle, the head
of the Eldorado Exploring Expedition, whose purpose, Marlow reports, was "to tear treasure out of the bowels of the land . . . with no
more moral purpose at the back of it than there is in burglars breaking
into a safe," "resembled a butcher in a poor neighbourhood and his
eyes had a look of sleepy cunning. He carried his fat paunch with
ostentation on his short legs" (32–33). There is an implicit connection
here between the "fat paunch" and the lack of "moral purpose." The
"pilgrims," Marlow's derogatory name for the Company workers that
accompany him downstream, have similar physiques. Again and
again, he uses descriptions like "a little fat man with sandy hair and
red whiskers" (41).

Marlow's implicit condemnation of fat can be connected to a transition in historical attitudes about body weight and its cultural significance. While in the early nineteenth century, weight and fat still stood for prosperity and power, by the late nineteenth century another attitude had emerged that equated body fat with corruption and laziness. Whereas historically thinness had signified scarcity, in a time of tremendous industrial expansion and rising standards of living, a fear of abundance developed.[34] According to Seid in *Never Too Thin,* "[T]echnological innovations, economic changes, and the ideology of efficiency all conspired to reinforce the slenderized ideal. The human body—both male and female—was to be as efficient, as effective, as economical, and as beautiful as the sleek new machines, as the rationalized workplace" (83). Despite what often seems an antiprogress, antiexpansionist stance, Marlow's body aesthetics and the qualities he takes the body to symbolize conform with this historical ideal.

Indeed, the ideology of efficiency is one of Marlow's strongest preoccupations, and as the thin body was taken to be much more efficient than the fat body, this has much to do with his preference. He repeatedly breaks into diatribes about the saving graces of efficiency and hard work, as in this characteristic passage: "I don't like work—no man does—but I like what is in the work—the chance to find yourself. Your own reality—for yourself—not for others—what no other man can ever know" (31). Marlow's most often-voiced complaint against the imperialist project is the inefficiency and laziness of its white participants, rather than its violence and cultural annihilation: "Th[eir] only real feeling was a desire to get appointed to a trading-post where ivory was to be had, so that they could earn percentages. They intrigued and slandered and hated each other only on that account—but as to effectually lifting a little finger—oh no" (27). Throughout the novel he dwells on inefficiency, and that inefficiency is indubitably equated with fat. At one point in his journey he mentions that he has "a white companion, not a bad chap, but rather too fleshy and with the exasperating habit of fainting on the hot hillsides miles away from the least bit of shade and water. Annoying, you know . . . I couldn't help asking him once what he meant by coming there at all. . . . he weighed sixteen stone" (23). Too much flesh is inefficient, "annoying," and makes one a burden. Marlow can't understand "what he meant by coming there at all," because efficiency demands a physical fitness that this "chap" lacks.

Inefficiency in the outposts and proceedings is immediately equated with what Marlow has named the "flabby devil": "On the fifteenth day, I . . . hobbled into the Central Station. . . . a neglected gap was all the gate it had, and the first glance at the place was enough to let you see the flabby devil was running that show" (24). The "flabby devil" becomes Marlow's controlling metaphor for the whole imperialist project. "I would become acquainted," he says, "with a flabby, pretending, weak-eyed devil of a rapacious and pitiless folly. How insidious he could be too" (20). Marlow has made flabbiness the figure for, the outward embodiment of, more inward characteristics that have moral connotations. Since *ravenous* and *voracious* are among the most common synonyms of *rapacious,* there is a clear connection between the devil's voracity and his flabbiness. Flabbiness is caused by morally flawed characteristics like voracity.

A necessary condition for efficiency in Marlow's narrative seems to be an anorexic attitude toward food, an ability to survive on little. He marvels that the Manager seems Manager only by virtue of his physical capacity for endurance, and he notes that "triumphant health in the general rout of constitutions is a kind of power in itself" (25). The Manager declares that "men who come out here should have no entrails," and Marlow gives him a grudging admiration for this, noting that with this utterance, "[Y]ou fancied you had seen things" (25). "No entrails," nothing coming in and nothing going out, seems the desired condition, signifying invulnerability and indestructability. Anorexics subscribe to this same ideal, which is a central part of the logic of the disease. If one had "no entrails" one would not have to eat. By not eating, anorexics deny they have entrails, and, by extension, that they have bodies at all. They see their ability not to eat as a form of power over their own bodies and the world around them.[35] It is this logic the Manager makes use of, whether he is anorexic or not. He further uses the ordering of food as a means of obtaining and maintaining power: "When annoyed at meal-times by the constant quarrels of the white men about precedence he ordered an immense round table to be made for which a special house had to be built. This was the station's mess room. Where he sat was the first place—the rest were nowhere"

(25). The Manager solves the question of precedence neatly through a hierarchical arrangement based on eating rituals, in which he occupies the head seat, reminding others of their dependence and vulnerability. Marlow articulates the traditional racist equation between blacks and embodiment, as well as his hierarchical assumptions, when he is further annoyed because, in addition to this reminder of the workers' dependence on the Manager for food, the Manager "allow[s] his 'boy'—an overfed young negro from the coast—to treat the white men, under his very eyes, with provoking insolence" (25). Fatness and the control of food operate here according to two symbolical systems: the earlier, that it signifies prosperity and power; and the later, that it signifies insolence and moral failure. Marlow's comment here is anti-fat as well as racist, pointing to his overwhelming prejudice toward fatness and all the things that it signifies to him. To an extreme degree, literal anorexics have internalized the sign system that Marlow uses in the text.

The antifat sign system Marlow deploys seems shared by his audience, for the frame narrator begins to emphasize what those on the ship experience as Marlow's disembodiment. Through their acceptance of his narrative authority and the symbols he makes use of, Marlow becomes "no more . . . than a voice" to his audience (30). Whereas this point marks one of Marlow's crises of narrative authority where he is certain of his inability to communicate, his audience seems to feel otherwise. Although Marlow has just exclaimed that "it is impossible to convey the life-sensation of any given epoch of one's existence," the frame narrator reports that "I listened on the watch for the sentence, for the word that would give me the clue to the faint uneasiness inspired by this narrative that seemed to shape itself without human lips in the heavy night air of the river" (30). Just as Marlow feels that Kurtz "presented himself as a voice" (48), the frame narrator feels the same way about Marlow and has the same faith in Marlow that Marlow has in Kurtz—that he will be able to provide a clue to the "faint uneasiness." Marlow seeks Kurtz because "I was curious to see whether this man who had come out equipped with moral ideas of some sort would climb to the top after all and how he would set about his work when there" (33). Here the frame narrator looks to Marlow to give a similar kind of answer: How would someone who has experienced all this interpret it? What answers would he have? Despite the fact that Marlow seems disembodied, because it has grown dark, this sense of disembodiment has much further significance. In *Heart of Darkness,* when audiences grant narrative authority, when they have come to see speakers as bearers of truth, they experience that authority as disembodied. For the frame narrator and Marlow, authoritative voices don't have bodies.

Marlow, despite all evidence to the contrary, designates Kurtz as an anorexic ideal of bodiless existence. He equates this ideal with a higher morality, an "idea at the back of it" that can "redeem" what seems immoral (10). He explains that "I had never imagined [Kurtz] as doing, you know, but as discoursing. I didn't say to myself 'Now I will never see him,' or 'Now I will never shake him by the hand,' but, 'Now I will never hear him'" (48). When Kurtz dies, Marlow still persists in saying, "[T]he voice was gone. What else had been there? But I am of course aware that next day the pilgrims buried something in a muddy hole" (69). He can only experience Kurtz's corpse as an abstract "something"; what is real to Marlow is "the voice." Kurtz, like the rest of the "flabby devils," is described as so "voracious" that it seemed as though he "had wanted to swallow all the air, all the earth, all the men before him." Yet he is "lank and with an uplifted arm . . . I could see the cage of his ribs all astir, the bones of his arm waving." From this description, clearly Marlow sees him as essentially different from the rest of the"rapacious" imperialists (59). In Marlow's sign system, lack of restraint leads to the pilgrims' paucity, as well as their deficient morality; and Kurtz also has "no restraint . . . a tree swayed by the wind" (51). Still, he escapes Marlow's condemnation and becomes his "choice of nightmares" (62). If one must have a nightmare, at least it shouldn't be fat. Since Kurtz's thinness makes him sufficiently superior in Marlow's eyes, Marlow sometimes forgets that "Mr. Kurtz lacked restraint in the gratification of his various lusts, that there was something wanting in him" (57). The fact that Kurtz has "no body" to a large extent dictates Marlow's "choice." He explains that all Kurtz's activity, all his acquisition of ivory that the others spoke so much about, was nothing, that "of all his gifts the one that stood out preeminently, that carried with it a sense of real presence, was his ability to talk, his words" (48). Paradoxically, what conveys a sense of "presence" to Marlow is not physical presence but words experienced as coming from a disembodied voice.

This perception of Kurtz mirrors the frame narrator's perception of Marlow, and each break in the narrative is filtered through a kind of screen that detaches words from body to produce more words. It seems necessary to obfuscate the body to generate the words. The second time Marlow experiences narrative crisis, the frame narrator's words (there are no words describing *his* body, so he is always a voice) replace Marlow's and return to his physicality: "Then a match flared, and Marlow's lean face appeared worn, hollow, with downward folds and dropped eyelids with an aspect of concentrated attention" (48). Although Marlow's "lean face" is a sign of his learned experience and marks a difference between him and his listeners, this description makes him more than a voice. When Marlow is silent, his body appears. When he speaks, his body disappears. To speak, the text suggests, one must not eat. To tear the veil from the "surface of things," one must not eat. Marlow doubts that his words will signify, precisely because he equates the "good appetites" he attributes to his audience with a perspective that would make it impossible for them to understand what he has learned from Kurtz: "This is the worst of trying to tell . . . Here you all are each moored with two good addresses . . . excellent appetites, and temperature normal" (48). "Excellent appetites," among other things, mark the audience as firmly grounded in a world that has no proximity to truth, that is "out of it." From such a perspective, Marlow fears, it is impossible to understand what he is trying to tell, since this perspective has such a firm belief in the "events of the surface." Those who can see beyond the surface have poor appetites. While Marlow fears that these men of appetite will not understand or will reject him, they actually seem to accept his position as the "lean learned sage" who will reveal truth.

If Marlow is granted narrative authority within the text, that authority has been questioned on feminist grounds, as well as on issues of race.[36] In these readings he is seen as ultimately upholding the very values he claims to critique. In her article "Too Beautiful Altogether," Johanna M. Smith argues that *Heart of Darkness* is "a story about manly adventure narrated and written by a man," and that "the collusion of imperialism and patriarchy [in] Marlow's narrative aims to 'col-

onize' and 'pacify' both savage darkness and women."[37] This colonization and pacification is achieved through Marlow's images of women
and "savages." These images tend to uphold imperialist and patriarchal stereotypes of the native cultures as "primitive" and of women as
"out of it." Nina Pelikan Strauss further sees *Heart of Darkness* as a
narrative predicated upon and made possible by the exclusion of
women. The text functions, in her view, as the establishment of a kind
of brotherhood between a male author, male characters, and male
readers.[38] I would add that those "brothers" are white, as the discussion of brotherhood in *Falk* makes clear. Both the image making that
Smith objects to and the exclusion that Strauss criticizes are explic-
able in terms of the anorexic logic I have analyzed. I argue elsewhere
that this attitude undergoes a shift in Conrad's work, and that the late
work is not as easily dismissed on these grounds. Conrad's ambivalence is readable even here, in *Heart of Darkness,* one of his first
works. Nadelhaft writes, referring to Marlow's disclaimer that "I don't
want to bother you much with what happened to me person-
ally"(*Heart of Darkness,* 11), that "the denigration of the 'personal' as
the proper subject for great literature haunts Conrad . . . This need
to disparage the personal and the specific nature of experience shapes
much of the prose style of *Heart of Darkness* and accounts for some
of its peculiar tension (*Joseph Conrad,* 44–45). Marlow's attempt to
attain and present a subjective and personal perspective that is also
transcendental, thereby claiming a privileged proximity to truth, is
part of the logic I call "anorexic." This posture results in the particular
images of women and natives he creates. Nadelhaft does not mention,
however, that Marlow's comment is then qualified by the frame narrator, who asserts that, in his devaluation of the personal, Marlow
"show[ed] in this remark the weakness of many tellers of tales who
seem so often unaware of what their audience would best like to hear"
(*Heart of Darkness,* 11). Clearly, Conrad was ambivalent toward the
idea that great literature is by definition impersonal and, as his later
work shows, toward the idea that such literature cannot include
women. The views expressed in *Heart of Darkness* align with the anorexic tradition that Smith and Strauss call "patriarchal." But the ideal
of impersonal literature, which is also a part of that logic, is questioned in Conrad's texts.

Most feminist readings that criticize Marlow focus on the four instances of discussion about or representation of women in the text.[39] *Heart of Darkness* reads as a nearly perfect demonstration of Lacan's "L-schema," in which a subject watches another subject unnoticed and assumes he has authority because of it, while he is in fact watched by someone else, whose watching calls that authority into question.[40] Marlow watches and critiques "the pilgrims" and their imperialist ideology, but as the L-schema demonstrates, we as readers watching Marlow observe that in his representations of women he replicates that same ideology. His fidelity to "the idea" that "redeems" the "conquest of the earth . . . [, which] is not a pretty thing when you look into it too much" (*Heart of Darkness*, 10), results in the famous lie to the Intended at the end of the novel, which keeps her "out of it" and thus maintains the order of the world as Marlow knows it. That world is ordered according to a strict separation by gender, a separation based on a theory of knowledge. In Marlow's designation of "haves" and "have nots," he ruminates that "it's queer how out of touch with truth women are. They live in a world of their own and there had never been anything like it and never can be. It is too beautiful altogether, and if they were to set it up it would go to pieces before the first sunset. Some confounded fact, we men have been living contentedly with ever since the day of creation, would start up and knock the whole thing over" (16). The attainment of truth, in Marlow's estimation, involves being "men enough to face the darkness" (10), and women are "out of it" (49), presumably because they lack the necessary "manliness." Their world is based on fantasy, not knowledge, a world created in opposition to "confounded fact[s]" and maintained only through ignorance. A further complication of Marlow's truth is that since nonwhites are themselves the essential "darkness" for Marlow, their access to truth is never a consideration.

Marlow's truth replicates the Victorian ideology of separate spheres, in which the white woman's role is to create a realm of domestic bliss to which the white man can return and recover from the brutality of the world of commerce.[41] Nonwhites, like the "overfed . . . negro from the coast" or the "native woman" whom the accountant forces to starch his shirts or Marlow's cannibal helmsman, exist only to serve. Marlow has some doubts about women but pushes social roles to the level of ontology, creating a seemingly unquestionable equation of women with nontruth and delusion that he finds in Kurtz's painting of "a woman draped and blindfolded carrying a lighted torch" (27). Yet the blindfold is significant, since it implies that it has been placed there—that female blindness is not innate but created. As the narrative proceeds, what seemed an absolute ontological statement becomes an ideology that it is necessary to impose: "Girl! What? Did I mention a girl? Oh, she is out of it—completely. They—the women I mean—are out of it—should be out of it. We must help them to stay in that beautiful world of their own lest ours gets worse" (49). Marlow's confusion at this point stems from the fact that he is working within a paradox. This passage immediately follows his sense of narrative failure, through which he realizes that "the worst of trying to tell" is that he is attempting to communicate to persons of "excellent appetite" an alien, anorexic perspective that he has learned from Kurtz. "Excellent appetite" marks their comfortable grounding in the world of "neighbors and policemen," a perspective that he is attempting to change by educating them.

Yet Marlow concurrently espouses the continuation of the very ideas that his narrative destroys. He breaks from what he thinks is a vain attempt to communicate a different perspective to a more strident insistence upon the ideology of separate spheres. This division is part of the very perspective he wants to break apart to communicate his truth. In the process of breaking he perhaps inadvertently indicates that the idea that women are "out of it" is itself ideological, and that he must come up with a story to explain it. Storytelling and image making, as he well knows through his criticism of the pilgrims' narrative that names the natives "rebels" and "enemies," help to create and impose ideology. The story becomes an interpretation that is mistaken for truth. Although Marlow sees and reveals imperialist ideology in images like the "bundles of acute angles" (21) that is an African worked to death by imperialist conquerors, he mistakes such barbarity as a necessary condition for human "civilization." He sees brutality as a truth that many are not "man enough" to face. But this is an interpretation of events that he misrecognizes, mistakes for necessity or truth.

This misrecognition leads him to assert that women "should be out of it." If the truth is that "civilization" is based upon the savagery of conquering "those with slightly flatter noses than ourselves," then the image of the "sombre and polished sarcophagus" that Marlow uses to describe the grand piano in the Intended's drawing room is appropriate, in his view, to this self-consuming society of cannibals who prey upon each other. Since the etymology of the word *sarcophagus* derives from the Greek word for "flesh eater," the piano, that embodiment of refined culture whose keys are made from the ivory extracted from the jungle by savage means, is the appropriate image for Marlow's truth. He becomes "anorexic" through insisting upon this truth in which he does not want to participate. He does not want to eat the flesh, to traffic with the imperialism he disparages. He does not want to participate in what he now sees as the process of "people hurrying through the streets to filch a little money from each other, to devour their infamous cookery, to gulp their unwholesome beer, to dream their insignificant and silly dreams" (70). At this point food and drink, symbols of ordinary human interaction, become tainted and impure. He makes the particular instance of his experience in the Congo into an ontology, a whole for human existence, reducing and collapsing history into a moment: "[W]e live in the flicker." Nineteen hundred years becomes "the other day" (9).

Yet he also actively upholds that civilization he so disdains through his lie to the Intended. He lies despite the fact that he has declared earlier that he "hate[s], detest[s] and can't bear a lie." Lies make him feel physically nauseous, "like biting something rotten would do." Lies have "a flavour of mortality"; they are what he "want[s] to forget" (29). It is the flavor, a physical sensation, that he wants to forget. Flavor and taste, gastronomical terms, are substituted for moral ones. From that substitution it is possible to glimpse an underlying sense, more personal, less abstract and intellectualized than Marlow's usual mode of philosophizing. He reacts to the world physically but wants to forget those sensations, to cut them out. Yet he risks the lie and the sensations it brings in order to keep women out, to keep them in "that beautiful world of their own." This need to keep women separate, cordoned off, marks his participation in the ideology he criticizes. It is the idea of separate spheres, one barbaric and one civilized, that allows imperialism to operate.

The "anorexic" cannibals, "savages" under Marlow's command on the steamboat, throw the idea of separate spheres into question. The cannibals are therefore a great mystery to Marlow, who can find no reason for their restrained behavior. Restraint is a large part of the anorexic sign system that decrees moral value and is associated with self-discipline and strength of will. The twenty cannibals on board his steamer are agreeable to Marlow because they are good workers: "Fine fellows—cannibals—in their place. They were men one could work with, and I am grateful to them. And, after all, they did not eat each other before my face" (36). What he doesn't see won't hurt him, is Marlow's attitude, as long as there is good work. But later he finds a much greater reason to respect the cannibals and dwells on that reason at some length. "It occurred to me," he explains, when a cannibal asks Marlow to "catch 'im," that is, one of the wailers on shore, "that he and his chaps must be very hungry, that they must have been growing increasingly hungry for at least this month past" (42). As the Company had provided the cannibals with pieces of brass wire they were supposed to trade for food, and villages had been hostile, Marlow realizes that "it didn't enter anybody's head to trouble how they would live" (42). Considering this further, he becomes quite perplexed:

Why in the name of all the gnawing devils of hunger they didn't go for us— they were thirty to five—and have a good tuck-in for once amazes me now when I think of it. They were big powerful men with not much capacity to weigh the consequences, with courage, with strength, even yet, though their skins were no longer glossy and their muscles no longer hard. . . . I looked at them with a swift quickening of interest—not because it occurred to me that I might be eaten by them before very long, though I own to you that just then I perceived—in a new light, as it were—how unwholesome the pilgrims looked, and I hoped, yes I positively hoped, that my aspect was not so—what shall I say?—so—unappetising. (42–43)

Marlow is especially daunted by this situation because cannibals are thought deficient in moral and physical restraint due to their eating practices. Yet they show a good deal more restraint than the "pilgrims," who carelessly make targets of anything that moves on shore.

The cannibals don't eat, for no discernible reason other than Marlow's half-joking speculation that it might have something to do with "how unwholesome the pilgrims looked." Since the pilgrims have been repeatedly described as fat and Marlow has been repeatedly described as thin, it can be assumed that to Marlow, their unwholesomeness is due to their fatness, and that he hopes he would be more "appetising," because he would make lean-cut chops rather than heavily marbled ones. But joking aside, what he calls the "dazzling fact" (43) of their restraint, their refusal to eat what would nourish them, is something he considers in serious moral terms:

Restraint! What possible restraint? Was it superstition, disgust, patience, fear—or some kind of primitive honor? No fear can stand up to hunger, no patience can wear it out, disgust simply does not exist where hunger is, and as to superstition, beliefs, and what you may call principles, they are less than chaff in a breeze. Don't you know the devilry of lingering starvation, its exasperating torment, its black thoughts, its sombre and brooding ferocity? Well, I do. It takes a man all his inborn strength to fight hunger properly. . . . But there was the fact facing me . . . like a ripple on an unfathomable enigma. (43)

This passage brings together many central preoccupations of the thin/fat motif. Hunger is presented in this passage as a force that goes beyond any system of values, that is "a sombre and brooding ferocity" stronger than any civilized ideals of restraint. Even men who are "men enough to face the darkness" (10), the passage suggests, cannot fight hunger. It takes something even more, "all a man's inborn strength." Restraint from hunger is defined here as the true test of strength and masculinity, of "true inner mettle." Femininity, then, would be defined by the opposite of restraint, by indulgence. Since it was thought that indulgence in food leads to fatness, fatness would be part of femininity, what makes the pilgrims "less men" than the cannibals. Restraint from eating is what "separates the men from the boys," and is therefore the ultimate sign of advanced civilization; for Marlow's bewilderment at the cannibals' abstention, "the fact facing [him] like a ripple on an unfathomable enigma," must arise from his assumption that cannibals have much less reason for restraint. Marlow, like the anorexic, misrecognizes renunciation as development, as refinement—as, in effect, masculinity. Marlow equates not eating with "higher life forms." The cannibals, who are more restrained and therefore more masculine, problematize that equation or cancel it out altogether.

Nonetheless, Marlow sticks to that equation, and the equation persists throughout early Conrad. In the early work, the view of history is that the anorexic condition is civilized, the very latest historical development. Anything else belongs to an earlier, more barbaric time. It is a state achieved only with great difficulty and is very precarious, and the civilized still retain traces of their former state. One must be "man enough" to face this dichotomy between civilization and savagery, not eating and eating in *Heart of Darkness*. From this perspective you must recognize

your remote kinship with this wild and passionate uproar. Ugly. Yes, it was ugly enough, but if you were man enough you would admit to yourself that there was in you just the faintest trace of a response to the terrible frankness of that noise . . . truth stripped of its cloak of time. . . . the man knows and can look on without a wink. But he must at least be as much of a man as these on the shore. He must meet that truth with his own true stuff—with his own inborn strength. Principles? Principles won't do. Acquisitions, clothes, pretty rags—rags that would fly off at the first good shake. (38)

The emphasis here on the "inborn strength" of men who are men is a repetition of the "inborn strength" that it takes for men to fight hunger. As in that passage, masculinity is defined as a man's ability to face the fact that he has within him "trace[s]" of what belonged to earlier phases of development, everything that as a civilized man he defines himself against: "wildness and passion," femininity, primitivism. Only a man can meet this horrifying "truth with his own true stuff." In the face of this truth the acquisitions of civilization become veils; principles are "pretty rags that would fly off at the first good shake"— feminine. The truth is masculine; what covers it, feminine. The truth is that masculinity carries some vestige, a "remote kinship," of femininity within it. Everyone is "wild at heart," a grim recognition true men can face—and also use to justify their colonialist enterprises through a "survival of the fittest" logic. True men know they could deteriorate into fatness and rapacity, and therefore learn to exercise the capacity for violence with discretion.

Thus, in Conrad's early work, fat is equated with femininity, but in a very different way than in the writings of Kafka, Eliot, Pound, and Williams. In Conrad, the connection is between fat and femininity, a quality, and not actual women. Men as well as women can be feminine. Femininity is paradoxical. It is associated with nature, the primitive, and the savage but also with civilization, which is, in *Heart of Darkness,* a fiction that veils truth: in other words, Kurtz's Intended and all she represents are the safe domestic sphere that manufactures comforting ideologies of human progress. Civilization, as a feminine fiction crucial to the lives of white women, covers up a truth of human brutality and lack of restraint that only "true men" can face. This lack of restraint is also coded as feminine and dark, so that true men recognize the terrible truth of the dark, feminine savage within. *Heart of Darkness* participates in the colonialist projection of unrestrained sexuality onto black women, equating them with bodily excess, so that white women can become disembodied "angels," as in the Intended who comes "floating toward [Marlow] in the dusk. . . . This fair hair, this pale visage, this pure brow, seemed surrounded by an ashy halo" (72–73). The feminine is thus split into light and dark, disembodiment and embodiment, fantasy and reality. The feminine as the flimsy fiction of civilization covers nature and simultaneously *is* nature defined as lack of restraint. Those who have no restraint are feminine and not "true men"; those who have no restraint eat, as well as plunder and kill; those who eat and plunder and kill without reason are fat. It is a complicated trajectory whose logic is an integral part of the colonialism Marlow critiques and is one of the ways he upholds its values.

The concrete historical situations that helped produce the particular anorexic attitudes expressed through Marlow demonstrate one level on which the logic operates. I have shown some ways in which economic circumstance contributed to a cultural aversion to materiality, how this aversion led to the aesthetic production of texts, and how that materiality and aesthetics were inflected by racial codes and gendered. Now I shift to an examination of the philosophical underpinnings of anorexic renunciation and its gender. The misrecognition of renunciation for cultural development in Conrad contains a view of history based on a particular theory of desire that is structured by the same anorexic logic as the previous discourse. Tracing that logic in an early Conrad text points to how he renegotiates it in his later work.

II. Fat Is Primitive:
Anorexia as Historical Progress in Falk

Falk takes as its subject the cultural equation between civilization and restraint that appears in *Heart of Darkness*. While the cannibals in that text behave like anorexics, problematizing Marlow's ideas about them, *Falk* is an extended exploration of the idea that cannibalism and primitivism are linked. The protagonist, Falk, is explicitly described in terms of his "life instincts," which are related to cannibalism. Sexuality and cannibalism are presented in an indissociable relation, part of the "appetites of the world" that, if one is modern, should be anorexically avoided. A reading of the text shows what Conrad conceives of as a model of desire—ultimately self-destructive and deconstructive—that establishes different phases in historical human development through which desire passes. This model is analogous to, but also in important ways different from, Freud's model of desire in the "Three Essays on the Theory of Sexuality." It makes early Conrad one of the clearest examples of the anorexic logic that equates development and progress with bodily renunciation in the modern literary tradition.

The text opens with a striking description of eating. The frame narrator reports:

Several of us, all more or less connected with the sea, were dining in a small river-hostelry. . . . the dinner was execrable, and all the feast was for the eyes. That flavour of salt-water which for so many of us had been the very water of life permeated our talk. He who hath known the bitterness of the Ocean shall have its taste for ever in his mouth. But one or two of us, pampered by the life of the land, complained of hunger. It was impossible to swallow any of that stuff.[42]

Here, already a kind of structural inversion is set up through the designation of the ocean as "the very water of life," since salt water is not amenable to the human body. These men are nourished differently than land dwellers, and their "execrable" dinner conflates past and present:

> The chops recalled times more ancient still. They brought forcibly to one's mind the night of ages when the primeval man, evolving the first rudiments of cookery from his dim consciousness, scorched lumps of flesh at a fire of sticks in the company of other good fellows; then, gorged and happy, sat him back among the gnawed bones to tell his artless tales of experience—the tales of hunger and hunt—and of women, perhaps! But luckily the wine happened to be as old as the waiter. So, comparatively empty, but upon the whole fairly happy, we sat back and told our artless tales. (234)

The present differs from the past in that the meat of "primeval man" is now inedible, the "good fellows" cannot bring themselves to "gorge" on "lumps of flesh" and must fill themselves with the less substantial and more refined "old wine."[43] The present speakers are "comparatively empty"; they have not gorged themselves; the meat is there, but they refuse to eat it. "The night of ages" in which one gorged on "lumps of flesh" is "brought forcibly" to mind by the chops, as if that past and its consumptive apparatus was something better forgotten. At this point I underscore the difference, in the text's time, between past gorging and present abstention. The "telling of artless tales" remains consistent, however, as does "the company of other good fellows." The act of eating or drinking, the act of incorporation, creates a fraternity in which "artless tales of experience" are told about other activities related to eating—"tales of hunger and hunt, and of women, perhaps." Women and sexual conquest belong to the same register, the same historical period, as the "hunger and hunt." Eating and hunting—food or women—and hunger constitute experience itself and are defined in this text as the basis for a community of "good fellows" formed through these acts and the kinds of exclusion these acts necessitate. Here one does not eat with the other, although one may very well eat the other, as indeed does happen.[44]

The "lumps of flesh" the primeval "good fellows" gorged themselves upon are transmuted into a description of the woman who becomes the object of the protagonist's "hunger and hunt." Significantly, the agency of this description is Schomberg, the hotel keeper obsessed with eating, who also appears in *Victory:* "'But for a fine lump of a girl, she's a fine lump of a girl.' He made a loud smacking noise with his thick lips. 'The finest lump of a girl that I ever . . .' he was going on with great unction," the narrator reports, "but for some reason or other broke off. I fancied myself throwing something at his head" (265). The description of a girl as a "lump," over whom one smacks one's lips as for a thick, juicy steak, is connected through repetition with the "lumps of flesh" that the "good fellows" gorge. Conrad makes explicit use of the "woman as food" metaphor here.[45] Schomberg's dispute with the protagonist doesn't have to do with his choice of sexual lump, for in the sexual sense he does consume, but with Falk's diet, which in Schomberg's view is curiously abstentious:

Rice and a little fish he buys for a few cents from the fishing-boats outside is what he lives on. You would hardly credit it—eh? A white man, too. . . . Falk wouldn't look at [the meat]. I do it for the sake of a lot of young white fellows here that hadn't a place where they could get a decent meal and eat it decently in good company. . . . A white man should eat like a white man, dash it all! . . . Ought to eat meat, must eat meat. I manage to get meat for my patrons all the year round. Don't I? I am not catering for a dam' lot of coolies: have another chop, captain. . . . No? (252)

Here the fraternity of "young white fellows" establishes itself again on the basis of the exclusion of racial and sexual others through eating rituals. Falk is indignantly seen as renouncing this brotherhood, because he won't eat the meat that establishes the community, and he subsists without it or the "good company" that goes with it, taking his meatless meals alone.

Falk has literally been a cannibal, forced to hunt down and consume a fellow shipmate on an inoperative ship drifting without food, and his aversion to meat is explained by this. Falk is described by the narrator as a "ruthless lover of the five senses" (293) and is connected with the "primeval men" of the opening passage. The emphasis on chronology is important, for Falk shows a tenacious "life instinct" that forms a mirror opposite to the protagonist of *Victory,* who exhibits an equally strong "death drive" and is described as "modern." Falk's connection with the primitive is made explicit, but his historical specificity is also insisted upon:

Self-preservation was his only concern. Not selfishness, but mere self-preservation. Selfishness presupposes consciousness, choice, the presence of other men; but his instinct acted as though he were the last of mankind nursing that law like the only spark of a sacred fire. I don't mean to say that living naked in a cavern would have satisfied him. Obviously he was the creature of the conditions to which he was born. No doubt self-preservation meant also the preservation of these conditions. But essentially it meant something much more simple, natural, and powerful. How shall I express it? It meant the preservation of the five senses of his body—let us say—taking it in its narrowest as well as in its widest meaning. (267–68)

Through his alliance with the "natural," the "five senses of his body," his identification with the body, Falk is identified with a previous world, as definitively nonmodern. Although it is clear that Falk is "the creature of the conditions to which he was born," that is, a creature of this later, differently formulated world, he also retains within him a drive that others, according to the text's formulation, seem to have lost. Through his "life instinct" he is seen "as though he were the last of mankind nursing that law like the only spark of a sacred fire." It is as if the cannibalistic Falk were the last cannibal. Paradoxically, through that cannibalistic nature, "the only spark of a sacred fire," he is the last of mankind with an instinct for self-preservation or a will to live. Identification with the body and the preservation of its five senses is cannibalistic and is equated with an earlier period of human development. Existence in the text's present, then, seems to indicate a nonidentification or renunciation of that body and its instincts toward self-preservation. The impossibility of maintaining this renunciation is made clear through a paradoxical structure: in the modern world the loss of the cannibalistic instinct, which is linked with self-preservation and has led to the extinction of self-preservation and thereby self-negation, is equated with the definitive condition of modernity, which is also self-negation. But these two negations cancel each other out: the negation of negation leads back into the abyssal structure of desire.

The first dimension of this paradox is further emphasized, as well as problematized, by the presentation of the object of Falk's hunger: "she was too generously alive; but she could have stood for an allegoric statue of the Earth. I don't mean the worn-out earth of our possession, but a young Earth, a virginal planet undisturbed by the vision of a future teeming with the monstrous forms of life, clamourous with the cruel battles of hunger and thought" (238). By implication the earth at an earlier state of human development was "too generously alive" and thereby somewhat horrific in that virginal excess that will eventually produce the "future teeming with monstrous forms of life." And in this "monstrous" future state, the time period of the text, hunger and thought have become opposed, the earth has become "clamourous" with the "cruel battles" between them. Through the logic of this opposition one cannot both think and eat, for each activity is at war with the other. The "virginal" phase of "young Earth" is associated with orality and cannibalism:

There was a sense of lurking gruesome horror somewhere in my mind, and it was mingled with clear and grotesque images. Schomberg's gastronomic tittle-tattle was responsible for these; and I half hoped I should never see Falk again. . . . [Falk's face] was immovably set and hungry, dominated like the whole man by the singleness of one instinct. He wanted to live. He had always wanted to live. So we all do—but in us the instinct serves a complex conception, and in him this instinct existed alone. There is in such simple development a gigantic force, like the pathos of a child's naive and uncontrolled desire. He wanted that girl, and the utmost that can be said for him was that he wanted that particular girl alone. I think I saw then the obscure beginning, the seed germinating in the soil of an unconscious need, the first shoot of that tree bearing now for a mature mankind the flower and the fruit, the infinite gradation in shades and in flavour of our discriminating love. He was a child. He was as frank as a child, too. He was hungry for the girl, terribly hungry, as he had been terribly hungry for food. Don't be shocked if I declare that in my belief it was the same need, the same pain, the same torture. We are in his case allowed to contemplate the foundation of all the emotions—that one joy which is to live, and the one sadness at the root of the innumerable torments. It was made plain by the way he talked. He had never suffered so. It was gnawing. (283–84)

There are striking similarities, as well as marked differences, between this passage, written in 1903, and Freud's "Three Essays on the Theory of Sexuality," written two years later. Conrad offers here a model of development that corresponds to Freud's, that seems to contain all the stages of the development of infantile sexuality set out in the "Three Essays," as well as the insight that the instinct itself, rather than its object, is the motivating force. Falk is here figured as a child but also as a man of another age, that is, from an earlier phase of human development, and his cannibalism is consistent with that age. According to the "authorities" in Freud's text, "[T]his aggressive element of the sexual instinct is in reality a relic of cannibalistic desires— that is, it is a contribution derived from the apparatus for obtaining mastery, which is concerned with the satisfaction of the other and, ontogenetically, the older of the great instinctual needs."[46] Cannibalism corresponds to the early oral phase of the libido, the stage of "cannibalistic pregenital sexual organization. Here sexual activity has not yet been separated from the ingestion of food. . . . the *object* of both activities is the same; the sexual *aim* consists in the incorporation of the object" (198). The language of Conrad's narrator—which describes desire and hunger in Falk as "the same need, the same pain, the same torture"—suggests that in Falk's primitive life instinct or libido, his wanting to live as the single driving force of his being, the same conflation can be seen. In Conrad's passage, however, this is linked to human development throughout history, not the life of a single individual.[47] "In us," Conrad's narrator says, "the instinct serves a complex conception, and in him this instinct existed alone." Falk exists in the earlier "singular" libidinal phase, a "gigantic force, like the pathos of a child's naive and uncontrolled desire." Not yet subjected to the later phases modern man experiences, Falk "wanted that girl" in the same way he had wanted to eat when starving on the ship—"he was hungry for the girl, terribly hungry, a he had been terribly hungry for food." In this hunger Falk is aligned with "the obscure beginning, the seed germinating in the soil of an unconscious need. . . . He was a child." Like the child in which a later man, like the narrator, can see earlier phases reflected, Falk's hunger and his cannibalism stand as the reminder or remainder of what modern man has presumably left behind. Yet that idea of development marks a typically anorexic form of "false consciousness" in its desire to deny and transcend bodily materiality by labeling it retrograde.

The one thing that differentiates Falk from the indiscriminate libido of a very young child—in Conrad's language, "the utmost that can be said for him"—is that he is at least discriminating in his choice of object: "he wanted that particular girl alone." The indiscriminate libido is the "seed germinating in the soil of an unconscious need, the first shoot of that tree bearing now for a mature mankind the flower and the fruit, the infinite gradation in shades and in flavour of our discriminating love." "Discriminating" is used in the sense of choice or taste while holding the sense of a systematic exclusion of one group by another within its horizon of meaning. In "mature mankind" there is differentiation and discrimination in choice of object, and Falk practices that discrimination that nonetheless retains its oral component, its "flavour." This discrimination or taste is the "utmost that can be said of him." It is this particular phrase that marks a difference between Conrad and Freud, and that signals the transition to *Victory*, a text that deals explicitly with the problematic nature of the "discriminating love" of "mature mankind." In the conventional reading, Falk's exclusive choice of object would be the good desire for the one, not the many.[48] In this reading, "the utmost that can be said of him" implies that at least Falk has discriminated in his childish hunger, and that the narrator is applauding him for this choice, his designation of a particular object, rather than a random consumption of all objects. But I offer an alternative reading of the line "the utmost that can be said for him was that he wanted that particular girl alone." It's not just that "discrimination" in object choice marks a superior or less primitive desire. Instead, the tone of this passage suggests that if Falk must desire or hunger at all, as he seems to, at least he is discriminating in his choice of food. The modern state, however, is to be without hunger.

Within this text, or if this text is read together with *Victory*, this phrase can also be interpreted as an indictment of desire in general. The implication is that on a certain level, the further evolution of "mature mankind" should be, paradoxically and impossibly, a development beyond any hunger altogether. This is, of course, a characteristically modernist position in that the philosophical skepticism posited as an alternative in Conrad is a repetition of similar attempts to renounce and transcend the flesh so prevalent in the Christian tradition of asceticism, as well as the Stoic and Cartesian philosophical traditions. Like Eliot in his call to replace the physical body with a poetic one, Conrad seems to argue for the progressive development of mankind away from the material, which is also a movement away from the feminine, and to locate that development in the modern period. A tendency that marks most modern writers is the perhaps willful ignorance of the many historical precedents for this development, like those discussed above, and its elevation to an ontology. In Conrad specifically, the texts are aware of the impossibility of such a development even as this development seems desired—the desire not to desire, the definitive form of anorexic desire. In the next chapter I examine the consequences of anorexic desire for women in the work of Jean Rhys: among them, how cultural constructions of materiality and the feminine situate female subjectivity in the black hole.

Chapter Four

Missing Persons
The Black Hole of the Feminine in Jean Rhys

Because a wound to the heart
Is also a wound to the mind.
Louise Glück,
"The Untrustworthy Speaker"

So far I have examined anorexia in terms of the cultural context that
has produced it. I explored an underlying logic or set of assumptions,
cultural valuations that privilege the masculine over the feminine,
spiritual and intellectual over the material, mind over body, thinness
over fatness. I have shown how a dominant strain of canonical modernism deploys these valuations in its theories of literary production
and artistic genesis, revealing a common mind-set that can produce
anorexia on the one hand and art on the other. Anorexia is a form of
expression based on the same values as high modernist literary art, so
that the text of the anorexic body stands as the literalization of the
modernist fascination with disembodiment, the desire not to desire.
The "great books" that have provided us with cultural heritage and
"meaning" have also given us anorexia.

Anorexic, high modernist values are all around us, and their continued prevalence, however discredited in the academy, still have a potent cultural function. Students, particularly women, who struggle
with the cultural devaluation of embodiment daily, and whose degree
of struggle depends on variables of race and class, find that devaluation again in the authority still given to so-called great literature. Every time they sit in a class that includes texts like *Heart of Darkness*,
they receive its anorexic values as truth, especially since these texts

are still often taught as sets of values we should identify with and accept. But while it is still important to read these texts to identify the political implications underlying them, it is equally important to explore texts that present alternatives. With this in mind, out of many possible alternatives I have chosen Jean Rhys, whose texts provide the reader with a compelling and relentless account of women's daily struggles with embodiment.

Rhys is exemplary for the complexity with which she engages the question of how a woman, along with her racial and class identities, is affected by an anorexic system of cultural valuation. What is the system and how does it function? What sustains it? What are the alternatives, and what, to use Rhys's language, is the "way out"? In its unflinching presentation of the ambivalence, confusion, and desperation the struggle with embodiment produces, Rhys reveals the psychology of why women can become anorexic. Her work stands as a fundamental expression of the effects of the anorexic logic, as well as the logic itself. While I have been concerned with charting that logic's horizon, in my reading of Rhys I start to explore some of its consequences and, following Rhys, begin a tentative stab at a way out.

Writing about Rhys is tremendously difficult for me, so much so that it took me a year and a half to do it. My first encounter with her was years ago in an honors class in college, where we read, tellingly, her novel *Wide Sargasso Sea* as part of a course on autobiography. Her real autobiography, *Smile Please,* was on reserve in the library, and because I hadn't had time to read the novel and was despairing of a paper topic, one afternoon I chanced upon it. I was struck by a powerful sensation, with an impact of physical force, an experience a naive reader often has. If you are lucky enough, you continue to feel what I felt upon encountering Rhys—a sense of complete, unproblematic identification, as if it were my life she had written, not hers. Certainly, because Rhys was a white West Indian who spent most of her adult years in England and France, the details of her life were different from mine, but the *feeling* behind the details, her overall sense of things, her worldview, was identical with my own. It was a moment of profound identification, where the words, that text, were much more real to me than almost any person I had ever met. It was nothing I could rationally make sense of, which made it difficult to tear her to pieces, to treat her academically, objectively, to parcel her out. It made me shake with rage to hear her discussed in class with so much triviality, so little passion, so little understanding: "And this is Rhys's relation to the literary tradition, blah, blah, blah . . ." I couldn't write about Rhys, could only state she was right. I didn't know it then, and am only beginning to make sense of it now, but the shared logic of the bond between us belongs to the anorexic horizon.

All Rhys's texts are haunted by "nothing," as was so commonplace in texts of the period, but Rhys's texts articulate a different form. Rhys's nothing is, to use the words of Arthur Kroker and Marilouise Kroker, a nothing of "cancelled identities and suffocating isolation"— the same nothing that produces anorexia.[1] As Judith Kegan Gardiner writes, "[Rhys] does not treat alienation as an existential fact but as the specific historical result of social polarizations about sex, class, and morality."[2] Yet, even as Rhys shows the historical origins of the constitution of her heroines' subjectivities, the nothingness they can fall into undercuts the social and political critiques the texts undeniably perform: like anorexia Rhys's critique ultimately consumes itself.[3] One cannot build an affirmative model for social change on nothing or on individual acts of self-consumption, no matter how critical of the status quo those acts might be.[4] For if there is nothing, only affirmation and triumph by redemption through flame and self-annihilation, as in Rhys's texts, we must consider this, like the anorexic paradigm, a problematic form of triumph.

In making this statement I leave myself open to charges that I, like "many feminist readers [who] are also wary of stories that are, like Rhys's, 'about victims,' . . . express impatience especially with characters who internalize the terms of their oppression, as if such characters had only to resolve to adopt a better attitude in order to surmount whatever obstacles stood in their paths."[5] The interplay between social context, victimhood, and self-empowerment is part of the double bind in Rhys's texts. She gives incisive psychological insight into how female identity, especially when compounded by racial- and class-based otherness, becomes a "black hole." The black hole as a consuming nothingness stands as a powerfully inflected metaphor for the Western fear of the feminine as "too much," identified by Bordo.[6] Rhys performs a powerful critique of the social forces that contribute to this fear. However, since Rhys remains in the anorexic position that does not examine the role of her own or her characters' internalization of such standards, she reduces the potentialities of both. Her texts leave us with a doorless universe where apocalyptic suicide is the only way out. Is it possible, since that universe is determined by profoundly masculinist social and literary conventions, to "adopt a better attitude"? Is there any alternative? It's not an easy question. As Rachel Bowlby writes, "[F]or Rhys, even more than with other writers, it does not seem easy to decide that her heroines' troubles are supposed to be caused by this or by that, by men, or madness, or the commodification of women in modern capitalism."[7]

Part of the inability to decide is attributable to the fact that Rhys's position, like that of the anorexic's, is articulated through an "agency of negation"—a position where, deprived of all alternatives, a woman says, "I negate what you make me [a powerless woman]. I will show I have power and agency by taking control of my body, the existence you say I do not own, by destroying it." The agency of negation is a willed destruction, a form of control that explains the anorexic's desperate need to "make out of your body your very own kingdom, where you are the tyrant, the absolute dictator" (Bruch, *Golden Cage*, 65). "Some feel," writes Bruch, that in anorexia, "for the first time there is a core to their personality . . . this accumulation of power giving [them] another kind of 'weight,' the right to be recognized as an individual" (5).[8] When, as is the case with Rhys's heroines, one clearly doesn't have "the right to be recognized as an individual" according to the dominant culture, the cultural process of "disrecognition" seems to contribute to both anorexia and the heroines' problems. Morag Macsween defines the hidden equivalency of masculinity and individuality and its incommensurability with traditional femininity as a major factor leading to anorexia when the historical context demands both simultaneously of women, and it is this cultural equation that Rhys is keenly attuned to.[9] As Molly Hite so persuasively shows in *The Other Side of the Story*, her analysis of how "categories of literary and social determination interpenetrate" in Rhys, the heroines assert themselves as major characters in a universe where they can only be minor ones (27). When one has no other choice, when self-destruction is the only possible form of agency offered, the act of reclaiming oneself through self-destruction characterizes the agency of negation. In this sense, Rhys is the paradigmatic anorexic, for she is anorexic in her simultaneous defiance of and accordance with cultural standards rather than, as in the male moderns discussed previously, primarily contributing to them.[10]

In male modernism the disparagement of the feminine as a distraction from truth, best exemplified in Conrad, also articulates the frame that makes women minor characters. Through the self-destructive agency of negation, both the anorexic and Rhys question the frame in which women are "soft and disgusting weights suspended round the necks of men, dragging them downwards," part of an anorexic logic that enforces cultural standards.[11] I make a distinction here between the anorexic logic, representative of the social context, and anorexic behavior, the reaction to and shaping of that context. Like the anorexic, Rhys is necessarily a figure of ambivalence for feminists, and preserving that ambivalence is a necessary gesture if we are to understand our own identifications with and investments in her work.

Partially because of feminist ambivalence, Rhys's work has recently been read more for its postcolonial context than for its critique of gender. Her work examines a model of relations between the sexes characterized by the anorexic logic that can be seen to demonstrate antagonisms between men and women generally, but Rhys also makes clear how, in Mary Lou Emery's words, "sexual and cultural conflict become coextensive."[12] Rhys's examinations of women's sometimes triply devalued position show ways in which race and class can make women's negative situatedness via gender and embodiment a good deal more powerful. Throughout, Rhys's texts focus on the anorexic cultural logic that conflates the feminine and the dark other into an embodiment that is despised.

As *Heart of Darkness* shows, at least since colonialist projects and the advent of white male exposure to "native women," these women's bodies were constructed as foreign territories, the savage otherness that made the further fiction of the desexualized "angel in the house" possible. Negative bodily associations with the feminine were twinned with darkness, and the virgin/whore dichotomy was often enacted along racial lines. Carnality and embodiment were split off from white women in the nineteenth century (which has continued into the present) and projected onto nonwhite women. This splitting means that the rape of a black woman by a white man gets no attention, since as the body of the savage other she is thereby appropriately colonized. Similarly, the rape of a white woman gets a good deal of attention if her attackers happen to be black (as in the case of the Central Park jogger), since the myth of white female purity can be used to construct voracious black male sexuality. Yet, even in fictions of white female purity, that splitting has never been entirely successful. From the Gibson girl of the 1920s to contemporary *Playboy* centerfolds and milk commercials, there has never been a complete dissociation of white women from their breasts and hips. Breasts and hips mean that if a white woman is raped by a white man, especially if he has money (like William Kennedy Smith), she will still be constructed as having "asked for it." The mix of patriarchal and colonialist assumptions characterizing all three situations connect the feminine and darkness with voracious sexuality and the body, assumptions Rhys's work renders increasingly disturbing for their violence and devastating affects on the lives of women. Women are thus positioned differently, but that difference is intertwined with cultural projections that forge inextricable links between women and their bodies. Some recent feminist criticism argues that an exclusive focus on difference risks missing, as Bordo writes, "important effects of the everyday deployment of mass cultural representations of masculinity, femininity, beauty, and success."[13] Rhys's work, among other things, addresses precisely those deployments and their effects.

I. Rhys's Life: Booze and Black Holes

Most recent feminist interpretations of Rhys attempt to utilize her work to articulate an alternative tradition to colonial, masculinist language and literary tradition.[14] Most of these readings are very convincing, and while I agree that the features on which they focus provide an alternative, there is always *another* tendency in Rhys operating simultaneously. To cast the debate in my own terms, in Rhys's texts there is the more overtly political tendency to hunger strike, as well as the more individualistic anorexic position—and I read the two positions as distinct. Feminists who read Rhys unproblematically in the affirmative, hunger-strike tradition must ignore one thing in her texts: the way female subjectivity is, as in anorexia, necessarily constituted as a black hole.

During the early twentieth century, women used the hunger strike effectively to get the vote. This strategy of political resistance to the dominant culture is often equated with anorexia.[15] While anorexia as a disease is frequently seen as a female protest against the dominant cultural standards, the anorexic and the hunger striker are not equivalent positions, as Elaine Showalter would have it: "the hunger strikes of militant women prisoners brilliantly put the symptomatology of anorexia nervosa to work in the service of a feminist cause."[16] On a clinical level the anorexic's actions reinforce the culture she resists, and on a literary level the anorexic position is clearly the domain of the male artist, defined in opposition to the female fatness of the contemporary culture. In resisting the feminization of the literary sphere, which they felt degraded their profession, makers of modernist manifestos, while cutting out the sociohistorical context and privileging art as an autonomous domain, also facilitated the very network of relations that they wished to make new. While anorexia is a strategy of resistance that leaves out the personal, the hunger strike includes it, even makes it its subject.

Rhys is ambivalent. While aspects of her work are clearly complicit with some of the terms of the dominant, anorexic literary tradition, she nonetheless manages to leave the personal in, forming an aesthetic criticized as too personal, too autobiographical despite the beauty of its "spare form." A work's relative degree of engagement with the personal has traditionally been a measure by which a work was deemed high literature or dismissed as popular trash. Even in recent Rhys criticism some are still disturbed that "the fiction is so heavily autobiographical." As Gardiner writes in *Rhys, Stead, Lessing, and the Politics of Empathy,* "[M]any negative responses to [Rhys's] work imply that living with her autobiographical characters is disconcerting, even embarrassing, for readers who blame their unease on her personality" (21), Gardiner argues that Rhys's status as an artist increases as she distances herself from that "personality": "[Rhys's] authorial self-concept changes, her identity as a woman writer matures, and the identifications she establishes between herself and her characters become more mediated" (23). Her comments reveal the extent to which even a feminist academic analysis is complicit in an anorexic logic that privileges impersonal distance and dictates literary merit. Distance does not necessarily lead to merit; so-called personal writing can be extremely powerful.

Because Rhys's writing is so personal, nearly every early critical study has focused either primarily or to a large extent on Rhys's biography, reading her novels as outgrowths of that life in a way that no reader would ever comfortably read Eliot, say, or Pound. As Gardiner writes in "Good Morning, Midnight; Goodnight, Modernism," "[B]e-cause much of her work has an obviously autobiographical base . . . she has been treated out of her historical context as an individual and pathological voice, the voice of a female victim" (233). This estimation of Rhys extends even to her biographer Carole Angier who writes in *Jean Rhys* that "her work is so personal that reading it is like being alone with her in a locked and shuttered room" (578).

Clearly, the modernist mandate for a poetics of impersonality that I analyze as a central part of an anorexic logic has little application to Rhys, for the personal—and its suppression in literary tradition—is always her subject.[17] For earlier critics this was almost uniformly a flaw that seriously compromised the artistic integrity of her work, while for the first feminist readers it was an asset.[18] To cast the debate into my own terms, what is cut out as "fat" in male modernists is the female point of view, the female half of the conversation. This is what Rhys includes. In a historical period in which women were struggling to find a voice, male fiction and aesthetic theory obsessively and an-orexically silenced it. Thus male moderns appropriate a lived female position in their aesthetics, using that anorexic position in support of the status quo based on an attempt to escape the "devouring femi-nine," or, as Rhys puts it so aptly in *Quartet,* the view that women are "loathsome, horrible—soft and disgusting weights suspended round the necks of men, dragging them downwards" (186). It is the figure of the devouring feminine, the "soft and disgusting [weight]," that the anorexic questions through her only choice, the agency of negation, but male moderns figuratively borrow the gesture of the anorexic's self-immolation in a way that doubly cancels her out.

Rhys's novels, and her life, subscribe to an anorexic logic that is self-canceling while simultaneously providing something that exceeds that cancellation. Both positions are in her texts, the hunger striker and the anorexic, assertion and cancellation. In her life, writing was her act of self-assertion. Her other actions, on the other hand, seemed to follow an almost deliberate pattern of self-sabotage. Rhys is anorexic in a different way from the other writers I analyze. While her work makes use of an anorexic aesthetic of spare form, she also reveals the cultural assumptions about masculinity and femininity, women and men, that inform that aesthetic. To the extent that Rhys configures female subjectivity, amplified by marginal race and class positions, as a black hole—a void, a cipher, an empty lack that cannot be filled—she shares with the male moderns an anorexic logic internalized from a social matrix that in her work also functions as a negative form of protest.

Because her life closely parallels the novels (although the two shouldn't be conflated), and because so much critical attention has been paid to her life, I briefly summarize the biography here.[19] What is interesting from my perspective are the life details that Rhys cuts out when writing her novels, what of the personal is included, and more important, what is excluded. The basic trajectory of her life is well known. Jean Rhys, christened Ella Gwendoline Rees Williams, was born in Dominica in the West Indies in 1890, where her father, who was Welsh, was a doctor. Her mother was Creole, descended from former colonialist slaveholders. Like Annette and Antoinette in *Wide Sargasso Sea,* both Rhys and her mother had an ambiguous position in the community—not white or black, not British or West Indian. Many studies focus on Rhys's failed relationship with her mother, for Minna Rees Williams seems to have been distant from Jean and largely inaccessible. Jean was born nine months after the death of an older sister, and the biographer Angier theorizes that Jean was meant as her replacement.[20] Deborah Kelly Kloepfer dedicates her study on Rhys and H. D. to an examination of "the ways in which the writing daughters have both refused and solicited the encounter with the mother, and how both her loss and her presence insistently ruptures the discourse of their texts." Kloepfer reads Rhys's work as revolving around the inscription and recovery of the maternal. The absent mother is also central to Lori Lawson's Lacanian reading of

Wide Sargasso Sea.[21] Rhys's childhood was spent in Dominica, where she was educated in a convent. Closer to her father than her mother, she was thought the difficult child because she was moody, full of intense feelings and what seemed strange concerns to her mother and aunts. She was so shy she often seemed to have bad manners. One of her mother's friends, a man near seventy, sexually abused her, but she never told anyone. At seventeen she was sent to England, to the Perse School for Girls in Cambridge. At her request, she then studied at the Academy of Dramatic Art until her teachers advised her father that her accent (her "nasty nigger's voice," as her aunt would call it) would inhibit an acting career. Her family wanted her to return to Dominica, but Rhys, determined to stay, in 1909 got a job in the chorus of a musical comedy with a second-rate troupe. The agent who hired her told Jean not to tell the other girls she'd been at the academy, pointing out a class discrepancy Rhys must have been aware of. The family protested, Jean insisted, and her father, as always, gave in.[22]

Working conditions were bad; the tours, long; and the pay, almost nothing. A year later, like many young actresses Rhys took a lover—a rich "English gentleman" named Lancelot Smith—quit the troupe, and became a "kept woman." When this relationship ended after a year and a half, Rhys was psychologically and emotionally devastated. She relied on men for money. Much of the material for *Voyage in the Dark* comes from this part of her life. She also made money as an artist's model and as a mannequin. In 1919, she married Jean Lenglet, a Dutch journalist who was involved in a number of dubious activities: he was a spy during the war and was later imprisoned for embezzlement. They had periods of extreme wealth and extreme poverty. Their first child, a son, died soon after birth, possibly due to neglect (he was left near an open window in the winter). They had one daughter, Maryvonne, who was largely brought up in boarding schools and by her father.

During Lenglet's prison stint, Rhys met Ford Madox Ford, whom many critics credit with developing her already "instinctive" talent for literary form. Ford became both teacher and lover, and was responsible for getting Rhys's first collection of stories, *The Left Bank*, published in 1927. During this time she divorced Lenglet. She drew on her relationship with Ford for the material in *Quartet*, which permanently estranged and angered him. In the twelve years following Ford's patronage—between 1927 and 1939—she produced most of her life's work. The final version of *Wide Sargasso Sea* and two collections of short stories came later, but the bulk of her work—four novels, eight long stories, a great deal of autobiographical writing, a lost novel, and a first draft of *Wide Sargasso Sea*—was written during this time. Sometime after her breakup with Smith, Rhys had started drinking seriously, and this became a lifelong habit. She was an alcoholic, and during and after her relationship with Ford she became violent. She was arrested several times in the thirties and forties for disturbing the peace.

In 1928, she married the literary agent Leslie Tilden Smith and lived with him until his death in 1945. He was responsible for getting most of this work published, and he made typescripts of her written drafts. In 1947, she married Smith's cousin, Max Hammer, who would also serve time in prison for embezzlement and fraud. Poverty had been a constant problem for Rhys and became an even greater constraint after Hammer's imprisonment. It was during this time that Rhys largely dropped from public view. When Selma Vas Dias tried to find the author of *Good Morning, Midnight* in 1948, so that she could adapt it as a radio monologue for the BBC, everyone thought Rhys was dead. But after the broadcast, Rhys began to emerge from obscurity. With the publication of *Wide Sargasso Sea* in 1966, she finally had some of the money and fame that had previously eluded her, although this didn't change her deep distrust of other people and the world in general. Her success was, she said, "too little, too late." She died in 1979.

These are the mundane facts of Rhys's life; the reality of her alcoholism and what in contemporary pop psychology is called "codependence" makes a much bleaker story. Rhys's feeling that she was a black hole underneath a more or less coherent surface may have served as a motivation to produce fiction but had devastating consequences. Constantly in need of reassurance, she demanded the utmost devotion from those around her while she repaid them with violence. As A. Alvarez unsympathetically put it, "Jean Rhys was one of the finest writers of the century but the best way to read her work is to know nothing about the woman who wrote it."[23] Rhys met with this kind of rejection throughout her life, which perhaps contributed to her violence. Some of these episodes, such as the one that landed her in Holloway prison, are what Rhys suppresses and cuts out of her fiction. However, as many critics have noted, perhaps problematically, the critical boundaries between Rhys's life and that of her protagonists are permeable.[24] Judged from a modernist perspective, her work is too autobiographical. Having read Rhys's biography and her letters, I do not question the closeness of her characters and their situation to her own life, but I do question why an autobiographical text should necessarily be criticized on that basis.[25] To read Rhys, we need to read her as a materially existent woman *as well as* an artist, although she herself might have wanted to keep those identities distinct. In his introduction to *Jean Rhys Letters,* Francis Wyndham writes, "[Rhys] firmly believed that an artist's work should be considered in separation from the facts of his or her life, even though the facts had provided the raw material for the work. . . . [Her novels,] though based on her own experience, were essentially works of the imagination which transcended that experience, and to exaggerate the connection between her writing and her life would, she feared, confuse rather than enlighten an appreciation of the former" (9). This emphasis on transcendence and Rhys's fear that discussions of her life would work against an appreciation of her work belong to the anorexic register of modernist criticism, best exemplified by Eliot's poetics of impersonality. A hierarchically organized distinction still operates between art and the raw material it is drawn from, a distinction that resembles the mind/body split: the mind is the agency of rational control and exclusion; the body is base materiality waiting for a shape.

I contend that Rhys's work cannot be read according to the dictates of this critical paradigm. Her work confounds the distinctions between art and life, mind and body, impersonal and personal that so inform modernist aesthetics. Had Rhys lived in a time when the critical paradigm was one that equally valued the personal, emotional, material—the "sordid subject matter" for which she was always condemned—she may not have felt the need for an opposition between her life and art. The autobiographical dimension of her work, her presentation of women's lived experience, creates the need to connect with and articulate our own experiences. We cannot make sense of

Rhys by adhering to the critical standard that says it is dangerous to read an artist's work in terms of her life or to read our own lives in that work. These standards cut out the author's experience of embodiment and how that embodiment is articulated textually, as well as negating a reader's personal, emotional identification with and relationship to the text. Similarly, a purely autobiographical analysis disregards the literary dimensions that are equally important to an informed understanding. In order for us to read Rhys, both autobiography and art must be part of the methodological focus. Both the critical standard that excises autobiography and a reading that disregards the literary partake of the anorexic logic that I have tracked in its various incarnations.

Crucial to my connection between the Rhys corpus and the anorexic *corps* is a feature that precedes those bodies as such. In her authoritative research on anorexia, still relied on as a definitive source today, Bruch is careful to point out that what we think of as anorexia—that is, women starving themselves to death in a quest for exaggerated thinness—is a *symptom* of a larger problem. A logic, a specific mind-set, precedes the onset of symptoms such as severe weight loss and refusal to eat. According to Bruch in *Eating Disorders*, "[N]oneating and associated weight loss [are] late features, secondary to underlying personality disturbances. . . . the main issue is a struggle for control, for a sense of identity, competence, and effectiveness. . . . Traditionally, the order has been reversed: anorexia nervosa is defined in somatic terms, as emaciation due to abstinence from food" (275). What Bruch calls an "underlying personality [disturbance]" characteristic of anorexics, I see as a logic that characterizes Rhys's texts. The same reaction to a cultural and historical context that is expressed through "abstinence from food" in a group of women we have come to call "anorexics" is expressed artistically in Rhys. But this is a different dynamic than that which characterized the relationship between Kafka, Eliot, Pound, Williams, Conrad, and anorexia that I analyzed earlier. Rhys is on "the other side" of the anorexic logic— she's the "base material" to which anorexic logic is applied, not a subscriber to this logic. As a result, the "struggle for control, for a sense of identity, competence, and effectiveness" that Bruch finds expressed through anorexia is also expressed in Rhys's texts. This logic takes different forms in the body of an anorexic and in Rhys: in anorexia the "author" creates an artistic object, the skeletal body through the operation of anorexic logic, while in Rhys's literary texts she conveys the same logic thematically. What the two forms share is a similar content. In Rhys's texts the same issues of control, identity, and competence find expression. For Rhys as a female artist, anorexia is always a paradox.

That paradox is embodied in the preface Ford wrote for Rhys's first publication, a collection of short stories called *The Left Bank*.[26] In this preface Ford muses about his boyhood in Paris, his opinion of Napoléon III, the Latin Quarter, and just about anything other than Rhys, whom he mentions only in the last four pages. He mentions her "remarkable technical gifts" (23), and by associating her with the left hand *(sinistra)*, he declares that she has "a terrifying insight and a terrific—an almost lurid!—passion for stating the case of the underdog" (24). "What struck me," Ford writes, "was the singular instinct for form possessed by this young lady, an instinct for form being possessed by singularly few writers of English and by almost no English women writers. . . . her business was with passion, hardship, emotions" (24–26). Rhys, according to Ford, had masculine form, which is "true art," but this instinct was turned toward formlessness—her "business" was with "passion, emotions." While his designation of Rhys's technical ability as "instinct" has clear gender implications that situate his perceptions in the long anorexic tradition equating women with the bodily instinct, Ford hit upon the paradox that structures the Rhys canon. She has an "instinct for form" located in the most paradigmatic ideals of the modernist tradition, a method of writing based almost exclusively on cutting, combined with subject matter— "passion, hardship emotions"—that had been cut from the modernist canon.

Rhys applied an anorexic method to subject matter that worked against the very precepts she employed. This is not to say that the process of cutting is intrinsically bad, a necessarily political gesture, but that in the high modernist tradition, as the Woolf epigraph to the second chapter notes, what usually got cut was the philosophically messier problems of materiality and the body. In a letter Rhys writes that "I've never got over my longing for clarity, and a smooth firm

foundation underneath the sound and the fury. I've learnt one generally gets this by cutting" (*Jean Rhys Letters,* 60). By characterizing
her emotional content as "sound and fury," or chaos, and opposing
this to the "clarity and a smooth firm foundation" that would ostensibly give the chaos of emotions shape, Rhys employs a formal strategy
that is anorexic in other modernists. In their work the strategy that
excised emotional chaos extends to content as well as form. Rhys does
not perform the same excision. Not surprisingly, while Rhys was uniformly praised for her style, until the 1970s her subjects were condemned. "I am always being told," she writes to Evelyn Scott in 1931,
"that until my work ceases being 'sordid and depressing' I haven't
much chance of selling. I used to find this rather stupid but through
much repetition I have come half to believe that it is so" (*Jean Rhys
Letters,* 21). Although her work is deemed "sordid and depressing"
because she writes about female experience outside marriage and
conveys the lived emotions associated with that experience, Rhys explains that "you see I like emotion, I approve of it" (*Jean Rhys Letters,*
45). In her approval she marks her distance from the program of impersonality advocated by the canonical modernist tradition, which decidedly did not approve. Rhys's moral language isolates a tendency
within formalist approaches to literature to disapprove of the thornier
material problems that real bodies, particularly bodies designated
"other," encounter daily—which Ford associated with Rhys's "lurid
passion for stating the case of the underdog." In Rhys's incisive critique of the social conditions that produce underdogs, she deploys
an anorexic critical method against itself, refusing to purge unseemly
content. But she is implicated in the very traditions she so passion-
ately questions to the extent that she articulates the precepts of the
anorexic philosophy that define female subjectivity as lack, nothingness, "impotent shadow," and that she presents those precepts as unchangeable realities from which her characters cannot escape.

   In "Jean Rhys: Poses of a Woman as Guest," Alicia Borinsky as-
tutely argues that the seeming opposition in Rhys's work between the
petite femme and the *femme convenable,* the unrespectable and the
respectable woman, the mistress and the wife, actually marks a convergence.[27] "Such convergences," she writes, "may indeed constitute
a clue to the condition of the feminine in Jean Rhys" (302)—a condi-

tion, I argue, of nothingness, of nonexistence. The convergence is based on Rhys's insight that the situation of the *petite femme,* one of placelessness and thereby facelessness, is not so different from the position of the *femme convenable.* The latter, in the seeming solidity of her place within the social structure, sacrifices that part of herself—the body, her sexuality—that the *petite femme* is allowed to embody, since it becomes the definition of her being. The *petite femme's* identity is reduced to the excess of the feminine that the social structure cannot contain. Borinsky writes:

> they are victims of a pact that is never quite questioned; they dress and act for a male gaze that will, inevitably, humiliate them in the end. They stay in hotels. The rooms are suitable frames for their lack of personal history. Hotel rooms are always renewed, their continuity is precisely the lack of traces they present to the person who stays, the assurance that whoever stays there will never own them completely but will be a *guest.* (299)

The *petites femmes'* "lack of personal history" makes them "guests" who rely on the generosity of those who have a place, of those who live inside the sanctioned social structure. As women who are seen to exist only as objects of sexual interest, they look to the men they sleep with, or might sleep with, to bestow a life upon them: "Without clothes, without the tension generated by the interest in being observed, these *petites femmes* would not exist" (Borinsky, "Jean Rhys," 301). Paradoxically, their existence depends on their interchangeability: "it was impossible," Marya thinks in *Quartet,* "when one looked at that bed, not to think of the succession of *petites femmes* who had extended themselves upon it, clad in carefully thought out pink or mauve chemises, full of tact and savoir faire and savoir vivre and all the rest of it" (111). Their metaphysical status is marked by hotel rooms, interchangeable, always the same room, and the rooms are metonyms for the women themselves: "Walking in the night. Back to the hotel. Always the same hotel. You press the button. The door opens. You go up the stairs. Always the same stairs, always the same room" (*GMM,* 32). Like the rooms they inhabit as guests, essentially unrooted, placeless, temporary, the women are interchangeable: "I have no pride—no pride, no name, no face, no country. I don't belong anywhere," Sasha explains (*GMM,* 44).

Rhys's protagonists, as Borinsky notes in her essay "Jean Rhys," are "always the same woman" (289) or, to alter the formulation slightly, are "five women in analogous situations" (Hite, *Other Side,* 22). Their faceless interchangeability is a necessary feature of the system that divides women neatly in two groups: "Lois is a good woman and you are a bad one; it's quite simple. These things are. That's what is meant by having principles. Nobody owes a fair deal to a prostitute. It isn't done. My dear girl, what would become of things if it were? Come, come to think it over. Intact or not intact, that's the first question. An income or not an income, that's the second" (*Quartet,* 161). If a man gave the *petite femme* a "fair deal," nothing would separate her from the *femme convenable.* The barrier that divides women into "good" ones and "bad" ones would collapse, revealing that the sex- and class-based structure that determines women's "value" has nothing to do with the women themselves but with the structure that designates their positions. As Hite puts it, in *The Other Side of the Story,* "Rhys demonstrates how both social and narrative conventions mandate that certain categories of women must be devalued if other categories of women are to assume importance"; within the oppositional structure mandated by those conventions, however, the difference between women always breaks down (32–33). A "good" woman cannot have sexuality; a "bad" woman is forced to define herself as all sexuality: "he was forcing her to be nothing but the little woman who lived in the Hôtel du Bosphore for the express purpose of being made love to. A *petite femme. . . .* he did it with such conviction that she, miserable weakling that she was, found herself trying to live up to his idea of her" (*Quartet,* 118). Rhys's texts show how a woman comes to define herself as either the *petite femme* or the *femme convenable;* why a woman tries "to live up to [a man's] idea of her"; and how by this lack of independent self-definition, a woman comes to represent the two sides of the same coin.

To "live up to his idea of her" as a being who exists "for the express purpose of being made love to," the *petite femme* goes shopping. She buys new clothes, a new hat, new stockings whenever she has the money. She thinks about having her hair dyed and "hang[s] on to that thought as you hang on to something when you are drowning. Shall I have it red? Shall I have it black?" (*GMM,* 52). Her life is an attempt to live up to this idea and express it through her appearance, a beauty that advertises itself, but that also expresses a sensuality, passion, and emotion that the *femme convenable* has been forced to suppress in order to mark her difference from the *petite femme*, to indicate her position on the respectable side of the line. Although Rhys's early texts don't mention it explicitly, the characteristics the *petite femme* is said to embody are usually attributed to nonwhites, revealing the convergence of patriarchal and colonialist perspectives. But the division between respectable and disrespectable, good and bad, procreative and sexual, legitimate and illegitimate begins to collapse when one examines the conventions that create the divide and see in them that women's bodies are used to constitute their identity and are divided into separate uses or functions. Whether women occupy a position within the social structure or haunt its margins, they are still defined and define themselves as an emptiness that only their relations with men can "redeem," fill, then give shape and thereby existence. To the extent that they both require the shape that relations to men provide to feel that they exist, to have a place that will drag them out of the darkness of undifferentiated space, the *femme convenable* and the *petite femme* are in the same boat. Octavio Paz defines the *Chingada* as the feminine principle whose "passivity, open to the outside world, causes her to lose her identity. . . . she loses her name; she is no one; she disappears into nothingness; she *is* Nothingness. And yet she is the cruel incarnation of the feminine condition."[28] Similarly, Rhys shows how women come to nothing in the terms of the dominant cultural logic. It is this radical openness, femininity, nothingness that the anorexic tries to close down when she seals her mouth, refusing to let anything in.

As Borinsky shows in her essay "Jean Rhys," Rhys explores this condition of openness, nothingness, the connection between the *petite femme* and the *femme convenable* in a short story called "Illusion." But while Borinsky concludes that "the apparent differences between the two women fade into a disturbing darkness" (302), I examine the implications of this conclusion for the problematic of female subjectivity in relation to the anorexic position: the ambivalence that oscillates between male identification and the semblance of conventional femininity.[29] The protagonist of "Illusion" is Miss Bruce, who is independently wealthy and has a career as a painter. She was "a tall, thin woman, with large bones and hands and feet. One thought of her as a shining example of what . . . British character and training can do. . . . Going on all the time all round her were the cult of beauty and the worship of physical love. . . . [She just] dismissed them from her thoughts . . . rather like some sturdy rock with impotent blue waves washing round it."[30] Miss Bruce is a "sturdy rock" that makes waves "impotent" by her dismissal of "the cult of beauty and the worship of physical love." Had she participated in these rites, the passage suggests, she would be in the "impotent" position herself. Strength comes from nonparticipation. With her money and career Miss Bruce defines herself as not-woman and marks her distinction from women by adopting the male gaze:

When pretty women passed her in the streets . . . La Femme, exquisitely perfumed and painted, feline, loved—[Miss Bruce] would look appraisingly with the artist's eye, and make a suitably critical remark. . . . As for the others, the *petites femmes,* anxiously consulting the mirrors of their bags . . . "Those unfortunate people!" would say Miss Bruce. Not in a hard way, but broad-mindedly, breezily: indeed with a thoroughly gentlemanly intonation. (30)

Miss Bruce with her "gentlemanly intonation" can adopt this intonation only by renouncing the conventionally feminine—the "exquisitely perfumed and painted, feline, loved." She can afford to be magnanimous to the *petites femmes* because, with her own income, she is never in danger of becoming like them, dependent on their sexual desirability for material sustenance. Yet despite her own income, to avoid objectification she must not emphasize the sexuality and reproductive potential—her body—that would place her in the same category as La Femme. As a result, "[S]he always wore a neat serge dress in the summer and a neat tweed costume in the winter, brown shoes with low heels and cotton stockings" (30). She wears no makeup and is always "sensibly," (i.e., asexually) dressed: "some strain in her made her value solidity and worth more than grace or fantasies" (32).

Yet, as the narrator unexpectedly discovers, the feminine proclivity toward "grace and fantasy" is not entirely absent from Miss Bruce's life. Instead, it has been exiled to her closet, where the narrator finds "a glow of colour, a riot of soft silks . . . everything that one did not expect . . . an evening dress of a very beautiful shade of old gold: near it another of flame colour . . . a flowered crepe de chine, positively flowered! . . . a neat little range of smaller boxes: Rouge Fascination, Rouge Mandarine . . . an outfit for a budding Manon Lescaut" (33). In contrast to what the narrator has imagined, Miss Bruce possesses the tools of the feminine trade, the clothes and makeup that emphasize the sensuality of the body that defines La Femme. They have been contained, however, confined to the solid boundaries of a closet, a repression the narrator identifies: "I knew it all: Miss Bruce, passing by a shop, with the perpetual hunger to be beautiful and that thirst to be loved which is the real curse of Eve, well hidden under her neat dress, more or less stifled, more or less unrecognized" (34).

Expressed in bodily terms of hunger and thirst, the narrator's analysis of a femininity "well hidden," the "real curse of Eve," seems reduced to an essentialist equation between women, their physical bodies, and a desire for love. The narrator appears to suggest that all women, regardless of their identificatory positions as masculine or feminine, retain an essential femininity underneath. Yet the narrator also shows that the cultural authorization as a subject that Miss Bruce enjoys results from her income and her renunciation, both of which make her masculine: "'Of course . . . I should never make such a fool of myself as to wear them. . . . Not bad hands and arms, that girl!' said Miss Bruce in her gentlemanly manner" (36).[31] The seeming disjunction in narrative position points to a distinction between a traditional essentialism that denies women being (the traditional feminine) and an essential subjectivity that has a feminine part. Miss Bruce's ability to assume the traditionally masculine subject position and comment on other women depends on her "gentlemanly manner," which in turn depends on her refusal to wear the brightly colored sensual gowns that would mark her with the sensuality that traditionally is "woman." Since Miss Bruce is largely successful in her assumption of the nonsensual masculine position, Rhys also suggests that femininity is a masquerade, a costume one puts on and takes off, like Sasha in *Good Morning, Midnight,* who reports that "it isn't my face, this tortured and tormented mask. I can take it off whenever I like and hang it up on a nail" (43).

Yet, if Miss Bruce has hung her face up on a nail, she does so, Rhys suggests, at a price. She hangs it up in a way that makes her similar to the *petites femmes* she seeks to distance herself from, for her male identification positions her similarly to them. Miss Bruce's position is anorexic in that she denigrates herself as nonbeing and tries to escape through an exorcism of the feminine. Like Miss Bruce, most women are taught that femininity is nonbeing and so might seem to entirely reject the feminine, but struggle to maintain it as well. If they believe the terms of traditional gender constructions, women either believe that their essence is negative, or that they have no essence—a choice between, in effect, Eve or the Lacanian signifier. Like the *petites femmes* who are faceless because interchangeable, because they have masked themselves according to a standard that makes them all the same, Miss Bruce in her adoption of the male gaze effaces herself as well. The anorexic position of male identification doesn't work because in its assumption of a position different from other women, it makes women not-women; but since they are still framed as women in the larger social context, if they are not women, then they are nothing. If they are women, they are defined as nothingness; if they refuse the feminine subject position but are not male, they have no subject position within the dominant culture. Rhys exposes the Freudian logic in which all three paths of feminine development lead, as Sasha says, to "what they call an impasse. . . . I try, but they always see through me. The passages will never lead anywhere, the doors will always be shut. I know" (*GMM*, 9, 31). Because it accepts the psychoanalytic definition of the feminine as lack ("unfortunate little people," Miss Bruce calls women), the anorexic position of male identification is as much an impasse as is femininity. Inhibited by the constraints and thinking of her historical period, Rhys could not imagine a way out of the Freudian scheme. It is a course we are still attempting to chart.

II. The "Problem with No Name" (Reprise): The Constitution of Female Subjectivity in the Black Hole

Her life is a hell, vacillating between an all-consuming need for male love and approval . . .

*to persistent feelings of inauthenticity when she
does achieve his love. Thus her whole identity
hangs in the balance of her love life. She is allowed to love herself only if a man finds her
worthy of love.*

*In a male-run society that defines women as an
inferior and parasitical class, a woman who
does not achieve male approval in some form is
doomed. To legitimate her existence, a woman
must be* more *than a woman, she must continually search for an out from her inferior definition; and men are the only ones in a position to
bestow on her this state of grace.*

Shulamith Firestone,
The Dialectic of Sex

Any reading of Rhys that examines both the formal principles shaping
her work and the principles structuring her subject matter must consider the paradigm analyzed in chapter 1: the cultural constitution of
the feminine as black hole; that cavernous, consuming nothingness
that will suck everything into itself if anything gets too close. The acceptance of this particular construction as a self-construction, along
with a racial identity that functioned much the same way, left Rhys
with a feeling throughout her life, as Angier writes, "of being wanted
by no one and belonging nowhere; of being nothing, not really existing at all. Like her heroines Jean often felt like a ghost" (*Jean Rhys*,
11); like Sasha, who explains that "I am empty of everything but the
thin, frail trunks of the trees and the thin, frail ghosts in my room"
(*GMM*, 56).[32] As Bowlby writes in *Still Crazy after All These Years*,
"[P]ersonal identities in the novel are . . . non-identities, without-
identities" (41), and this nonidentity is intimately related to what
Bowlby terms a "narrative principle of undifferentiation that extends
to objects, places, times and to the phrases which mark them out"
(37). The underlying conception of feminine subjectivity in the black
hole structures the "narrative principle of undifferentiation." Because
she exists in a frame where there are no boundaries and thereby no
identities, everything is the same, a repetition in Rhys's texts: hotel
rooms, people, the routines that structure the heroines' existences. In

her autobiography Rhys writes, "I could imagine the house wasn't a house at all, but a person. . . . I do not know [other people]. . . . I see them as trees walking."[33] People are houses or trees, trees or houses are people—it makes little difference.

In a related sense, Rhys's heroines are often "empty ghosts," whose spiritual, emotional, or intellectual ghostliness is physically displaced on male figures like the *commis voyageur* in *Good Morning, Midnight,* who is "thin as a skeleton. He has a bird-like face and sunken, dark eyes . . . a paper man, a ghost, something that doesn't exist" (14, 35), or the figure in *After Leaving Mr. Mackenzie:* "His face was cadaverous, his nose long and drooping. He smiled continually as he danced, displaying very yellow teeth. . . . as he leaned over the table his face was all bones and hollows in the light of the lamp striking upwards, like a skeleton's face."[34] These male skeletons with no bodies haunt the margins of these texts as the obverse of female bodies with no subjectivities, women who are empty, only their bodies, "instrument[s], something to be made use of" (*GMM,* 58). The skeleton men physically figure the emptiness within the heroines, so that the characters enact the traditional view that men lack bodies, and women, souls.

Men aren't the only skeletons. For Rhys the emptiness also extends to a bouquet of "flowers . . . like the incalculable raising its head, uselessly and wildly, for one moment before it sinks down, beaten, into the darkness. Like skulls on long, thin necks. Plunging wildly when the wind blows, to the end of the curtain, which is their nothingness" (*GMM,* 131). The only agency ever allowed a Rhys heroine is attributed to flowers here, which are "like the incalculable raising its head, uselessly and wildly, for one moment before it sinks down, beaten, into darkness." The "incalculable" that manifests itself in the flowers, allowing them to raise their heads one last time before fading into nothing, mirrors the movement of Julia's spirit in *After Leaving Mr. Mackenzie:*

she was crying now because she remembered that her life had been a long succession of humiliations and mistakes and pains and ridiculous efforts. Everybody's life was like that. At the same time, in a miraculous manner, some essence of her was shooting upwards like a flame. She was great. She was a defiant flame shooting upwards not to plead but to threaten. Then the flame sank down again, useless, having reached nothing. (131)

The Rhys heroine, in this case, Julia, has an "essence" that always reaches "nothing." She has a brief moment as a "defiant flame," but this agency is short-lived, not long enough to accomplish anything. As Bowlby puts it in *Still Crazy after All These Years,* "[I]t is as though there were a continuous possibility of slumping back into some state of undifferentiation from which the attempt at a particular story—of this woman, these places, these times—has only artificially and momentarily managed to emerge" (35). Julia's sense of emptiness and nonexistence makes her only momentarily capable of "shooting upwards," distinguishing herself from the undifferentiated blankness from which she emerges. She, like other Rhys heroines, is without agency. The sole exception is Antoinette in *Wide Sargasso Sea,* who takes the flame imagery she identifies with and literalizes it when she enacts the only agency allowed her: burning down Thornfield Hall while she leaps to her death. Even though identity in Rhys is determined contextually rather than essentially, the one definitive action a heroine takes involves self-annihilation by flame, since she is denied the reconceptualization of "conventional notions of the individual" when she is removed from the Caribbean context so important to her.[35]

These heroines suffer from a sense of ghostly nothingness that at times recalls the existential dramas performed in male writers like Conrad: "And I felt as if all my life and all myself were floating away from me like smoke and there was nothing to lay hold of—nothing. And it was a beastly feeling, a foul feeling, like looking over the edge of the world" (*After Leaving Mr. Mackenzie,* 53). Sounding like Marlow in *Heart of Darkness* struggling with death "in an impalpable greyness with nothing underfoot, with nothing around, without spectators, without clamour, without glory,"[36] Rhys's heroines' lives that float away, that dissipate into nothing, form a familiar modernist trope, as does their figuration of nothing: "That was the first time you were afraid of nothing—that day when you were catching butterflies—when you had reached the patch of sunlight. You were not afraid in the shadow, but you were afraid in the sun . . . the last time you were happy about nothing; the first time you were afraid about nothing. Which came first?" (*After Leaving Mr. Mackenzie,* 160). Although the nothingness about which Rhys writes seems familiar, she provides a gender-specific nothingness directly related to the designation of women as bodies with nothing within, a nothingness that grants them a place in the cultural matrix only according to bodily reproductive or sexual potential. Rhys shows that while women's nothingness comes from within, it also comes from without, determined by their status within a specific social and historical context. The Caribbean context with its history of slavery adds even greater weight when the "productivity" of female slaves is considered—as a further context for Rhys's sense of the feminine.

Sasha in *Good Morning, Midnight* is the culmination of the series of self-conscious heroines who think they have no right to exist unless they are part of the bodily network of commodification and desire. She constructs internal dialogues about how others perceive her: "Qu'est-ce qu'elle fout ici, la vieille? What the devil (translating it politely) is she doing here, that old woman? What is she doing here, the stranger, the alien, the old one? . . . I quite agree too, quite. I have seen that in people's eyes all my life. I am asking myself all the time what the devil I am doing here. All the time" (54). Particularly as an older, unmarried woman with little money, Sasha sees herself as an excess that the cultural machine would like to discard. Her sense of placelessness, alienation, not belonging, is part of an internalization of the rejection that she attributes to others, and following their cue, she rejects herself—"I quite agree." Sasha echoes the Rhys of *Smile Please,* who writes, "I would never be part of anything. I would never really belong anywhere, and I knew it, and all my life would be the same, trying to belong, and failing. Always something would go wrong. I am a stranger and I always will be" (100).[37]

Rhys's women need acceptance from others, particularly men, to feel that they have the right to exist, and without it, they don't feel as if they do. They give men the godlike power either to bestow existence upon them or to deny it. Their existence seems dependent upon the ability to attract a man's love, which will fill the ghostly emptiness or strangeness they feel within. In *After Leaving Mr. Mackenzie,* the description of a woman who "was a shadow, kept alive by a flame of hatred for somebody who had long ago forgotten all about her" is characteristic of the way Rhys's texts reveal how women are constituted as shadows only granted existence in relation to men (15). Yet, to some extent, this is a position, which women still buy, that Rhys's heroines construct themselves.[38] In *Voyage in the Dark*, Anna explains that "I was so nervous about how I looked that three-quarters of me was in a prison, wandering round and round in a circle. If he had said that I looked all right or that I was pretty, it would have set me free."[39] She grants the male subject the power to "free" her from her prison of self-doubt through approving of her appearance. As in the perennial cultural myth of the femme fatale, she thinks his approval will give her a kind of agency, since it will draw men to her, thereby confirming her existence. As she finds out in the end, this kind of agency is the most transparent illusion and results in a rejection and abandonment that flings her further into nothingness. Anna's ability to attract men sexually, which is represented as a form of control, controls them only to the extent that they make use of her body, then abandon her.

The femme fatale is an extremely problematic concept, evoked again in our so-called postfeminist culture as a legitimate source of female power. The April 1993 issue of *Vanity Fair* features a cover graced by Sharon Stone, the latest in the series of women supposedly granted power by their ability to control men sexually. This piece includes a quotation from the "power feminist" Camille Paglia, who says that "women *are* bitches! . . . Woman is the bitch goddess of the universe. *Basic Instinct* has to be seen as the return of the femme fatale, which points up woman's dominance of the sexual realm . . . that interrogation scene in the police station. . . . There you see it: all those men around her, and a fully sexual woman turns them to jelly! The men are enslaved by their own sexuality!"[40] Although women may not have power, perhaps due to changes in the social and historical context that have given them more control over their economic destinies, at this point they are free from the devastation women suffer in Rhys as a result of this particular myth of agency. Yet the idea that women are granted agency through their sexuality has always obscured the power relations that determine that sexuality. If Rhys's work does nothing else, it provides an unquestionable refutation of the argument that women control men through sex. In Rhys if men turn to jelly they do so only momentarily, then feel hatred and indifference toward the object who has made them jelly, made them soft or flabby. The slavery is on the female side: a woman radically dependent upon men to confer her existence is virtually annihilated by the inevitable rejection. Yet this formulation does not necessarily cry "victim." Fully aware of her political disempowerment, the female subject desperately searches for an alternative position, and both anorexia and the femme fatale seem to offer some semblance of power: the first, over the self; the latter, over the other. The same logic that affirms the power and control of the anorexic position affirms the power and control of the femme fatale. Initially embraced, consciously or unconsciously, as a form of empowerment, both positions are equally destructive to the women who hold them. Understanding this dynamic is crucial to understanding Rhys.

The annihilation of subjectivity the Rhys heroines suffer is a position some find difficult to understand. For example, Wyndham writes in his introduction to *Jean Rhys Letters:*

Mysteriously, ever since the end of her first love affair [Rhys] had also been cursed by a kind of spiritual sickness—a feeling of belonging nowhere, of being ill at ease and out of place in her surroundings wherever these happened to be, a stranger in an indifferent, even hostile, world. She may have wanted to think that this crippling sense of alienation was merely that of a native West Indian exiled in a cold foreign land, but in fact she believed that the whole earth had become inhospitable to her *after the shock of that humdrum betrayal* [emphasis added]. All that had happened was that a kind, rather fatherly businessman, who had picked up a pretty chorus girl with a disconcertingly vague manner, decided after a year or so to pension her off. (10–11)

I hope that this chapter will have given this mystery an intelligible frame. It is hard to believe Wyndham's interpretation was written relatively recently (1984), for the blindness it demonstrates toward gender dynamics, particularly the one I analyze here, seems spectacularly anachronistic. If Wyndham's perspective is representative, some readers of Rhys are reading her with a particular set of assumptions about romantic relations. Anna in *Voyage in the Dark* and Rhys in her life seem to have experienced the relationship with this businessman as the murder of their soul, the annihilation of their existence and of the sense of safety and belonging all too recently granted them. "All that had happened," Wyndham writes, "was that a kind, rather fatherly businessman . . . had picked up a . . . chorus girl . . . [and pensioned] her off," as if this behavior is commonplace, so much a part of the daily network of heterosexual relations, *that it barely deserves comment.* As if unaware of the ideas disseminated by the women's movement, Wyndham reveals a lack of understanding of the devastating, compelling problems of a woman who has thought herself valued, "loved" as a sexual object, and who is then abandoned. If, in accordance with the cultural prescriptions for femininity, a woman's whole sense of value, worth, and existence in the world is determined by her relation to men, their rejection and abandonment of her *feels* anything but "humdrum." The rhetoric of "power feminism," the idea that women now have full equality, opportunity, and choice, is glibly tossed about in the postfeminist world, as is the argument that "all that has changed." However, a discussion with therapists whose files are swollen with dossiers on women whose emotional lives are still structured according to traditional femininity—the openness, nothingness that Paz describes—or with doctors who routinely prescribe antidepressants and other mood-altering drugs to women so stricken would show that the social construction of feminine subjectivity has not come "a long way, baby" since the time of Rhys's "humdrum betrayal."

This dynamic of subjectivity in the black hole requires further examination, especially in terms of Rhys's analysis of its connection to consumer culture. In her autobiography, *Smile Please,* Rhys writes of praying to God for beauty (as has Anna in *Voyage in the Dark*): "Staying in Castries for the wedding was a young man called Mr. Kennaway. When he watches me I can see that he doesn't think I am pretty. O God, let me be pretty when I grow up. Let me be, let me be. That's what is in his eyes: 'Not a pretty little girl'" (44–45). But Rhys's sense of deficiency, of not belonging, is always momentarily cured by a new outfit and the hope that it brings: "Auntie B had made me some dresses I liked, a Liberty bodice had been ordered for me from England, my stockings no longer drooped and I no longer thought of myself as an outcast" (45). This central deficiency the heroines feel within themselves makes them into the quintessential consumer subjects, always in need of some new prop that will help them fit in, make them desirable, an "outcast" no longer.

Since she accepts the social reduction of women to faceless, interchangeable bodies, when the Rhys heroine struggles to constitute herself, it is as a consumer subject who exists by virtue of her need to attract the men who will help her belong, give her a sense of place: "She began to imagine herself in a new black dress and a little black hat with a veil that just shadowed her eyes. After all, why give up hope when so many people had loved her? . . . 'My darling . . . My lovely girl . . . *Mon amour . . . Mon petit amour*'" (*After Leaving Mr. Mackenzie*, 181–82). Only the love of a man, ostensibly attracted by "a little black hat with a veil that just shadowed her eyes," can provide hope, a motivation to keep going and interact with the outside world. When there is no man, there is nothing: "There was a monsieur, but the monsieur has gone. There was more than one monsieur, but they have all gone. . . . I'll lie in bed all day, pull the curtains and shut the damned world out" (*GMM*, 81). Every time a heroine finds herself at the end of a chain of disastrous circumstances, failed relationships with men that deprive her of subjectivity, rather than granting it, she tries to start the cycle all over again—the only form of agency she knows—or she does nothing.

As the Rhys heroine is keenly aware, this sense of nonexistence remedied only by male approval fuels the whole consumer cycle. One requires goods to attract a man, to attract a man to exist, and a man to pay for the goods: "Just when you need it there's no money. . . . Tomorrow I'll go to the Galeries Lafayette, choose a dress, go along to the Printemps, buy gloves, buy scent, buy lipstick . . . buy anything cheap. Just the sensation of spending, that's the point" (*GMM*, 144–45). "The sensation of spending" brings about a new hope that says, "'If I could buy this, then of course I'd be quite different.' Keep hope alive and you can do anything, and that's the way the world goes round, that's the way they keep the world rolling. So much hope for each person. And damn cleverly done, too" (*Voyage in the Dark*, 130). "Cleverly done," because it keeps the heroines running on a treadmill they can never get off, the cycle is fed by that which seems to confer existence but which creates more emptiness: "the world is so-and-so and nothing can change it. For ever and for ever turning and nothing, nothing can change it" (*Voyage in the Dark,* 43). If women did not see themselves as black holes in need of a man to fill their lack, in need of goods to create the body to attract the man, who would buy the goods? Yet the goods and men never seem to do the trick. Beyond the new dress, the new hair, and the monsieur who goes, there is only an undifferentiated state of blankness where "you know that there is no past, no future, there is only this blackness, changing faintly, slowly, but always the same," so that "when I think 'tomorrow' there is a gap in my head, a blank—as if I were falling through emptiness. Tomorrow never comes" (*GMM,* 172, 159). But is the constitution of female subjectivity in the black hole a form of cannibalism, a consumption of the other, or is it anorexia, a form of self-consumption? The unanswered question of whether these empty gaps come from the heroines themselves, from the men that manipulate them, from literary convention, or all three, implies that the interrelation among these forces creates the gendered nothingness haunting Rhys's texts, as well as the necessity for her "narrative principle of undifferentiation."

III. Jean Rhys, Sexual Harassment, and the Academy: Manifestations of the "First Death," or Clipping Your Students' Wings

Long before the issues became feminist commonplaces, Rhys's fiction explored women's experience of embodiment in a culture constructed according to the terms described above that equate the male with mind/being and the female with body/nonbeing, and the sexual double standard and subjectivity constructions that result from those terms. Recent feminist work looks at how race and class inflect that sexual standard and makes nonwhite or working-class women even more vulnerable to the sexual abuse related to those constructions. Much of Rhys's fiction, as well as her personal sense of nonbeing, was motivated by what we now call "sexual harassment," a phenomenon that continues to affect women's lives long after the experience itself, and that had no name at the time Rhys was writing. Sexual harassment was simply a lived reality, an integral part of the relations between men and women that, because unnamed, was never questioned. The experience articulated in the short story "Goodbye Marcus, Goodbye Rose" was a crucial determinant in Rhys's identity formation. Rhys becomes a ghost to herself, alienated and split off from herself, in an experience of sexual harassment narrated in this tale and written in diary form in her "Black Exercise Book." The skeleton of "Goodbye Marcus, Goodbye Rose" comes directly from the diary, with whole passages repeated word for word. Thus, it offers an insight into the sense of nothingness that haunts both her characters and her life, a particular form of nothingness that has haunted my own life, as well as the lives of other women who only now feel authorized to articulate the previously unnameable forces that have structured the narratives of their lives.[41] In the backlash culture of the midnineties, however, there is increasing pressure to remain silent.

Remaining silent is precisely what Rhys didn't do, and for this we owe her. Rhys's experience was recorded in diary version first, what she calls her "record of facts." An old friend of Rhys's mother's, a war hero about seventy years old, stopped in Dominica with his wife on the way back to England. The family had represented him in hyperbolic terms as "the hero of numberless adventures" and as "an almost fabulous person."[42] Rhys longed to meet him, and as he "spoke very politely to her, [and] included her in the conversation, treat[ing] her 'with deference, exactly as if [she] were grown up,'" Rhys "'was captivated . . . and [she] went on being captivated'" (*Jean Rhys*, 27). He asked Rhys to take him on a tour of the town, and she felt flattered. During this outing, they stopped for a while in the Botanical Gardens, sitting on a secluded bench. After an interlude of pleasant conversation, he asked her how old she was. When she replied, "[F]ourteen," he responded, "[Q]uite old enough to have a lover," and placed his hand under her shirt. According to the diary, "[I]t travelled downwards, a cool, masterful hand, until stopped by the waist belt. . . . this is a mistake . . . a mistake . . . if I sit quite still & don't move he'll take his hand away & won't realize he touched me." She felt, she writes, "dreadfully attracted, dreadfully repelled."[43] He never touched her physically again, but when the walks continued at her mother's insistence that she must not be "rude," the relationship took the form of an intellectual seduction: "Mostly he talked about me, me, me. It was intoxicating . . . irresistible." From there the conversations took a decidedly Sadeian turn. In *Jean Rhys,* Angier describes "[A]lways he would return to . . . the same themes: submission, punishment, cruelty. That was love, he told her, that was making love: not kindness, but violence and cruelty. She would only be allowed to rebel enough to make it more fun to force her to submit. She would have to obey his will. And always in the end she would have to be punished" (28).

Although the conversations bothered Rhys, what bothered her more was that she listened to them. There must be something wrong with her, she thought, for doing so: "I only struggled feebly," Rhys writes, "what he had seen in me was there. . . . that could only mean that he'd seen at once that [I] was not a good girl—who would object—but a wicked one—who would listen. He must know. He knew. It was so." Soon after, the man and his wife left Dominica to return to England. Ten years later, he "died an easy death at the age of eighty, respected and loved by all. And I? . . . I became very good at blotting things out, refusing to think about them. . . . it went out of my memory like a stone."[44] But though the incident may have gone "out of her memory like a stone" ("stone" suggests, to the contrary, an immovable presence), her self-conception remained articulated along the trajectory this man's actions seemed to suggest. She was "wicked. . . . It was so."

"Goodbye Marcus, Goodbye Rose" explores the consequences of this self-construction. Closely paralleling the diary, the narrator reports that Captain Cardew "was not only a very handsome old man but a hero who had fought bravely in some long ago war. . . . it had been impressed on her how kind it was of him to bother with a little girl like herself" (*CSS,* 285). Phoebe's lack of subjectivity, her diminished form as "a little girl," is supplemented by Captain Cardew, who has an important "place," and who therefore can bestow upon her the social importance she lacks. Phoebe is attracted to the captain as a person of social importance who is also physically attractive. She is flattered that a person of importance wants to spend time talking to her, because this suggests that she herself is a person of importance. Initially, Captain Cardew offers Phoebe a kind of confidence, but like the confidence of the femme fatale, it is illusory, dearly bought.[45] As in the diary, in the story Captain Cardew asks, "[H]ow old are you?" and, upon receiving a response, proclaims her "'old enough to have a lover!' His hand, which had been lying quietly by his side, darted towards her, dived inside her blouse and clamped itself around one very small breast" (*CSS*, 286). His action produces a deep sense of ambivalence in Phoebe, who freezes and decides that, in her disempowered position, it is best to disregard what happened:

> Phoebe remained perfectly still. "He's making a great mistake, a great mistake," she thought. "If I don't move he'll take his hand away without really noticing what he's done." . . . He talked of usual things in a usual voice and she made up her mind that she would tell nobody of what had happened. Nobody. It was not a thing you could possibly talk about. Also no one would believe exactly how it happened, and whether they believed her or not she would be blamed. (286)

"It was not a thing you could possibly talk about," because, with the configuration of power structuring their positions, and with the codes that define Phoebe as a maturing girl, as a sexual body, there was nothing to talk about and no name for what had happened. She was an enticement, he acted, nature asserted itself. "She would be blamed," because, within the system a female body determines that she is always responsible for that embodiment and its consequences.

The alternative position to embodiment offered to women is that of the anorexic or the seeming anorexic. In Rhys's story, when the walks continue, Captain Cardew "never touch[es] her again"; instead, he tells her stories:

> Someone—was it Byron?—had said that women were never so unattractive as when they were eating and it was still most unfashionable for them to eat heartily. He'd watch in wonder as the ethereal creatures pecked daintily, then sent away almost untouched plates. One day [Byron] had seen a maid taking a tray laden with food up to the bedrooms and the mystery was explained. But these stories were only intervals in the ceaseless talk of love, various ways of making love, various sorts of love. He'd explain that love was not kind and gentle, as she had imagined, but violent. Violence, even cruelty, was an essential part of it. (287)

Either women must be "ethereal creatures" who express their disembodiment, their noncarnal natures through refusal of food, or embodied, they must be objects of violent love. Similar images persist in contemporary constructions of the female body. The most popular recent models seem to fall into the category of either the "postmodern body" of Kristen McMenamy, the "rail-thin, almost absurdly angled woman, all mouth and legs, a paradigm of the postmodern beauty aesthetic," or the pornographic body of the Guess? model, all breasts and blonde hair, slipping her dress strap off her shoulder or drawing back the beads that curtain her fantasy boudoir.[46] In Captain Cardew's representation of Byron's view of female embodiment, the fashionable anorexic is a fake, someone who puts on the mask of food refusal but reveals her essential, embodied nature when she is caught eating. Her punishment for that nature is violence and cruelty, an anger enacted upon her body as if to punish it for its existence. Phoebe learns from her talks with the captain that a woman is not allowed to exist bodily, and if she does, then she is bad and will be punished.

When Captain Cardew leaves, she defines herself according to these terms: "she . . . began to wonder how he had been so sure, not only that she'd never tell anybody but that she'd make no effort at all to stop him talking. That could only mean that he'd seen at once that she was not a good girl. . . . He knew. It was so" (*CSS*, 288–89). The initial confidence he had given her, the flattering attention to the "little girl like herself" that he uses to draw her in, ends in causing her to think about herself as fundamentally "bad"—which can mean "invalid, void"; "failing to reach an acceptable standard"; "not fresh, spoiled"; "morally objectionable"; "inadequate or unsuited to a purpose"; or "incorrect, faulty."[47] Phoebe comes to fully accept herself as "morally objectionable" and "faulty" in terms of the cultural construction of proper female sexual behavior. According to that construction, she "[fails] to reach an acceptable standard," and in terms of the purity a good girl is supposed to offer a husband is "spoiled." Phoebe combines all these definitions to construct herself as "invalid, void"— a black hole.[48]

The only screen she has to cover that hole, what makes it endurable, is the fiction of power offered by the position of the femme fatale. Captain Cardew makes her feel significant through his attentions. She feels insignificant in the first place because the cultural matrix situates her as valueless, in need of attention to meaningfully exist.[49] He gives her a sense of power or value through constructing her as a sexual subject, as a woman reduced to man's sexual use, "the little woman who lived in the Hotel du Bosphore for the express purpose of being made love to" (Rhys, *Quartet,* 118). This later position, Marya's in *Quartet,* is something that she *accepts herself,* that she wills upon herself. If, as Borinsky writes in her essay "Jean Rhys," Rhys's stories are really about "the same woman," then Captain Cardew's constitution of Phoebe as a being for sex underlies Marya's acceptance of the position of the *petite femme* (288–302). Phoebe ambivalently accepts this position, falling for the fiction of power it offers:

Wasn't it quite difficult being a wicked girl. . . . the thought of some vague irreparable loss saddened her. Then she told herself that anyway she needn't bother any longer about whether she'd get married or not. . . . She could hardly believe that only a few weeks ago she, like all the others, had secretly made lists of her trousseau, decided on the names of her three children. Jack. Marcus. And Rose. Now good-bye Marcus. Goodbye Rose. The prospect before her might be difficult and uncertain but it was far more exciting. (*CSS,* 289–90)

Deprived of the traditional destiny for women by her wickedness, Phoebe sees the elimination of that destiny as a liberation from worry about social failure, worry that she will be an old maid. Although "difficult and uncertain," the future, she thinks, actually has more to offer in terms of excitement, for she will not be the traditional wife and mother but the mistress, the femme fatale who tempts and controls men through her sexuality and gets them to do things they would not do otherwise. But the rest of Rhys's novels expose this control for the chimera it is, showing how it systematically drains women's bodies and souls until they are ghosts, entirely empty. Excitement becomes repetition, placelessness, an endless succession of hotel rooms and an abject dependence on men who make use of a woman's body and then pay her off with as little as possible. Through her experience with Captain Cardew, Phoebe comes to define herself as bad, unworthy of the one acceptable subject position that society offered, and begins her pilgrimage as a ghost.

Significantly, the experience with Captain Cardew deprives her not only of the possibility of goodness defined in social terms but also of

the ability to write. Because she has no connection to either herself
or the world around her, she no longer feels she has anything to say:
"On hot fine nights she'd often lie there in her nightgown looking up
at the huge brilliant stars. She'd once tried to write a poem about
them but had not got beyond the first line: 'My stars. Familiar jewels.'
But that night she knew that she would never finish it. They were not
jewels. They were not familiar. They were cold, infinitely far away,
quite indifferent" (288). Through her experience, Phoebe is fundamentally dispossessed. Nothing, including herself, belongs to her any
longer. She is deprived of a sense of agency, of the power to own, of
the ability to say "my stars" or to say anything. Most of all, she cannot
tell what happened to her, since "no one would believe exactly how it
happened, and whether they believed her or not she would be
blamed." She is consigned to the position of the dispossessed, to the
position of silence.[50]

Both the story "Goodbye Marcus, Goodbye Rose" and Rhys's self-
conception are based on the kind of incident that occurs on a regular
basis and in the most unexpected situations.[51] In the context of an
often cynical so-called political correctness that can characterize public attitudes toward gender issues in the 1990s, today harassment
takes forms that are not always as blatant as what Rhys experienced,
but that affect women in similar ways.[52] While violent experiences
such as rape contribute to the development of a subjectivity haunted
by the particular form of feminine nothingness seen in Rhys's work,
other, more subtle experiences can function in the same way. Guided
by Rhys, my own experiences of sexual harassment give me a strong
identification with Rhys's text, a powerful framework from which I
can embody them, make them intelligible in daily experience, rather
than anomalies or aberrations. The personal, political, and literary
come together in the resonances between my text and Rhys's, between our texts and many others.[53] And those resonances clarify how
the personal struggles of women, with their cultural designation as
nonbeing, reflect the gendered political space of Western culture.
One experience in particular gives me a way of understanding why
and how Rhys constituted female subjectivity as a black hole from
which there seems no escape.

What I offer is a narrative of a daily, ordinary experience, set in an

academic context, in which neither individual concerned is explicitly
at fault. It is a narrative that takes place, however, within the fundamentally hierarchical, sexist frame that gives female students a kind
of illusory power and sense of themselves only through their sexual
attractiveness, and that gives male professors the license and agency
to relate to female students in a manner characterized by sexual overtones. As in the Rhys text, with parallel subject positions to those of
young girl and captain, this frame ensures that both student and professor consider those overtones complimentary, rather than a form of
sexual harassment.[54] The immensely difficult question is that, within
and because of this frame, if both parties encouraged this kind of interaction, can it be called "harassment"?

Starting at the age of twenty, as an undergraduate I worked closely
with a particular professor. Like many other young women of that age
who have internalized the complex, unspoken, but immensely powerful set of rules governing male/female, professor/student relationships, I saw him as an authority, someone whose work I admired very
much, and whom I naively invested with a great sense of knowledge
about the many mysteries of life. I was attracted to his ease, his easy-
going manner that seemed to break down the kind of hierarchical
relationship between professor and student that seemed inexplicable
and annoying when I was younger and had not yet had any students
myself. Like Captain Cardew, he seemed to treat students as equals,
to consider seriously what they had to say, and to present himself as a
congenial mentor and even as a friend. "People are people," his attitude seemed to say, regardless of the position they occupy within the
context of power relationships that constitute any academic situation.
To a young female student, who for that reason has little power, an
apparently antihierarchical attitude is very attractive. Like Phoebe I
was flattered that he would "bother with a girl like myself," and this
gave me a sense of importance and confidence I otherwise would not
have had.

But part of the breakdown of traditional boundaries that seemed
to characterize his approach was a charming flirtatiousness to at least
some of his female students. This was not intended as a harmful gesture but as an openness and even as a compliment. Also, I must add
in all honesty that I found him physically attractive, as Phoebe had

found Captain Cardew attractive. This attractiveness, the mystique that surrounds the artist, and the usual authority a student grants her professors, combined with the personal recognition and attention he extended to students, were devastating. Like thousands of students before me, I developed a crush on my professor.

To the individual concerned and to other members of the faculty, this crush was obvious, and they seemed to find it mildly amusing. As with Phoebe, whose sense of herself was bolstered by the attentions of Captain Cardew, I was grateful for any personal attention my professor would give me, and I regularly went to his office hours and talked to him as much as I could. I think I remember that, in the lack of judgment twenty-year-olds have in these matters, I even knitted him a scarf for Christmas—a monstrous, uneven, horrible thing that he probably threw away as soon as he received it. I don't know, but I do know I made my feelings painfully obvious. I never made any explicit advances; I just hung around him. His reaction was not to encourage an advance, nor did he make one himself, at least not initially. But he did treat me as someone special, not as just another student— that was what got me. He did encourage a kind of friendship, and he didn't tell me to knock it off. He casually flirted with me, exchanging various pleasantries and even indulging the intense conversations that undergraduates seem to have a proclivity for. Sometimes he would tell me how much I was like his wife. Once in a while, we went to lunch. He encouraged my work, listened to my problems and anxieties, and wrote me letters of recommendation for scholarships. Throughout, there was an underlying sexual tension that marked our interactions, which made me think that he supported my work and enjoyed talking with me because I was physically attractive, rather than because he really respected either my work or conversation.

One moment in particular stands out. In the spring of my senior year, faced with graduation in the summer and an uncertain future, I went to his office in a particularly exacerbated state of distress. He listened to me for a couple of hours and offered what advice he could. As I got up to go, feeling better than when I had come in, he grabbed me by the arm, turned me around, and kissed me hard on the mouth. I asked, "What was that for?" and he replied, "Because I wanted to."[55] I remember feeling confused and disturbed. As with Phoebe, who felt that "it was not a thing you could possibly talk about," since "whether they believed her or not she would be blamed," I never questioned what his response claimed: the unquestionable right to act toward me however he chose. Accustomed to treatment as, even seeing myself as, a sexual being a priori, as a body, rather than a mind, I could say nothing. He could do "as he wanted" because, as a body, not a person, I had no agency that could question him. Because of his authority, it wouldn't have occurred to me, which is why some legal definitions of harassment as "unwanted advances" incorrectly assume that both persons are acting equally as free agents. And like Rhys, I assumed to a certain extent that there was something essentially wrong with me, something tainted or polluted, because I was defined as body, as sex. It was an impossible circle: I got attention for sexual attractiveness, and this made me then interact accordingly. But that same attractiveness was used to discount me as a person, and it was the recognition of my value as a person—of which I was uncertain—that I was after in the first place. Yet, because I had willingly put myself in that position, I also felt to a certain extent that there was something fatally flawed within me. If I was treated as body, not being, there must be something in me that deserved it, that solicited this response.

When our relationship became the subject of a literary work he wrote based on our experiences, he gave me a copy with a note scrawled across the top—"Leslie, thank-you for [inspiring] this writing. I hope you like it as much as I do." He signed his name. The work in its draft form was graphic, making explicit reference to events that involved more than a kiss: "taking his penis into her mouth / and then she felt it stuck there like an eternal toothache." That he would write and give me a copy with a note such as this shows the degree to which he did not realize that his actions in any way could be construed as harassment. Again, he thought his behavior toward me was complimentary.

I, however, had begun studying feminist theory in earnest and was starting to think this behavior was anything but complimentary. The incident that triggered the work was a fight we had about the Chinese women writers we had been studying in his seminar, whose writing was about entrapment, sexual exploitation, and the longing for expanded boundaries. I was powerfully affected and upset by the content of this writing and expressed my feelings. He said something like "What's the matter—they died years ago." My dawning consciousness that these Chinese women's situation was very relevant to my relationship with him made me respond with a kind of anger that shocked him so much that he tried to figure it out through writing about it. His work more or less presented women's subordinate position in society vis-à-vis men as inevitable and placed me in a "long line of women" whispering secrets in each others's ears across the centuries (the resonance with Rochester's designation of Antoinette as part of a "long, long line" of women who "know the secret and will not tell it" [*Wide Sargasso Sea*, 172] shows the persistence of this trope). Reading the work, I saw clearly for the first time how he actually saw me. I felt simultaneously betrayed, hurt, and immensely stupid.

From the perspective of Rhys's novels, his actions were an abuse of a power conferred upon him by a masculinist power structure that grants women agency only in sexual terms and so makes them willing accomplices to this kind of interaction. From his perspective, as I read it, he had a little fun with a cute girl who'd had a crush on him for a number of years. He thought, I think, that the personal attention he gave me was complimentary—the established professor taking the coed seriously enough to make her a subject of his work and to spend time talking to her. I never tried to explain to him that the work was offensive and angered me very much because it put me in the position of muse, of inspiring writing although I considered myself a writer, and because he had placed me in "a long line of women" who couldn't do anything about the social dynamics that diminished them. I never tried to explain that the final, more sexualized turn the relationship took was just an extension of years of my feeling that despite his position as my teacher, mentor, and faculty supervisor on various projects, his interaction with me had far more to do with what I looked like than how I wrote.

I never tried to explain that the basis of his interaction with me, which forced me to take the position of the embodied feminine, diminished me in ways very difficult to name. I lived a dichotomy, within which I kept thinking, "I could swear to God I do exist (the position of the writer), but everyone keeps telling me that existence is contingent upon my relation to men (the muse position), and sometimes I believe them." Like Rhys's characters, I wanted to fly, but my wings were clipped—not by the "evil other" but by a structure to which we were both subject.[56] In this particular configuration, I could only momentarily and partially experience myself as Rhys's "flamboyant flame," as genuinely alive. This affected my writing, although I continued to do it. It was an unsolvable paradox: on one level my writer mentor encouraged me to write, whereas on another more subtle and pervasive level he treated me as body, nonagent, nonbeing. Nonbeing can't write, can't say "my stars" or say anything at all. Like Rhys, I was struggling to articulate myself when I wasn't even sure that I was alive. I felt alienated from myself and from that "fatal flaw" of sex that I hid inside, but that he and others could see, which made me a muse, not a writer. I experienced a dichotomy that reflected simultaneously a belief in my own essential emptiness and a sense of being. My sense of being was continually contradicted, for in our interaction vis-à-vis the positions my professor and I took up so very easily, like Rhys's characters, I wore the mask of the feminine, the embodied, sexualized position of nonbeing.

I never explained that this form of interaction had caused me a great deal of pain and had made me a ghost to myself, an essential emptiness. I felt that this would be so far outside the paradigm he used to construct the world that there would simply be no way of reaching him. I felt guilty and foolish, thinking that from his perspective, I had been acting the part of the ditsy coed for a very long time— if he had been treating me like a sexual object, well, I had presented myself that way. Furthermore, compared to some of his colleagues, his behavior was restrained.

I felt that it was easier just to let the matter drop, to leave it behind. And I still felt some kind of loyalty to him. I still do. Since he was an important part of my earlier life, I would still like to call him a friend. But I never left the ambivalence of those experiences behind. They left me feeling as if I had an amputated limb, a numbed, dull place, a silence I had swallowed. The dynamic that characterized our relationship was structured in such a way as to take away my dignity as an articulate, thinking, feeling human being. Furthermore, I willingly participated in this dynamic, since, to the naive and immature woman, it seems to offer a kind of power that masks the dehumanization actually taking place. The question is: What constitutes appropriate behavior between male professors and female students in general or, for that matter, between female professors and their students? In the context within which such behavior was situated and the differences in age and maturity, was my professor responsible for drawing appropriate boundaries? Was Captain Cardew in Rhys's story?

Another professor commented that he had never heard of harassment in the department: "Affairs, yes. Marriages, yes. Harassment, no." But my situation raises the question of whether an affair or even a quasi-affair like mine can be called harassment. From my perspective, I say, "Yes it was, but he didn't mean it to be harassment." Nonetheless, his intentionality is not really the issue here, since it is the whole context of professorial empowerment brought to play in the sexual register that is at question—a context so pervasive that it passes for normalcy. Since the context determines the frame in which individual incidents are played out, a focus on this context, rather than on specific instances, helps address the real issues that underlie them.

As Rhys's work and my own experience show, sexual harassment is not a question of incidents but of the social dynamics that allow incidents to happen, and that give them a particular form. And when those dynamics empower one group of people at the expense of another in ways that are very subtle because they are so much a part of the social fabric that constitutes daily reality, an examination of those dynamics is the only way to confront the issue. Common sense dictates that any investigation related to sexual harassment needs to address those dynamics and how they pertain to individual situations.

From the perspective of one set of assumptions about the world— the business-as-usual perspective that says, "Boys will be boys," and "If women ask for it, what's the harm"—my experience with this professor wasn't harassment at all. From the perspective of some versions of feminist theory, I had constructed myself according to the dictates of a system that made me a willing participant in my own harassment. And from my own perspective, torn between the arguments of those two worlds, both of which are a part of me, I know only that my narrative recounts a set of incidents that occurs daily. Nearly every week I have students come to me with their own stories, most recently a twenty-year-old undergraduate who got a note from her professor with his address, phone number, and the assertion that he was "available for dating." Every time the topic of sexual harassment comes up in conversation, all the women present have their own versions. What is the meaning of those experiences, and what frame will be used to interpret similar experiences as awareness shifts and sexual harassment becomes a problem, rather than the norm? When male sexual prerogative and authority no longer constitute the norm of the academic (and other) environments? When female students experience themselves as empowered subjects, rather than as empowered only if they are objects of sexual interest? As beings instead of ghosts?

I was a student in a period when the professor's interaction with me was a part of business as usual. This context made me feel that articulating any objections to my experience would result in hostility, antagonism, and dismissal, or, as Rhys puts it, simple disbelief. The inability to articulate is crucial because my inability to speak made me experience myself as a numbed ghost. I was not a victim, as the new movement in power feminism would have it.[57] If I felt that I had missing limbs, these were limbs I had at least partially amputated myself. I was emotionally frozen and did not regain a sense of feeling until I articulated my experience. Whether or not such experiences, forged in relation to the anorexic logic that sometimes leads to anorexia, rather than texts, will be interpreted as harassment or as business as usual remains to be seen. I do know that, now more than ever, in a hostile political climate that encourages silence, such experiences bring together questions we must continue to address. They are questions that Rhys, sixty years or more ahead of her time, had already articulated in "Goodbye Marcus, Goodbye Rose." In her last novel, *Wide Sargasso Sea*, she attempts a tentative answer, a way out we have only begun to see.

IV. Beyond Negation (?): Wide Sargasso Sea

In *Smile, Please,* Rhys puts herself on trial and attempts to justify her existence to the prosecution. She declares that "if I stop writing my life will have been an abject failure. It is that already to other people. But it could be an abject failure to myself. I will not have earned death" (133). Self-consciously aware that this statement is somewhat clichéd, Rhys has the prosecution respond that *"you are aware of course that what you are writing is childish, has been said before"* (133). It has *"been said before,"* but Rhys means it. And with *Wide Sargasso Sea,* she earns the death she doesn't feel she deserves. In *Wide Sargasso Sea* the ghosts of nothing turn into a qualified something through an agency of negation figured by flame. Rhys uses this trope for the "essence" that, in the other texts, "sank down again, useless, having reached nothing." Here the flame catches fire.

In *Wide Sargasso Sea* the heroine seems to have been consumed or cannibalized by her husband. Yet the text is as much about anorexia, self-consumption, as it is about consumption by the other and the relationship between them. Rhys's much acclaimed last novel, it represents a contextualization of the personal missing from her other works. For this reason, among others, it is the most popular, most often hailed as her "triumph" or "masterwork" that succeeds where the other novels fail.[58] For it is *Wide Sargasso Sea* that is the most definitively modern in the high modernist, anorexic sense: a tendency toward the metaphoric pole in prose style, an elaborate structure of literary allusion, and a presentation of character that relies on history and depth, rather than the everyday details of empirical perception.[59] *Wide Sargasso Sea* is indisputably the most beautiful, the most aesthetic, of Rhys's longer texts and also the most anorexic in its use of the agency of negation. Like the anorexic who seems to resist ideology while ultimately affirming it as she literally incorporates its standards into her flesh, radically internalizing its values, *Wide Sargasso Sea* seems to resist the logic of white male European colonialist domination. But with its insistence on the empty ringing of the modernist "nothing, nothing," the text adheres to the same logic of the black hole—central to the logic of anorexia—that supports the values it seems to protest, and like anorexia, it is a failed protest. Yet perhaps there is a residue, some way in which it is not entirely co-opted. "Fire purifies everything," according to the typically modernist metaphysics of the flame seen in Kafka, but it always leaves something behind. Careful study of Rhys, who both supports and deconstructs modernist values, shows what the ideals of high modernism do to disempowered subjects, and why we must be most wary of the most beautiful products, the most fully achieved art. Combining a use and a deconstruction of those ideals—read in its relation to the literary text that frames it, Charlotte Brontë's *Jane Eyre*—*Wide Sargasso Sea* perhaps does something else with nothing.

Wide Sargasso Sea is an intertextual study of *Jane Eyre* set primarily in the Caribbean. The significance of the setting is that it articulates, according to Emery, "the complex interrelationship between the condition of oppressed races and cultures under European imperialism and the masculine oppression and silencing of women within European society," conditions different but similar in ways very important to Rhys (*Rhys at "World's End,"* 62). One similarity is the power of naming and ownership given to Rochester under English law. In Rhys's version, Rochester names her "Bertha," which is not her real name. She is the madwoman who was Rochester's first wife, and she narrates the events before and after they go to England. There is also a middle section from Rochester's point of view. The novel tells the other side of the story, the side that Antoinette herself proclaims: "there is always the other side, always" (128). *Wide Sargasso Sea* is the voice of the repressed other of the first text, the story, as Joyce Carol Oates puts it in her introduction to *Jane Eyre,* of "the appropriation, colonization, exploitation, and destruction of a pastoral tropical world by a wholly alien, English sensibility."[60] It is the text where Antoinette gets to speak her piece in dialogue with Rochester, so that the English sensibility presented as the norm in *Jane Eyre* is reduced to a particular point of view, its colonizing aspects unmasked. For Rhys, what is appropriated and exploited is not just the land and the indigenous peoples but also the subjectivity of the female other whose ways of knowing, thinking, and feeling are affiliated with that land, with place instead of conventions of individual essence. The Caribbean context draws attention to ways in which marginal subjectivities are often forged in response to trauma, through, according to Emery, "a search for community and place that results from colonial and sexual exile" (*Rhys at "World's End,"* 174). Struggling with competing modes of subjectivity but constituted as a subject according to the precepts of English sensibility through her marriage to Rochester, Antoinette accepts a nothingness she redeems in the end. The novel exposes, in Emery's words, "the conventions of marriage and romance within fiction as coercive institutions through which feminine identity is constituted while female subjectivity is denied" (176). In response to that denial, Antoinette can only act through an agency of negation that nonetheless produces *something,* and that complicates the anorexic position.

I am one of those people who has never liked *Jane Eyre.* In my view, like a dog or a cat person, you are either a *Wuthering Heights* person or a *Jane Eyre* person. For me, and, I suspect, for most of us in the anorexic position who have at some point embraced the agency of negation as our only alternative, *Wuthering Heights* presents more familiar terrain.[61] But read with Rhys, the story begun in *Jane Eyre* becomes something else altogether. Instead of staging a competition between women, between the two Mrs. Rochesters, Rhys's text provides a forum for their interrelation, giving figuration to that repressed excess that will bring the whole house down in a way that even Catherine and Heathcliff could not.[62]

Wide Sargasso Sea is a sustained examination of the destruction of a woman's spirit by love.[63] That destruction is articulated in Antoinette's theory of existence and death that Rochester reports in his narrative. "There are always two deaths," she says, "the real one and the one people know about" (128). For Antoinette, the "real" death is not the physical death but the spiritual one. "The one people know about" is physical. The "real" death occurs sometimes long before the physical death and is the result of subjectivity in the black hole. Anorexics, like the zombie women or walking dead throughout Rhys, are powerful examples of such ghostly subjectivities although anorexics often literally drift into nothingness. In *Wide Sargasso Sea* the "real" death occurs in connection to the male agency that, because it gains definition as agency by reference to the female as not-agency, can grant "life" by extension or proximity—and can take it away as well. "If I could die," says Antoinette to Rochester before the break in their relationship, "now, when I am happy. Would you do that? You wouldn't have to kill me. Say die and I will die" (92). She is only happy when she has his love, since that love grants her existence, and as the proprietor of that existence, he "wouldn't have to kill [her]," because she will do it herself, annihilate herself if he just gives the word. Because, as with the heroines of the previous novels, Antoinette's sense of existence is conferred by men, they are also given the power to take it away. She tells Rochester, "I never wished to live before I knew you. . . . Why did you make me want to live? Why did you do that to me?" "Because I wished it," Rochester replies, fully accepting his position as the proprietor, literally and figuratively, of her existence, "isn't that enough?" "Yes, it is enough," she answers, "but if one day you didn't wish it. What should I do then?" (91–92). On the material level Antoinette, who had inherited thirty thousand pounds from her stepfather, loses it all in her marriage to Rochester. Her existence becomes his property: "I have no money of my own at all, everything I had belongs to him" (110). Therefore, when, as she suspected, he doesn't wish to make her live, Rochester has the power to deny her individual agency on both a spiritual and material level, and in a system that defines existence as agency, this gives him the power to deny her existence. According to Antoinette, she is a ghost before she meets Rochester. He brings her to life and then makes her a ghost again—what she calls the "real" death.

As Rhys's work continually shows, for a woman to be articulated in the social network as anything but a ghost, she needs the love of a man to give her a position, to drag her from the black hole of nonexistence. Rochester invokes this power, as well as its source: "I tell you she loves no one, anyone. I could not touch her. Excepting as the hurricane will touch that tree—and break it. You say I did? No. That was love's fierce play. Now I'll do it. . . . She'll not dress up and smile at herself in that damnable looking glass. . . . Vain, silly creature. Made for loving? Yes, but she'll have no lover, for I don't want her and she'll see no other" (165). As Rochester correctly perceives, he possesses the ability to "break" Antoinette.[64] He is enraged because if she loves "anyone," not exclusively him, that shows an agency that extends beyond him that he then must "break" to confer his own subjecthood. He seeks to deprive her of the one thing that seems to give her agency, to keep her alive—her status as a being "made for loving." By taking her out of the network of love relations—which, since she is his property, he may do—he renders her existence superfluous, turns her into a ghost. The paradox he struggles with here is that, as a being for love, she can love and be loved by anyone. Her love maintains no exclusive attachment. Her love, her body, which seems his property because he brought it to life, actually exceeds him. She does not need him to exist; it could be anyone that allows her to do so. He says, "She'll not dress up and smile at herself in that damnable looking glass," because, without her status as a being for love and the hope of this being that the looking glass offers, she is deprived of being altogether. If she fits a certain form, then there is always hope she can attract a man to make her exist, as happened with Antoinette's mother, Annette, who, Antoinette imagines, "had to hope every time she passed a looking glass" (18). Annette's hopes of life are answered when Mr. Mason appears and marries her, for without him, "yes, she would have died, I thought, if she had not met him" (36). Isolated as "individuals" because of connections to colonialism and slave ownership but not granted individual existence within the colonial context, Annette and Antoinette belong nowhere, and in the interlocking terms of colonialist and patriarchal structures, really cannot be. The existence these men seem to grant so beneficently is taken from both Antoinette and her mother through first the "real" death and then "the one people know about."

The "real" death is represented in the novel by a parrot, which in West Indian legends symbolizes the soul. This parrot, unlike others, has a limited but significant vocabulary. "Our parrot was called Coco," Antoinette reports. "[H]e didn't talk very well. He could say *Qui est là? Qui est là?*" Although he had been somewhat independent when he had possession of his wings, "after Mr. Mason clipped his wings he grew very bad tempered" (41). Significantly, it is Mr. Mason who clips his wings, and this clipping is responsible for Coco's death by flames. The parrot, too, dies two deaths, one when his wings are clipped and another when the house is set on fire by, as Mr. Mason puts it, "a handful of drunken negroes" (38). As the house goes up in flames, Coco is spotted "on the *glacis* railings with his feathers alight. He made an effort to fly down but his clipped wings failed him and he fell screeching" (43). Antoinette's mother and then Antoinette follow a similar pattern and end up screaming *"Qui est là"* as well. Both originally "parrot" masculinist, colonialist assumptions through their marriages, but despite this (or as the result), both get "clipped wings." Their spirits are "broken . . . as the hurricane will touch that tree." Traveling a trajectory her daughter will closely repeat, furious that

Mr. Mason had not listened to her and that therefore her son, Pierre, was killed in the fire, Annette breaks out violently against her husband. As a result, she is proclaimed mad and is abandoned by him, confined to a house with a caretaker who repeatedly rapes her. She dies an obscure death several years later. So much for Annette's hope of existence through Mr. Mason's love.

In a similar manner, Rochester vows to deprive Antoinette of any hope, any existence he has granted her. Originally indifferent to Rochester and his "love," "very soon she was as eager for what's called loving as [he] was—more lost and drowned afterwards" (92). Rochester "brought [Antoinette] to life" in a sexual way and then uses that "life" to deprive her far more radically of life. As Christophine, the Martinican woman who is Antoinette's nurse and mentor, as well as her closest friend, explains it, "'You fool the girl. You make her think you can't see the sun for looking at her.' It was like that, I thought. It was like that. . . . 'And then,' she went on in her judge's voice, 'you make love to her till she drunk with it, no rum could make her drunk like that, till she can't do without it. It's *she* can't see the sun any more. Only you she see. But all you want is to break her up'" (152–53). The attention that originally brings Antoinette to life, that gives her a sense that she is loved and therefore worthwhile, then makes her dependent on this sense. She therefore emotionally discloses herself to Rochester and makes him the center of her existence, so that she "can't see the sun any more. Only [him] she see." Rochester then "break[s] her up" by withdrawing his love and thereby her sense of existence. Brought from indifference painfully into life, she is even more painfully thrown into the death "people [don't] know about."

Rochester shrinks from love as from a force that would devour him, turning it back on itself so that it devours her:

No more damned magic. You hate me and I hate you. We'll see who hates best. But first, first I will destroy your hatred. Now. My hate is colder, stronger, and you'll have no hate to warm yourself. You will have nothing. I did it too. I saw the hate go out of her eyes. I forced it out. And with the hate her beauty. She was only a ghost. A ghost in the grey daylight. Nothing left but hopelessness. *'Say die and I will die. Say die and watch me die.'* (170)

Since Rochester sees love as a hostile force that threatens to consume him, he takes Antoinette up on her promise to "die" at his bidding.

He leaves her not even "a flame of hatred" to keep her alive, no flame, no beauty, only the "real" death, the death of being that leaves only the ghost, the hopelessness of no further lovers, the empty nothing. Ironically, he experiences Antoinette in her nothing, a nothingness constructed in response to both sexual and colonial exile, as *too much*. He reacts to her as to an overwhelming emotional force, the force of a black hole, that will drag him in and engulf him. He associates her with the landscape around him, which he experiences as too radically alive: "Everything is too much . . . too much blue, too much purple, too much green. The flowers too red, the mountains too high, the hills too near. And the woman is a stranger" (70). As strange to him as the alien landscape that is "too much," Antoinette is experienced as "too much" as well. In this designation Rochester charts the cultural logic that the anorexic has internalized and reacts against in her self-immolation, an action Antoinette repeats when she tells Rochester to "say die and I will die." As Bordo writes, "[T]he mythology/ideology of the devouring, insatiable female . . . is the internalized image the anorexic has of her female self. . . . Hungering. Voracious. Extravagantly and excessively needful. Without restraint. Always wanting. Always wanting too much affection, reassurance, emotional and sexual contact and attention."[65] Since Rochester understands Antoinette as a being who is excessive, connected to a landscape that is excessive, he will only talk to her "if [she] promise[s] to be reasonable," which means nonemotional. He is threatened by both her "too much" and the correspondent "too much" of the landscape, which makes him "feel that this place is my enemy and on [her] side" (*Wide Sargasso Sea,* 129). Sexual contact is experienced as a "feeling of suffocation" (137), and to escape it, he deflects the love back toward her, so that instead of consuming him, it will consume her: "no more damned magic. We'll see who hates best. . . . you will have nothing" (170). He has granted existence and he takes it away. "Die," he says, and she does. Almost.

For Antoinette is the only Rhys heroine whose flame (unlike Julia's "essence of her shooting upwards like a flame . . . not to plead but to threaten. Then the flame sank down again, useless, having reached nothing" [*After Leaving Mr. Mackenzie,* 131]) reaches something, rather than nothing. It is no accident that the word *flame,* the symbol of agency in Rhys, also means "sweetheart" or "lover"—there is no essence for these women without lovers. Yet, however negative that agency is, Antoinette does something; she produces an effect, so that hers is the only fire never extinguished. "I will write my name in fire red," Antoinette says, embroidering at the convent, and she does (*Wide Sargasso Sea,* 53). Her signature is fire. "Time has no meaning," she explains, imprisoned in Thornfield Hall. "But something you can touch and hold like my red dress, that has a meaning . . . the colour of fire and sunset. The colour of flamboyant flowers. If you are buried under a flamboyant tree . . . your soul is lifted up when it flowers. Everyone wants that" (185).[66] Antoinette insists on her materially tangible red dress as a badge of her identity and claims that she can't be known for who she is without it. The dress symbolizes her sexuality, makes her "look intemperate and unchaste . . . that man told me so" (186), and it is precisely this dress that is connected with the flame that symbolizes agency: "I let the dress fall on the floor, and looked from the fire to the dress and from the dress to the fire. . . . I looked at the dress on the floor and it was as if the fire had spread across the room. It was beautiful and it reminded me of something I must do. I will remember I thought. I will remember quite soon now" (186, 187). The "something [she] must do," the destruction of Thornfield Hall by fire, is connected with her sexuality, her identity as a being for love; for if she does exist for love alone, that love is strong enough to destroy all that raises itself around it and to "lift her soul up." Destroy—and enable.

A woman's existence as a being for love is predicated on the assumption that she will compete with other women to secure that love, so that she will then be allowed to exist. In the literary frame of *Jane Eyre* and *Wide Sargasso Sea,* there is ostensibly a competition between Antoinette/Bertha and Jane, for Antoinette is the obstacle that must be removed before Jane can realize herself and her position through Rochester. Women compete, the tradition goes, and some make it, and some don't. According to Rochester in *Wide Sargasso Sea,* the ones that don't, the ones who are the excess that can't be placed, form a peculiar community:

Very soon she'll join all the others who know the secret and will not tell it. Or cannot. Or try and fail because they do not know enough. They can be recognized. White faces, dazed eyes, aimless gestures, high-pitched laughter.

The way they walk and talk and scream or try to kill (themselves or you) if you laugh back at them. Yes, they've got to be watched. For the time comes when they try to kill, then disappear. But others are waiting to take their places, it's a long, long line. She's one of them. I too can wait—for the day when she is only a memory to be avoided, locked away (172).

Although Rochester attempts to distinguish between Antoinette and her kind and other women, in Rochester's tradition is there really any "kind" other than "one of them"? Rhys's texts suggest not. As with the deconstruction of the opposition between the *femme convenable* and the *petite femme,* within the framework of the anorexic philosophical, literary, and religious traditions, "it's a long, long line." Each woman constructed as "loved" becomes "one of them"—the lost ones love "broke," because the "love" masks an anorexic ambivalence toward the feminine. Differences between women in this tradition are a function of their roles and positions, and underneath those roles lies an anorexic contempt for and hatred of the feminine, which is not to say that women are essentially the same. Rather, for Rhys, women are both the same and different; it is deviation from prescribed roles that is punished by accusations of madness. The "love" offered by Rochester that made the role of British wife seductive to Antoinette is nothing seemingly but the *pharmakon,* the remedy that is also a poison. But Antoinette can do something about this ghost-making love: "They try to kill, then disappear." But, Rhys's text inquires, does anything ever "disappear"? Isn't it just repressed, "avoided, locked away"? The "flames," the female spirits that flare up in Rhys's other texts join in conflagration here—forming what? A negative community? "Now at last I know why I was brought here and what I have to do. . . . I shielded [the flame] with my hand and it burned up again to light me along the dark passage" (190). What Antoinette/Bertha has to do is more than conveniently step aside. It can be said that Antoinette's action enables a recognition that destabilizes Rochester's anorexic paradigm, based on projections of being and lack. Antoinette/Bertha doesn't step aside, defined against Jane, thwarted and consumed by jealousy, as in Brontë's text. Instead, she enables us to question the safety and sanctity of Rochester's house and to see that life will go on beyond its destruction. There are alternatives to the system of British colonialist mastery, and Antoinette clears a space that makes those

alternatives imaginable. Inside the house it is hard to imagine anything else. Antoinette in her nonassimilability points to alternatives.

Rhys's text, read in relation to Brontë's, conceivably proposes a
different form of love relationship than the "deadly" one she experienced. She calls into question Rochester's cultural designation as
"being" and shows how that designation has hurt Rochester as well.
Antoinette's action, though problematic in its self-destruction, decenters Rochester from a subject position that was never actually centered, a de-centeredness that he sensed; so threatened, he then felt
he had to defend this position by "killing" Antoinette. The fiction of
his identity as self-sufficient, a masterful presence, is already questioned by economic circumstances, and his position as a second son
is rendered palpable; thus, he doesn't have to act the part any longer.
In other words, Rochester is only acting out the role of being that
the anorexic cultural scripts foist upon him. Those scripts designate
masculinity, whiteness, and the mind as signifiers of being while their
opposites, femininity, blackness, and the body, are signifiers of nonbeing, of base materiality. What Rochester points out is that these designations are cultural scripts he tries only half-heartedly to follow in his
courtship of Antoinette: "I played the part I was expected to play. She
never had anything to do with me at all. Every movement I made was
an effort of will and sometimes I wondered that no one noticed
this. . . . But I must have given a faultless performance. If I saw an
expression of doubt or curiosity it was on a black face not a white one"
(*Wide Sargasso Sea*, 76–77).

Rochester performs his role of colonialist master, the centered,
self-sufficient subject. He realizes that this mastery and sufficiency is
a masquerade, that, to borrow Kaja Silverman's formulations of male
subjectivity, "lack of being is the irreducible condition of subjectivity"—a lack that is then projected onto women and racial others.[67] It
is Rochester's perception of his lack and misrecognition of that lack
as an individual deficiency, rather than a fundamental social condition, the failure to recognize that masculine self-sufficiency is a performance for all men, that leads him to find himself wanting and then
turn on Antoinette, whose projected deficiencies then function to
shore up his own. Because the white faces seem to buy his masquerade, the doubt on the "black face[s]" can't matter, since those faces

are nonbeing according to the script. Rochester's performance is directed to a white male audience and is accepted as his personal essence, rather than a performance, making him one of the boys, even though his status is dependent upon Antoinette's money. He feels deficient, since he knows he is not in essence being, but rather that he plays the part of being, the self-sufficient *is*.

Rhys suggests a paradigm that without literal destruction, we might utilize to get beyond the impasse to which the construction of male being and female nonbeing inevitably leads. In her destruction of the father's house, his house of being, his house of cards, Antoinette clears a space for a more mutual relation based on something other than antagonistic struggle. In her use of the agency of negation, she, like the anorexic, makes her present absence known. She points out the problems in the structure she destroys—her body, the house that imprisons her. She doesn't merely disappear. She lingers. She grows. What was negative becomes affirmative. Nothing becomes something.

Of course, this reading of the two texts depends on my reading *Jane Eyre* entirely through Rhys. *Jane Eyre* is very problematic from the perspective of the frame I have just constructed to read it. As Gayatri Spivak writes:

in this fictive England, [Bertha/Antoinette] must play out her role, act out the transformation of her "self" into that fictive Other, set fire to the house and kill herself, so that Jane Eyre can become the feminist individualist heroine of British fiction. I must read this as an allegory of the general epistemic violence of imperialism, the construction of a self-immolating colonial subject for the glorification of the social mission of the colonizer. At least Rhys sees to it that the woman from the colonies is not sacrificed as an insane animal for her sister's consolidation.[68]

I don't question Spivak's reading of *Jane Eyre*, yet, since I argue that Antoinette's action provides a space where gender relations can be reconfigured, my reading could be seen as the sacrifice of the other to the "feminist individualist heroine." Why should Antoinette, designated as unassimilable other by Rochester and his anorexic framework of assumptions that constructs her as "too much," have to "act out the transformation of her 'self'" and do something like burn the house down that brands her as crazy, much better out of the way, so that Jane and others like her can live differently? Is it because she is West Indian as well as female that she serves as a sacrifice to enable her white sisters?

But, as I think Spivak suggests, what if the two women are not opposed in Rhys's text as they are in Brontë's? What if they are inter-related, in an analogue to what Borinsky has shown about the decon-struction of the opposition between the *petite femme* and the *femme convenable* in Rhys? What if Antoinette and Jane are not opposed but share similar metaphysical positions within the anorexic logic that Rochester figures as the "long line"? In Rochester's reading, Jane would be the "good" woman outside that line, designating some women "good" and others "bad," branding some (nonwhite women) with all the negative metaphysical weight of corporeality while disem-bodying others (white women). This separation creates a shared space between them in which each might want a way out of her predesig-nated position, for cultural designation as either embodiment or dis-embodiment makes significant problems in lived existence. The "bad" women in the line know the "secret" is that they are not essentially opposed to "good" women any more than women are essentially op-posed to men or lovers to beloveds. Because of discrepancies in power according to their relative proximity to white men, women are disempowered in different ways. And if women are fictively con-structed as needing the love of a white man to have cultural value, it follows that the power white men hold, though very real from a mate-rial perspective, is no less fictive, and its construction can change, as Antoinette's action reveals. A relationship with a white man provides the *illusion* of safety, symbolized by the house, as Grace Poole says in *Wide Sargasso Sea:* "the house is big and safe, a shelter from the world outside which, say what you like, can be a black and cruel world to a woman" (178). Yet Antoinette must burn that house down be-cause she knows, from her experience of marriage, that the "safe house" marriage is said to provide is no real alternative to "the world outside." Her action reveals that the world outside and the house amount to the same thing, that no one else can provide a woman with safety, and that revelation empowers. Just as the position of the *petite femme* and the *femme convenable* amount to the same thing, the sub-

ject positions of lover and beloved amount to the same thing. The
lover bestows a false existence upon the beloved, false because it isn't
his to bestow. The lover's existence, Rhys reveals, is just as precarious
as the existence of the one he is supposed to bring to life through his
love. In destabilizing the white male colonialist fiction of presence
based on the anorexic equation between disembodiment and empowerment and full humanity, Rhys's text brings white and nonwhite
women out of the shadows of embodiment, where they are negated.

In fact, the slipperiness of his position threatens Rochester, and
that threat, not any essential maliciousness, makes him turn on Antoinette and turn her into a "ghost." Rochester, agonized, knows there is
no safety he can offer, and the pressure to do so, which reminds him
of his own insufficiency, drives him from Antoinette, makes him experience her as "suffocation": "'You are safe,' I'd say. She'd liked that—
to be told 'you are safe.' Or I'd touch her face gently and touch tears.
Tears—nothing! Words—less than nothing. As for the happiness I
gave her, that was worse than nothing" (93). Rochester is also made
ghostly by the impossible pressure of his designation as being. Trying
to play to an impossible standard leads him to empty himself, interpreting his failure to meet the standard as proof that he is "nothing."
His bitterness comes from a crippling sense of insufficiency, his inability to give Antoinette safety or happiness, so that he must feel his
words reassuring her of safety are "less than nothing," and the happiness he senses he cannot bestow is "worse than nothing." Impossibly,
as the white male subject, as the paradigm of being, he is supposed
to be able to give happiness and existence to another. When he finds
he can't, creating a sense of insufficiency that scares him, he is desperate and turns that insufficiency back toward her. Rhys reveals a structure where dehumanization does occur, but that dehumanization
works more than one way. The malleability of the metaphysical frame
that masquerades as stable truth, ostensibly the cause of the problem
(Rochester's uneasiness and therefore viciousness), also enables the
frame to change, releasing both parties from roles that make them
ghostly. This is a crucial insight. Their positions—fixed as mind or
body, humanity or animality, masculine or feminine, rather than as
combinations of both—are powerful social fictions. Thus, it is finding

elements of the other within and interpreting that otherness as personal failure that drives Rochester to the spiritual immolation Antoinette suffers.

If, Rhys suggests, in a radical insight that has not been much discussed, *his* position were not constructed, impossibly, as being, he would not have the same desperate emotional need to defend it. So, instead of annihilating the other, creating an emptiness to shore up the emptiness of his own position, the two could relate to each other from a subject position that recognizes both its being and lack, its wholeness and its fragmentation, its masculine and its feminine. Through her agency of negation Antoinette reveals, as Silverman writes in *Male Subjectivity at the Margins,* that "female subjectivity represents the site at which the male subject deposits his lack" (46), and that the fiction of male self-sufficiency in fact masks an "irreducible lack" (38). Her nothingness, her self-immolation, becomes something.

This is why I cannot read Antoinette's self-immolation as merely destructively stepping aside to give Jane her legitimate place. Instead, through "burning down [his] house," she fractures the illusion of safety that the relationship to a white male subject provides, and she offers the chance to configure love relationships from a different position in which no one is safe, and both can admit it. Antoinette clears a space within which both subjects operate from a sense of mutual deficiency, thereby disrupting the power relation within which one subject is defined as sufficiency and the other as deficiency. She destroys and realizes herself in flame, just as the anorexic burns her own body from within. Both, tragically, use the agency of negation to disavow what the cultural system, the signifying chain, has made them. But in this disavowal they clear the antagonistic space of being and nonbeing. They are the force that cannot be denied, pathologized, swept under. Their position is not a viable political alternative, but to the extent that, poised at a historical moment of tremendous upheaval and change, we can read the text they have provided, we can learn to construct ourselves otherwise, can learn the lesson and go on. Rhys was ahead of her time. She can enable us to do something different in ours.

The politics of the personal expressed so clearly in Rhys, the dialectic of male being and female nonbeing, emotionally and physically disabled her throughout her life. These same politics, which she articulates, which she names, many now "believe." They have disabled many of us in the personal politics of our own lives, but we have tired of cutting off our own limbs. I read and articulate the politics of my own experience through reading Rhys, and her discourse has enabled me, rather than disabled. She has shown, all too clearly, the ways in which women are disempowered and the ways they disempower themselves. Her exchange with me has become my exchange with others, for what I have spoken can lead others to speak. If literature is dying, this must be literature that does not count on these voices coming so vibrantly alive after a long and numbing ghostliness. Like the concentric circles spreading out from the stone that Antoinette, "like a boy," throws into the pool, the "beautiful place" that makes Rochester "want what it *hides*—that is not nothing" (*Wide Sargasso Sea*, 87), our discourse joins, merges, grows, and grows. The secret is not that we are nothing—we've always been told that—but rather that we can speak.

As I have been enabled to speak through Rhys, the exchange with her texts can be a model for an exchange between women, and between women and men. Further, rereading canonical high modernists like Eliot, Pound, Kafka, Williams, and Conrad from the point of view of the anorexic logic identifies a substructure that has devalued the problem of embodiment and any historical, lived relation to it. Rereading these central cultural maps facilitates thinking otherwise. From this different exchange between readers and texts proceeds a crescendo of voices, telling different stories, regaining our sanity, regaining our lives, so we don't "burn the house down" in the end. This powerful form of exchange and understanding that rereading literature makes possible is the reason that I read, the reason that I write, the reason that I teach. In the community of voices that combines the literary, the academic, and the personal, we begin again to live. By rereading the standards, then telling my stories and Rhys's stories, and how our stories figure into cultural stories about women and men, I tell a story that replaces the old anorexic tale based on emptiness and self-denial. Characters may be linguistic constructs, but so are we. Books have brought me to life and will bring life to others as well, our stories spreading in ever-widening circles that reach out to include within them more and more and more, recovering our disowned parts, discarded limbs, and releasing ourselves from nothingness.

We cannot condemn or even criticize Jean Rhys for the nothingness that she lived. She provides devastating insight into the sexual conventions that shape male and female relations and the social construction of masculine and feminine, race- and class-based subject positions. But neither can we valorize what she says in every text. Anorexics live in Rhys's bleak, undifferentiated world, embracing an agency of negation. It is a terrible space. The time has come to construct something else. Her world, without access to liberation movements that could provide a way out of individual pain, was the despair and terror of a world in which "the doors will always be shut" (*GMM*, 31). It is still possible to read our world this way, but it is slowly, despite backlash, becoming possible not to. Formulating an antidote to the anorexic logic, I've made use of Rhys's forms, forms of discourse traditionally denoted "trivial": the personal, the emotional, the genuinely felt. It may be called "the criticism of confession," "*moi* criticism," "individualism run rampant,"[69] but these labels disregard connections between the fragmented voices of disparate I's, speaking pains previously silenced.

Bodies in pieces: I'd like to hold on to each one. Heal the scar between "theory" and "living" that often surfaces in practice, the privilege sometimes extended to cynical toughness, unemotional prose, theory without organs, detachable floating minds. Anorexic language, whistling through space, empty as trees. We've been Hegelian "shadows" long enough. We've been anorexic long enough.

Notes

Preface

1. The common assumption that the anorexic logic affects only white women has erased the experiences of gay women and women of color who, as members of the dominant culture, may struggle with anorexic thinking as much or sometimes more than white heterosexual women. For example, until recently, medical research and scholarship on eating disorders assumed a white heterosexual female subject.

1. Clarice Got Her Gun

1. Since I discuss women's masculine identification, the problem of the serial killer Buffalo Bill's feminine identification is not fully worked out in this analogy. Lecter explains that "Billy is not a real transsexual, but he thinks he is, he tries to be . . . Billy hates his own identity. He thinks that makes him a transsexual, but his pathology is a thousand times more savage and more terrifying." The film attempts to detach Bill's violence from his feminine identification, as when Clarice states, "No. Transsexuals are passive," in order to equate violence and masculinity. See Elizabeth Young, "*The Silence of the Lambs* and the Flaying of Feminist Theory," *Camera Obscura* 27 (1991), p. 9.

2. I assume that violence differs across culture, race, and class in significant ways. That the victim we see, Catherine, is a senator's daughter makes this case more sensational.

3. It has been pointed out to me that my language here has an unfortunate echo of the anti-abortion propaganda film *Silent Scream*. My use of this

language is not in any way related, and I argue that it is questionable whether or not a fetus can "scream," while it is clear that women can and do.

4. Thanks to Lawrence DeValencia for suggesting *The Silence of the Lambs* analogy to my project.

5. On connections between eating disorders and sexual abuse, see Susan C. Wooley, "Sexual Abuse and Eating Disorders: The Concealed Debate," in *Feminist Perspectives on Eating Disorders,* ed. Patricia Fallon, et al. (New York: Guilford Press, 1994), pp. 171–211. Wooley argues that at least 60 percent of women with eating disorders have also been sexually abused and details some of the reasons why this fact isn't discussed more often by professionals.

6. This line is dialogue from the movie. Clarice is explaining to Hannibal what woke her the morning she attempted to rescue the spring lambs headed for slaughter, and what continues to wake her.

7. Morag Macsween, *Anorexic Bodies* (London: Routledge, 1993), p. 252.

8. In this formulation I am indebted to Robin Harders.

9. Nike advertisement, *Vogue,* British ed. (March 1994).

10. In this attempt I owe a great deal to the French feminist tradition and the formulation of *écriture feminine,* especially Hélène Cixous and Catherine Clément, *The Newly Born Woman,* trans. Betsy Wing (Minneapolis: Univ. of Minnesota Press), 1986.

11. See Macsween's conclusion that "anorexia transforms the social meanings of the body . . . an individual transformation of social meaning . . . the individual woman cannot negate a social meaning" (*Anorexic Bodies,* p. 250). Also see Becky W. Thompson, *A Hunger So Wide and So Deep* (Minneapolis: Univ. of Minnesota Press, 1994), especially chapter 1, on how eating disorders are equally a response to the injustices of racism, classism, and heterosexism as they are responses to gender inequality.

12. See Thompson, *A Hunger So Wide and So Deep,* whose work is groundbreaking for its inclusion of these previously marginalized women.

13. Susan Bordo, *Unbearable Weight* (Berkeley: Univ. of California Press, 1993); and Macsween, *Anorexic Bodies.*

14. Ellen Wiley Todd, "Kenneth Hayes Miller and Reginald Marsh on Fourteenth Street, 1920–1940," in *Gender and American History since 1890,* ed. Barbara Melosh (New York: Routledge, 1993), pp. 127–54.

15. *Los Angeles Times,* Sunday, December 6, 1992; and Jennefer Shute, *Lifesize* (New York: Houghton Mifflin, 1992).

16. Thomas Laqueur, *Making Sex: Body and Gender from the Greeks to Freud* (Cambridge: Harvard Univ. Press, 1990).

17. Gillian Brown, "Anorexia, Humanism, and Feminism," *The Yale Jour-*

nal of Criticism 5, no. 1 (1991), pp. 189–215; Sandra M. Gilbert, "Hunger Pains," *University Publishing* 8 (fall 1979), pp. 1, 11–12; Hilde Bruch, *The Golden Cage: The Enigma of Anorexia Nervosa* (New York: Vintage, 1979); idem, *Eating Disorders: Obesity, Anorexia Nervosa and the Person Within* (New York: Basic, 1973); and idem, *Conversations with Anorexics,* ed. Danita Czyzewski and Melanie A. Suhr (New York: Basic, 1988).

18. William Withey Gull, "Anorexia Nervosa (Apepsia Hysterica, Anorexia Hysterica)," in *A Collection of the Published Writings of William Withey Gull,* ed. Theodore Dyke Acland (London: New Sydenham Society, 1896), pp. 305, 307.

19. Cited in Naomi Wolf, *The Beauty Myth: How Images of Beauty Are Used against Women* (New York: Morrow, 1991), p. 182. There is a dearth of new statistics; inquiries to the American Anorexia and Bulimia Association and other related organizations did not turn up more recent statistics.

20. See Joan Jacobs Brumberg, *Fasting Girls: The History of Anorexia Nervosa* (Cambridge: Harvard Univ. Press, 1988), pp. 8–40; Roberta Pollack Seid, *Never Too Thin: Why Women Are at War with Their Bodies* (New York: Prentice Hall, 1989), pp. 137–86; Kim Chernin, *The Obsession: Reflections on the Tyranny of Slenderness* (New York: Perennial Library, 1981), pp. 20–28; Wolf, *Beauty Myth,* pp. 181–87; Richard Gordon, *Anorexia and Bulimia: Anatomy of a Social Epidemic* (London: Basil Blackwell, 1990), pp. 102–15; and Susan Bordo, "Reading the Slender Body," in *Body/Politics: Women and the Discourses of Science,* ed. Mary Jacobus, Evelyn Fox Keller, and Sally Shuttleworth (London: Routledge, 1990), pp. 83–112.

21. Cited in Wolf, *Beauty Myth,* p. 182.

22. Quoted in Macsween, *Anorexic Bodies,* p. 247.

23. See Bruch, *Golden Cage,* especially pp. 15–18, 25–26, 38–39, 58–59, 68–73, 85, 93.

24. René Descartes, *Meditations on First Philosophy,* trans. Laurence J. Lafleur (New York: Macmillan, 1985), p. 22.

25. Chernin, *Obsession,* pp. 146–47.

26. I should add here that the body is also historically associated with nonwhites and labor, significantly complicating the cultural symbology for women of color who are also working class.

27. In anorexia the gendered configuration of the mind/body split is clear. Bruch writes that in her patients "sooner or later a remark about the other self slips out, whether it is 'a dictator who dominates me' . . . or 'the little man who objects when I eat.' . . . When they define this separate aspect, this different person always seems to be a male" (*Golden Cage,* p. 58).

28. Quoted in ibid., p. 15.

29. Quoted in ibid., p. 18.

30. Plato, *The Symposium,* trans. Walter Hamilton (New York: Penguin Classics, 1987), pp. 94, 92.

31. Luce Irigaray, "Women on the Market," in *This Sex Which is Not One,* trans. Catherine Porter (Ithaca: Cornell Univ. Press, 1985). See also her critique of Plato in *Speculum of the Other Woman,* trans. Gillian C. Gill (Ithaca: Cornell Univ. Press, 1985), pp. 243–353. See also her provocative analysis of language in *je, tu, nous: Toward a Culture of Difference,* trans. Alison Martin (New York: Routledge, 1993).

32. G. W. F. Hegel, *The Phenomenology of Spirit,* trans. A. V. Miller (Oxford: Oxford Univ. Press, 1977), p. 270.

33. Along with Bordo, Wolf, and others, I read anorexia at least partially as a self-sacrifice on the part of women to the masculine philosophical, literary, and popular ideals of Western culture.

34. G. W. F. Hegel, *The Philosophy of Right,* trans. T. M. Knox (Oxford: Oxford Univ. Press, 1942), p. 114.

35. Freud is a highly complex and ambiguous figure for this kind of analysis, since some of his insights have been essential to feminist theory in its formulations of female subjectivity and particularly film theory and constructions of the male gaze. This analysis does not preclude the positive aspects of Freud or attempt to reduce all of his theory to the aspects I present here. Instead, I articulate that aspect of Freud, historically determined, that is congruent with the philosophic logic I analyze. Many essays that I cite are highly ambivalent and also emphasize the constructedness of gender along with a more "naturalized" emphasis. The most influential feminist theorist who incorporates Freud's insights in feminist theory is Juliet Mitchell, whose *Psychoanalysis and Feminism* (Harmondsworth: Penguin, 1974) launched a school of feminist theory that is one of the most powerful today. A recent example of feminist theory that involves a reinterpretation of Freud is Teresa Brennan, *The Interpretation of the Flesh: Freud and Femininity* (New York: Routledge, 1992).

36. Sigmund Freud, *Sexuality and the Psychology of Love,* ed. Phillip Rieff (New York: Collier, 1963), p. 198.

37. In what can only seem like a betrayal to readers who admired *The Beauty Myth,* in her new book, *Fire with Fire* (New York: Random, 1993), Wolf argues that "the meaning of being a woman changed forever" in the Anita Hill–Clarence Thomas hearings. According to Wolf, conditions have now "shifted to put much of the attainment of equality in women's own grasp" (*Fire with Fire,* xv), calling, in large, sweeping terms, most feminist critiques of patriarchy "victim feminism." Many feminists have interpreted Wolf's positions in *Fire with Fire* as opportunistic and as an integral part of

the backlash that Wolf herself critiqued in *The Beauty Myth*. See especially bell hooks, *Outlaw Culture: Resisting Representations* (New York: Routledge, 1994), chap. 8. I agree with hooks's reading.

38. I argue here, as elsewhere, that cultural standards of female beauty in the United States tend to presume whiteness, and that particularly under pressures of assimilation, women of color are likely to be affected by them. Thompson writes how her case studies of women of color and lesbians "reveal the social inequalities that whittle away at a woman's ability to identify her body as her own" (*Hunger So Wide*, p. 20), inequalities that include sometimes virulent racism and homophobia, which sometimes cause women to disavow their colored or homosexual bodies, seeing their devalued bodies as the sources of their pain.

39. Nike advertisement, *Vogue*, (June 1992).

40. In spring 1995, in the popular media a form of backlash appeared that legislates against the strong, successful career woman. Movies that exemplify this backlash, like *Disclosure* or *The Last Seduction,* and fashion's return to fifties-style dresses and jackets, along with the appeal to female power in the form of femme fatale sexuality, rather than power in the workplace—all undermine the image of individual female success. This "family values," back-to-the-home trend has been met in the most recent Nike advertisements (for instance in *Vanity Fair,* March 1995) with text copy that reads, "Pursue pleasure. No matter how damn hard it may be," in an ad that equates working out with pleasure—a radical departure from the individual achievement ethos of the eighties.

41. Self-esteem is the topic of Gloria Steinem's book, *The Revolution from Within* (Boston: Little, Brown, 1992). Steinem writes that "even I, who had spent the previous dozen years working on external barriers to women's equality, had to admit there were internal ones, too" (p. 3).

42. Barbara Ehrenreich, "The New Anger," (paper presented at the Women's Studies First Annual Regents Lecture, University of California, Irvine, February 10, 1993).

43. Toni Morrison, *Beloved* (New York: Plume, 1987), p. 133.

44. I'm not saying that consumer culture isn't interested in constructing the male body and subjectivity as well. It's just that in the sociohistorical context articulated so clearly by Julia Kristeva—that "a woman, that cannot *be:* it is even what doesn't fit into *being*" ("La femme, ce n'est jamais ça," *Tel quel* 39 [fall 1974])—advertising deploys itself differently to the male or female subject. Since in the postmodern, being as a category is under question, and the construction of the subject through consumer goods fuels the economy, there is no doubt that this analysis would have to include men and the

male body (there are males with eating disorders). But the (non)subject is likely to respond differently if one has aligned oneself or been aligned with the position of nonbeing from the beginning.

45. "Blonde Ambition," *Flex* (April 1994), p. 141.

46. Michel Foucault, *The History of Sexuality*, trans. Robert Hurley, vol. 1 (New York: Random, 1978), p. 6.

47. Robert Marzec and I came up with the term *schizophrenic liberation* when struggling to account for the contradictory messages these images presented. Marzec's work on the disinterested subject has been instrumental in helping me think through my own work on the anorexic logic.

48. Slavoj Zizek, *The Sublime Object of Ideology* (London: Verso, 1989), p. 33.

49. See Jacques Derrida, *The Post Card: Socrates to Freud and Beyond* (Chicago: Univ. of Chicago Press, 1987). The allusion is to systems of signification, which are continually undermined from within, although they try to pin meaning down to a fixed absolute. Therefore, the dense network of cultural meanings, which would seem to fix female bodybuilders, for instance, and to make them readable in a particular way, can always be read in more than one way, leaving some potential for subversion of the dominant cultural logic.

50. Susan Bordo, "Anorexia Nervosa: Psychopathology as the Crystallization of Culture," in *Feminism and Foucault: Reflections on Resistance,* ed. Irene Diamond and Lee Quinby (Boston: Northeastern Univ. Press, 1988), p. 94.

51. Quoted in ibid., p. 105.

52. See especially *The Edible Woman* and *Lady Oracle.*

53. I am using "alienation effect" in the Brechtian sense. Brecht defines "alienation effect" as "alienations [that] are designed to free socially-conditioned phenomena from that stamp of familiarity which protects them against our grasp. . . . a representation that alienates is one which allows us to recognize its subject, but at the same time makes it seem unfamiliar" (*Brecht on Theatre*, trans. John Willett [London: Methuen, 1957], p. 192).

54. Noelle Caskey, "Interpreting Anorexia Nervosa," in *The Female Body in Western Culture: Contemporary Perspectives,* ed. Susan Rubin Suleiman (Cambridge: Harvard Univ. Press, 1986), p. 187.

55. Louise Glück, "Dedication to Hunger," in *Descending Figure* (New York: Ecco Press, 1980), p. 29.

56. See note 8 above.

57. Eavan Boland, "Anorexic," in *Introducing Eavan Boland: Poems* (Princeton: Ontario Review Press, 1981), pp. 52–53.

58. Carol F. Karlsen, *The Devil in the Shape of a Woman: Witchcraft in Colonial New England* (New York: Vintage, 1987), p. 155.

59. Quoted in Bordo, "Anorexia Nervosa," p. 95.

60. See also ibid., p. 92.

61. *Webster's Ninth New Collegiate Dictionary,* s.v. "heresy."

62. Quoted in Chernin, *Obsession,* p. 195.

63. *Webster's Ninth,* s.v. "wiles" and "pap."

64. Let me emphasize that the equation between men and abstemiousness is an ideological construct rarely practiced. A reader who read this in draft form protested what seemed like an acceptance on my part of the men-as-less-needy mythology.

65. See also Sandra M. Gilbert and Susan Gubar, *The Madwoman in the Attic* (New Haven: Yale Univ. Press, 1979), pp. 45–92.

66. For a firsthand account of the hunger-strike procedure, see E. Sylvia Pankhurst, *The Suffragette Movement: An Intimate Account of Persons and Ideals* (London: Longmans, Green, 1931), pp. 301–19, 342–46, 438–54.

67. See, for instance, Wolf, *Beauty Myth,* pp. 188–91.

68. Writers like Susan Bordo, bell hooks, Michele Wallace, Cornel West, Audre Lorde, Adrienne Rich, Gloria Anzaldua, and Becky W. Thompson are just a few of the many others whose writing attempts to "recover" these bodies. Indeed, the "turn to the personal," although protested, is a large enough movement to draw media attention. See chapter 4.

69. That some female bodies are hated more than others is a point that I should emphasize more fully than I have.

70. Bell hooks's *Teaching to Transgress* (New York: Routledge, 1994) contributes significantly to this conversation.

71. Susan Bordo, "The Feminist as Other" (paper presented at the State University of New York, Binghamton, April 3, 1994).

2. From Female Disease to Textual Ideal

1. Mark Anderson, "Anorexia and Modernism, or How I Learned to Diet in All Directions," *Discourse* 11.1 (fall–winter 1988–89), pp. 28–41. Maud Ellmann's *Hunger Artists: Starving, Writing, and Imprisonment* (Cambridge: Harvard Univ. Press, 1993) is one of the first important books to explore the connection. Her work is, according to the author, "neither a history of starvation nor a work of anthropology, psychoanalysis, or sociology, although it plunders those disciplines at different times. It is best described as a 'phenomenology' in the sense that Gaston Bachelard has used the term, because its aim is not to find the cause of self-starvation but to follow the

adventures of its metaphors" (p. 15). Ellmann's work is then about language. She explicitly defines herself against the tradition my own work falls within:

"The body" . . . is an awkward term to use these days because it has become the latest shibboleth of literary theory, particularly west of the Rockies, where essays on the body are churned out of PCs with the same demonic rigor that the bodies of their authors are submitted to the tortures of the gym. Indeed, the theorization of the body has become the academic version of the "workout." In criticism, the cult of the body has arisen in defense against poststructuralism, and especially against the fear that "history" and "real life" have been overlooked in favor of a dangerous Gallic fascination with the signifier. In this context the body has come to represent the last bastion of materiality: if history is nothing but a narrative, "a tale like any other too often heard," and if the universe is merely an effect of rhetoric, the body seems to stand for an incontestable reality, a throbbing substance in a wilderness of signs. This book, by way of warning, is concerned with *dis*embodiment, not bodies; with the deconstruction of the flesh; and with writing and starvation as the arts of discarnation. (pp. 3–4)

To the extent that I share some of the concerns that Ellmann mentions, particularly "the fear that 'history' and 'real life' have been overlooked in favor of a dangerous Gallic fascination with the signifier," I stand guilty as charged. Ellmann succinctly characterizes the anxieties of the discourse my work is situated within. I claim, though, that this tendency in literary criticism and in my own work is informed by a deconstructive understanding of "history" and "real life," as well as "the body," and that we are attempting to negotiate what might seem like an impasse between material theories and deconstructive theories. I, too, am specifically concerned with the logic of disembodiment but in a very different sense than Ellmann, for the Western preoccupation with disembodiment in literature, philosophy, psychology, and poststructuralist theory is precisely that logic I have named "anorexic." Ellmann utilizes a narrower definition of the term. Furthermore, as she has perceptively noted and as I have argued, most of us writing on this particular topic are ourselves caught in the grips of its logic, our "essays on the body churned out of PCs with the same demonic rigor that [our] bodies . . . are submitted to [in] the tortures of the gym." My work attempts to theorize the sources and trajectory of that "demonic rigor" to arrive at an understanding of how, in the postmodern economy of the "wilderness of signs," our bodies are produced by those signs in order to negotiate some path of resistance.

2. See Jean-Michel Rabate, *Language, Sexuality, and Ideology in Ezra Pound's "Cantos"* (London: Macmillan, 1986), p. 219. Rabate argues that for Pound, although phallic assertion is the "cutting tool" that will eliminate the "bloated [feminine] flesh," it "needs the 'cutting' quality of thought, which dissociates, dissects the 'clots' which become clogs." Rabate interprets this cutting as castration, which then "opens the way to phallic drives." The criti-

cal process is the mediator between flesh and phallus as not-flesh. By definition, then, the "feminine" is the flesh that "clogs" and needs to be eliminated
before the seminal, phallic creative processes can occur.

3. See Sandra M. Gilbert and Susan Gubar, *No Man's Land: The Place of
the Woman Writer in the Twentieth Century,* vol. 1 (New Haven: Yale Univ.
Press, 1988), especially "Tradition and the Female Talent: Modernism and
Masculinism," pp. 125–62.

4. See, for instance, Hilde Bruch, *Eating Disorders: Obesity, Anorexia
Nervosa and the Person Within* (New York: Basic, 1973), chaps. 2 and 3;
and Joan Jacobs Brumberg, *Fasting Girls: The History of Anorexia Nervosa*
(Cambridge: Harvard Univ. Press, 1988), chap. 1, on how the disease cannot
be considered as either biological or sociological/cultural in an oppositional
way. Such an opposition cannot explain the etiology of anorexia, since anorexia combines the biological, sociological, and cultural in an overdeter-
mined way.

5. The first physician to write about and name anorexia nervosa was Sir
William Withey Gull, a prominent British surgeon who discussed the disease
in an article in *Lancet* in 1874. The French physician Charles Lasegue began
discussing anorexia in his writings at roughly the same time, but unlike Gull,
who confined his discussions of etiology to somatic causes, Lasegue emphasized the psychological dimensions of the disease. Gull did note, however, in
a manner typical of Victorian medical discourse that defined female adoles-
cence in terms of hysteria, that "the want of appetite is, I believe, due to a
morbid mental state. . . . that mental states may destroy appetite is notorious,
and it will be admitted that young women at the ages named are specially
obnoxious to mental perversity" (*A Collection of the Published Writings of
William Withey Gull,* ed. Theodore Dyke Acland [London: New Sydenham
Society, 1896], p. 311). Many feminist scholars, however, see the disease as
concretely expressing the norms demanded of women, which function as a
means of social control. For instance, Susan Bordo argues that "many of
these behaviors [anorexia and bulimia] are outside the norm. . . . But preoccupation with fat, diet, and slenderness are not. Indeed, such preoccupations
may function as one of the most powerful 'normalizing' strategies of our century, ensuring the production of self-monitoring and self-disciplining 'docile
bodies,' sensitive to any departure from social norms, and habituated to self-
improvement and transformation in service of these norms" ("Reading the
Slender Body," in *Body/Politics: Women and the Discourses of Science,* ed.
Mary Jacobus, Evelyn Fox Keller, and Sally Shuttleworth [London:
Routledge, 1990], p. 85). Anorexia, in this argument, is an expression of the
culture's deepest pathologies, rather than an individual deviation. See also
Susan Bordo, "Anorexia Nervosa: Psychopathology as the Crystallization of

Culture," in *Feminism and Foucault: Reflections on Resistance,* ed. Irene Diamond and Lee Quinby (Boston: Northeastern Univ. Press, 1988), pp. 87–117.

6. See Caroline Walker Bynum, "Fast, Feast, and Flesh: The Religious Significance of Food to Medieval Women," *Representations* 11 (1985), pp. 1–25; and idem., *Holy Feast and Holy Fast: The Religious Significance of Food to Medieval Women* (Berkeley: Univ. of California Press, 1987). See also Rudolph M. Bell, *Holy Anorexia* (Chicago: University of Chicago Press, 1985). Bell, a medievalist, argues that medieval holy women like Catherine of Siena engaged in anorexic behavior patterns like those we see today, creating a psychological continuity in the quest for female liberation from a repressive patriarchy across the centuries. The problem with his argument is that it assumes a fixed female psychology that has remained consistent across the centuries.

7. See Barbara Ehrenreich and Deirdre English, *For Her Own Good: 150 Years of the Experts' Advice to Women* (New York: Doubleday, 1978).

8. Helena Michie, *The Flesh Made Word: Female Figures and Women's Bodies* (Oxford: Oxford Univ. Press, 1987), p. 16. See especially the chapter "Ladylike Anorexia: Hunger, Sexuality, and Etiquette in the Nineteenth Century," pp. 12–29.

9. See bell hooks, "Selling Hot Pussy: Representations of Black Female Sexuality in the Cultural Marketplace," in *Black Looks: Race and Representation* (Boston: South End Press, 1992). Hooks connects the early nineteenth-century construction of Sarah Bartmann to twentieth-century constructions of Josephine Baker and Tina Turner that are based on the same racist logic.

10. Aristotle, *De Anima* and "On the Generation of Animals," in *The Basic Works of Aristotle,* ed. Richard McKeon, trans. Arthur Platt (New York: Random, 1941), pp. 555, 561.

11. Hilde Bruch, *Conversations with Anorexics,* ed. Danita Czyzewski and Melanie A. Suhr (New York: Basic, 1988), p. 120. Subsequent references in this paragraph refer to this text. Bruch's *Golden Cage: The Enigma of Anorexia Nervosa* (New York: Vintage, 1979) was the first major book on anorexia, and her *Eating Disorders* (1973) is still referred to as a standard.

12. Richard A. Gordon, *Anorexia and Bulimia: The Anatomy of a Social Epidemic* (London: Basil Blackwell, 1990), p. 83.

13. Frank Lentriccia, *Ariel and the Police* (Madison: Univ. of Wisconsin Press, 1988), p. 137.

14. Ezra Pound, *Gaudier-Brzeska: A Memoir* (New York: New Directions, 1970), pp. 88, 92.

15. The idea of bodily renunciation as leading to greater literary produc-

tion has a romantic heritage. Lord Byron, for example, who in his own time was an enormously influential figure in popular culture, made the struggle between body and mind a central one. According to Brumberg, "Byron starved his body in order to keep his brain clear. He existed on biscuits and soda water for days and took no animal food. According to memoirs written by acquaintances, the poet had a 'horror of fat'; to his mind, fat symbolized lethargy, dullness, and stupidity. Byron feared that if he ate normally he would lose his creativity. Only through abstinence could his mind exercise and improve. In short, Byron was a model of exquisite slenderness and his sensibilities about fat were embraced by legions of young women" (*Fasting Girls,* p. 183). This romantic sensibility regarding fat and its relationship to literary productivity is central to the modern conception but becomes increasingly tropological and textual, displaced onto texts. There is a preoccupation in the modern with "becoming text," so that the textual body actually replaces the literal one. This logic was only nascent in the romantic period.

16. Quoted in Anderson, "Anorexia and Modernism," p. 32.

17. Malcolm Pasley, "The Act of Writing and the Text: The Genesis of Kafka's Manuscripts," trans. Susan Lhota, in *Reading Kafka: Prague, Politics, and the Fin de Siècle,* ed. Mark Anderson (New York: Schocken, 1989), p. 214.

18. See Brumberg, *Fasting Girls,* especially chap. 3, "The Debate over Fasting Girls."

19. Franz Kafka, "A Hunger Artist," in *Selected Stories of Franz Kafka,* trans. Willa Muir and Edwin Muir (New York: Modern Library, 1952), p. 188.

20. See Mark Anderson, "Unsigned Letters to Milena Jesenska," in *Reading Kafka,* pp. 244–45.

21. Slavoj Zizek, *The Sublime Object of Ideology* (London: Verso, 1989), p. 30.

22. In a lecture on Kafka at the University of California, Irvine (April 5, 1993), Professor Gail Hartz said that Kafka "gives us the dust, fleas, and food scraps of twentieth-century life." His writing gives us the repressed material of the modern, but in his life and his philosophy of writing he worked incessantly to repress that materiality.

23. Erich Heller, "Kafka's True Will," in *Letters to Felice,* by Franz Kafka, ed. Erich Heller and Jurgen Born, trans. James Stern and Elisabeth Duckworth (New York: Schocken, 1973), pp. xii–xiii.

24. Franz Kafka, *Letters to Felice,* p. 304.

25. Jacques Derrida, "The Rhetorics of Cannibalism" (seminar, University of California, Irvine, 1990–91).

26. Quoted in Heller, "Kafka's True Will," p. viii.

27. It is an interesting historical footnote that Kafka says that "secretly I don't believe this illness to be tuberculosis," since it probably wasn't. His journals and letters reveal a long history of difficulty eating, coupled with a pervasive logic that proclaimed the need to transcend the daily aspects of material existence to produce art. Probably, Kafka did suffer from anorexia nervosa and was misdiagnosed as having tuberculosis—a common misdiagnosis often made by medical professionals of the time unfamiliar with anorexia. Specialists in anorexia today have written that Kafka probably suffered from this disease, rather than tuberculosis. See especially Manfred M. Fichter, "The Anorexia Nervosa of Franz Kafka," *The International Journal of Eating Disorders,* no. 2 (1987), pp. 367–77. I am not primarily interested in whether or not Kafka was in fact an anorexic. Rather, because in my approach I critically reproduce the anorexic logic, I am interested in what belonged to Kafka's mind, not his body. I read the body as an outward sign of a pervasive logic, the body as created by culture and the mind, so that my analytical interests lie primarily in these areas.

28. The various figures I examine can be situated along this spectrum. Eliot, Pound, and Williams participate in failed attempts to eliminate or incorporate "feminine weight"; Kafka is haunted by it; Conrad refuses and then embraces it; and Jean Rhys makes the female experience of embodiment her main subject.

29. Franz Kafka, "The Metamorphosis," in *The Complete Stories,* ed. Nahum N. Glatzer, trans. Willa Muir and Edwin Muir (New York: Schocken, 1971), p. 139.

30. Reiner Stach, "Kafka's Egoless Woman: Otto Weininger's *Sex and Character,*" trans. Neil Donahue, in *Reading Kafka,* pp. 149–69.

31. Quoted in ibid., p. 157.

32. Ezra Pound, *Selected Letters of Ezra Pound, 1907–1941* (New York: New Directions, 1950), p. 170.

33. T. S. Eliot, *"The Waste Land": A Facsimile and Transcript of the Original Drafts Including the Annotations of Ezra Pound* (New York: Harcourt, Brace, Jovanovich, 1971), pp. 23, 25. Quotations from both transcript and final versions are from this source.

34. T. S. Eliot, *Ash Wednesday,* in *"The Waste Land" and Other Poems* (New York: Harcourt, Brace, World, 1962), p. 59.

35. See Thorstein Veblen, *The Theory of the Leisure Class* (1899; reprint, New York: Random, 1934).

36. Eliot's preoccupation with female sexuality is historically grounded, for the women's movement of the second decade of the twentieth century made female sexuality a central issue. These first "feminists" were divided: some made suffrage the only issue, while others brought female sexuality

and birth control into the foreground. It was a very public and hotly debated topic in all spheres at the time. As Nancy F. Cott writes, "[O]lder suffragists hastened to disavow any connection between the vote for women and sexual promiscuity, for free love was a bogey that anti-suffragists had been warning about for decades. Indeed, anti-suffrage writers of the early 1910's very quickly discerned that Feminism was even more alarming than suffragism because of its combined emphasis on women's economic dependence and sex rights along with the vote. . . . By ancient cultural tradition, the loosing of women's sexual desire from men's control released the fiendish contents of Pandora's box" (*The Grounding of Modern Feminism* [New Haven: Yale Univ. Press, 1987], p. 44). In his writing, particularly in *The Waste Land,* Eliot seems often to be reacting to his perceptions of these "fiendish contents."

37. Maud Ellmann, *The Poetics of Impersonality: T. S. Eliot and Ezra Pound* (London: Harvester Press, 1987), p. 165.

38. Of course, in the literal, empirical world men have just as many "spreading" bodies as women and can hardly stand for the ideal. In this particular context, I refer to the figurative representation, rather than the literal manifestation.

39. Ezra Pound, "Doggerel Section of Letter to Marianne Moore," in *The Gender of Modernism,* ed. Bonnie Kime Scott (Bloomington: Indiana Univ. Press, 1990), pp. 362–63.

40. Ezra Pound, quoted in Rabate, *Language, Sexuality, and Ideology,* p. 217.

41. See Abelard, *Historia calamitatum,* in *The Letters of Abelard and Heloise,* trans. Betty Radice (New York: Penguin, 1974), pp. 57–106.

42. Sigmund Freud, *Civilization and Its Discontents,* trans. James Strachey (New York: Norton, 1961), pp. 50–51.

43. See, for instance, Sigmund Freud, "'Civilized' Sexual Morality and Modern Nervousness," in *Sexuality and the Psychology of Love,* ed. Philip Rieff (New York: Macmillan, 1963), pp. 20–40, in which Freud argues that the artist is highly sexually active, and that this activity enhances and enables his work. This early piece (1908) contradicts the statement from the much later *Civilization and Its Discontents* (1930). The early work argues that suppressing the libido results in a great loss of energy that would be freed through activity, and that the "lost energy" due to sexual activity and interaction with women is not "expedient" to the claims of civilization. What I call the anorexic logic of literary modernism combines both positions in that the anorexic who suppresses libido through that very act of suppression figured as fasting (rather than sublimation) frees that energy for a higher form of production.

44. Ezra Pound, *The Cantos of Ezra Pound* (New York: New Directions, 1973), p. 193. For the translations of Greek and Latin that appear in this canto, I rely on Carroll F. Terrell, *A Companion to the "Cantos" of Ezra Pound* (Berkeley: Univ. of California Press, 1980), pp. 160–62.

45. Quoted in Bryce Conrad, *Refiguring America: A Study of William Carlos Williams's "In the American Grain."* (Chicago: Univ. of Illinois Press, 1990), p. 106.

46. T. S. Eliot, "Tradition and the Individual Talent," in *Selected Essays* (New York: Harcourt, Brace, Jovanovich, 1950), p. 7–8.

47. The pronoun used here is deliberately "his," for I argue that, since literary modernism sees a privileged male position—that of the anorexic— as the necessary precursor for the production of "true" art, women, stereotyped as nonanorexic, are excluded from the artistic domain.

48. Again I use the masculine pronoun to emphasize that in high modernism the anorexic position from which artist creates is continually gendered male.

49. Despite the status of imagism as one of the first identifiable "modernisms," in *The Pound Era* (Berkeley: Univ. of California Press, 1971), Hugh Kenner reads it as one of the "clots" in Pound's energies, an anomaly that would be better off excised: "from the directed force and constellated *virtu* of the 'Osiris' articles, through the pulsating universe of Fenollosa's essay . . . and thence into the *Cantos,* runs a steady preoccupation with persistently patterned energies. Lodged in that current, an enigmatic stone called 'Imagism' created and continues to create its distracting turbulence" (p. 173). Why imagism is lodged as a stone, is not clear, except that Kenner wishes to claim for Pound a primacy that an association with other imagists like Richard Aldington, H.D. or Amy Lowell would seem in his mind to preclude: "[Imagism] had come to mean very little more than a way of designating short *vers libre* poems in English. But [Pound's] 'doctrine of the image' . . . remains vital. . . . it is folly to pretend, in the way of historians with books to fill, that [Lowell, H.D., Aldington] were of Pound's stature. Vorticism implied his alliance with his own kind: Gaudier, Lewis" (pp. 178, 191). But the criterion that Kenner uses to establish Pound's higher "stature" sounds remarkably like the vocabulary associated with imagism. As he reads Pound's "Return," these are some of the words he uses to establish the "true artist": "sharp meters," "sharp images," "imagistically sharp and metrically cut," "sculptured stasis," "fragmentary effect" (pp. 190–91). He claims that Pound's "doctrine of the image," rather than the "technical hygiene" of F. S. Flint's imagism, "made possible the *Cantos* and *Paterson,* long works that with the work of T. S. Eliot are the Symbolist heritage in English," the post-Symbolist verse of which "Pound's imagism set out to reform by deleting its self-

indulgences, intensifying its virtues, and elevating the glimpse into the vision
. . . delivering post-Symbolist poetry from its pictorialist impasse" (pp. 183,
185, 186). Here again is the metaphor of midwifery, a birth achieved through
cutting, through the circumvention of the feminine as reproductive fat. And
here again is a rhetoric (although imagism claimed to be antirhetorical, "objective") of gender enacted in Kenner's reading of Pound, his establishment
of Pound as "genius": "deleting . . . self-indulgences, . . . elevating the
glimpse into the vision," for "Pound's Imagism is energy, is effort. It does not
appease itself by reproducing what is seen, but by setting some other seen
thing into relation. The mind that found 'petals on a wet, black bough' had
been active" (p. 186). Pound produces, rather than reproduces, creates
something new, rather than merely replicates, implying the old trope of masculine spiritual production, rather than feminine material reproduction. His
imagism is active, rather than passive; vital energy, rather than placid stasis;
masculine, rather than feminine. His imagism makes it possible for male
writers to give birth to "the *Cantos* and *Paterson.*" Never "self-indulgent,"
never easily "appeased," both words associated with misogynist stereotypes
of women, Pound is not content with passively "glimpsing" but must rather
elevate that "glimpse into . . . vision." In Kenner's rhetoric, vision is only attainable through a particularly gender-coded deletion of the feminine. On
imagism's antirhetorical stance, see John T. Gage, *In the Arresting Eye: The
Rhetoric of Imagism* (Baton Rouge: Louisiana State Univ. Press, 1981), especially chap. 2.

50. Natan Zach, "Imagism and Vorticism," in *Modernism, 1890–1930,* ed.
Malcolm Bradbury and James McFarlane (New York: Penguin, 1978), p.
238.

51. Brumberg cites Gilbert and Gubar's discussion of anorexia in *The
Madwoman in the Attic,* as well as Elaine Showalter's *The Female Malady,*
as examples of this tendency to glorify anorexia as a political strategy of resistance to the dominant patriarchal culture. I agree with Brumberg that this
is a problematic position for the reasons already cited.

52. William Carlos Williams, *In the American Grain* (New York: New
Directions, 1956), p. 179 (hereafter cited as *American Grain*).

53. Quoted in Conrad, *Refiguring America,* p. 106.

54. Quoted in ibid.

55. Williams, *American Grain.* The passage quoted is not located on a
numbered page but stands as a kind of epigraph at the beginning of the book
before the table of contents. I am assuming that it is placed there as a kind
of summary, meant to declare Williams's intentions. While this might then
function as a commentary on method, on what has been attempted, it is by
no means clear that the essays reveal the "true character" Williams says he

seeks. His alternative histories never seem to claim the same status, and his ambivalent stance toward the characters he seems to identify with rather have the effect of offering another point of view without claiming that this view is "truth." Paradoxically, then, while the essays don't seem as uncomplicated as this declared intention, as just another view they also cannot function as the shared ground for community and identity Williams seeks to establish through his newly constructed myths.

56. William Carlos Williams, author's note to *Paterson* (New York: New Directions), 1963. Page numbers are not given in the author's note to this edition, but the quotation is from the third page of that text.

57. Andreas Huyssen, "Mass Culture as Woman: Modernism's Other," *Studies in Entertainment,* ed. Tania Modleski (Bloomington: Indiana Univ. Press, 1986), p. 191.

58. William Carlos Williams, "Queen Anne's Lace," in *American Poetry,* ed. Gay Wilson Allen, Walter B. Rideout, and James K. Robinson (New York: Harper, 1965), pp. 741–42.

3. "Should Be Out of It"

1. Albert Guerard, foreword to *"Typhoon" and Other Tales,* by Joseph Conrad (New York: Signet, 1962), p. vii.

2. Joseph Conrad, author's note to *Heart of Darkness,* ed. Robert Kimbrough (New York: Norton, 1988), p. 3. All references are from this critical edition.

3. Ian Watt, *Conrad in the Nineteenth Century* (Berkeley: Univ. of California Press, 1979), pp. 93, 98.

4. Joseph Conrad, *Heart of Darkness,* p. 9. On Conrad and narration, see Royal Roussel, *The Metaphysics of Darkness* (Baltimore: Johns Hopkins Univ. Press, 1971); Suresh Ravel, *The Art of Failure: Conrad's Fiction* (Boston: Allen and Unwin, 1986); and Edward W. Said, "Conrad: The Presentation of Narrative," in *Critical Essays on Joseph Conrad,* ed. Ted Billey (Boston: G. K. Hall, 1987), pp. 27–47. Roussel discusses a shift in Conrad's work that derives from the problem raised by the detached narrators like Marlow who insist upon the unreality of existence, the fact that "it is impossible to make a recognition of the self's ephemerality the rationale of its continued existence" (p. 139). Roussel argues that as a result of this impossibility, in the later work Conrad drops the detached narrator and his search for an ontological ground for the subject, attending instead to the "incidents of the surface" or what I have been referring to as "the personal." It is not that Conrad is no longer "man enough to face the darkness," but rather that his

perspective changes to include as valid "the surface" he had formerly wanted to dispense with. I recast the shift from ironic detachment to a kind of political and emotional engagement with "the personal" as a progression from an anorexic logic to one more inclusive of and positively inclined toward things "feminine."

5. J. Hillis Miller, "*Heart of Darkness* Revisited," in *"Heart of Darkness": A Case Study in Contemporary Criticism,* ed. Ross C. Murfin (New York: St. Martin's, 1989), p. 212. Conrad's statement of his goal to "make you see" is from the famous preface to *The Nigger of the "Narcissus."*

6. Quoted in Jefferey Meyers, *Joseph Conrad: A Biography* (New York: Scribner's, 1991), p. 150.

7. Joseph Conrad, "Typhoon," in *"Typhoon" and Other Tales,* p. 250.

8. Joseph Conrad, *The Secret Agent* (New York: Penguin Classics, 1988), pp. 244, 242.

9. Quoted in Meyers, *Joseph Conrad,* p. 165.

10. On this aspect of the women's movement, see Nancy F. Cott, *The Grounding of Modern Feminism* (New Haven: Yale Univ. Press, 1987), pp. 41–50. Cott explains that public discussion of female desire and sexuality and its liberation from male control was seen as a threat to the social order: "In the very years that feminists were articulating this threat, the thrill and the fear female sexual assertiveness posed to male control was translated into mass culture by the vamp star of the silent screen, Theda Bara. She reigned supreme from 1913 to 1916, her role emblematic of the simultaneous allure and threat to the social order contained in the female erotic" (pp. 44–45). After centuries of silence the open discussion of the female erotic by women themselves must have contributed to the period's uneasiness about materiality and the body's status, particularly the female body.

11. Roberta Pollack Seid, *Never Too Thin: Why Women Are at War with Their Bodies* (New York: Prentice Hall, 1989), p. 82.

12. In a seminar on European decadence (University of California, Irvine, 1989), Barbara Spackman emphasized the connection between anxiety about the body's uselessness in the modern context and the futurists, who, in an attempt to save the body from obsolescence, turned the body into a machine.

13. Quoted in Meyers, *Joseph Conrad,* p. 166.

14. Quoted in ibid., p. 171.

15. On Conrad and his various illnesses, see ibid., pp. 23–28, 104–8, 130–31, 140–41, 258–59; Bernard Meyer, *Joseph Conrad: A Psychoanalytic Biography* (Princeton: Princeton Univ. Press, 1967), pp. 63 n, 104, 120, 166, 183, 219, 269; and Fredrick R. Karl, *Joseph Conrad: The Three Lives* (New York:

Farrar, Straus, and Giroux, 1979), pp. 46–48, 51–52, 62–63, 68–72, 92–94, 96–97, 111–12, 194–95, 239–41, 284–85, 293–98, 345–46, 423–25, 496–99, 572–79, 667–70, 749–50, 809–10, 903–4.

16. G. Jean-Aubry, *Joseph Conrad: Life and Letters,* vol. 1 (New York: Doubleday, 1927), p. 232.

17. The "seminal" analysis of this trope in Western culture is Luce Irigaray's "'Mechanics' of Fluids," in *This Sex Which Is Not One,* trans. Catherine Porter (Ithaca: Cornell Univ. Press, 1985), pp. 106–18.

18. Aristotle, "On the Generation of Animals," in *The Basic Works of Aristotle,* ed. Richard McKeon, trans. Arthur Platt (New York: Random, 1941), p. 678.

19. On Poradowski, see Meyers, *Joseph Conrad,* pp. 93–97; on Jane Anderson, see ibid., pp. 293–311.

20. Meyers, for instance, writes that "Conrad wanted and needed a sacrificial wife and surrogate mother," citing a letter Conrad wrote to an editor after his first son's birth: "I really ought to have a nurse—since my wife must also look after the other child" (ibid., p. 143).

21. Quoted in ibid., p. 142.

22. Jessie Conrad, *Joseph Conrad as I Knew Him* (London: William Heineman, 1926), p. 45.

23. In the *Heart of Darkness* manuscript included in the Kimbrough edition of that novel, Marlow says, referring to the Roman conquests as opposed to contemporary imperialism, that "the best of them is that they didn't get up pretty fictions about it" (p. 10).

24. On the emergent connection between obesity and the lower classes, Seid writes that "in a curious inversion of popular imagery, the poor and lower classes began to be seen as stocky and plump rather than as thin and undernourished—or rather, plumpness began to be associated more insistently with the lower classes" (*Never Too Thin,* p. 91). The quotations from Morrell, Woolf, and Wells are from Meyers, *Joseph Conrad,* p. 144.

25. Quoted in Meyers, *Joseph Conrad,* p. 226.

26. Ruth L. Nadelhaft, *Joseph Conrad* (Atlantic Highlands, N.J.: Humanities, 1991), p. 9.

27. Thomas Moser, *Joseph Conrad: Achievement and Decline* (Cambridge: Harvard Univ. Press, 1957), p. 99.

28. Noelle Caskey, "Interpreting Anorexia Nervosa," in *The Female Body in Western Culture* (Cambridge: Harvard Univ. Press, 1986), p. 175.

29. According to some studies the average twenty-year-old woman has 28.7 percent body fat, while the average man of the same age has 11 percent; other, more conservative estimates are 22 percent for women and 15 percent for men. My source is Seid, *Never Too Thin,* p. 175.

30. Often people are so influenced by these codes that husbands write to "Dear Abby" complaining that they love their wives, but that these women are so fat that they will have to get rid of them. An exemplary letter to "Dear Abby," quoted in Kim Chernin, *The Obsession: Reflections on the Tyranny of Slenderness* (New York: Perennial Library, 1981) reads as follows: "My wife gained ten to 15 pounds while pregnant with our son 11 years ago. She has never been able to lose that weight despite many dieting attempts. . . . I weigh the same as when I graduated from college. I have tried every method I can think of to encourage her to lose weight—incentives, insults, praise, punishment, joint exercise, and threats. . . . Otherwise she is a great wife and wonderful mother. I do love her, and have no desire to see our marriage end. However, I cannot accept her as she is no matter how hard I try. . . . This problem is continually on my mind, and I am afraid that a permanent separation will eventually be the result" (pp. 111–12).

31. Naomi Wolf, *The Beauty Myth* (New York: Morrow, 1991), p. 191.

32. Seid notes that the establishment mandate that "thin is in" and furthermore is necessary to national health was one mandate left unquestioned in this country by the counterculture of the sixties (see *Never Too Thin*, chap. 7). The preference for thinness in Conrad is one ideological formation he leaves unquestioned, while he subjects so many others to scrutiny.

33. On the thin body as signifying an intellectual nature and the relationship between this signification and contemporary anorexia, see Chernin, *Obsession*, especially, pp. 56–65; Caskey, "Interpreting Anorexia Nervosa," especially, pp. 184–87; and Wolf, *Beauty Myth*, pp. 179–217.

34. See Seid, *Never Too Thin*, pp. 81–102.

35. See Hilde Bruch, *Eating Disorders: Obesity, Anorexia Nervosa and the Person Within* (New York: Basic, 1973), pp. 211–27; and Joan Jacobs Brumberg, *Fasting Girls: The History of Anorexia Nervosa* (Cambridge: Harvard Univ. Press, 1988), chap. 1.

36. On Conrad and race, see Chinua Achebe, "An Image of Africa: Racism in Conrad's *Heart of Darkness*," *The Massachusetts Review* 18 (1977), pp. 782–94; Hunt Hawkins, "The Issue of Racism in *Heart of Darkness*," *Conradiana* 14 (1982), pp. 163–72; and Benita Parry, *Conrad and Imperialism: Ideological Boundaries and Visionary Frontiers* (London: Macmillan, 1983).

37. Johanna M. Smith, "Too Beautiful Altogether: Patriarchal Ideology in *Heart of Darkness*, in *"Heart of Darkness": A Case Study*, p. 180.

38. Nina Pelikan Strauss, "The Exclusion of the Intended from Secret Sharing in Conrad's *Heart of Darkness*," *Novel* (winter 1987), pp. 123–37.

39. See Susan Ludvall Brodie, "Conrad's Feminine Perspective," *Conradiana* 14, no. 2 (1984); Nadelhaft, *Joseph Conrad;* Smith, "Too Beautiful

Altogether"; Strauss, "Exclusion of the Intended"; and Zohreh T. Sullivan, "Theory for the Untheoretical," *College English* 53, no. 5 (1991). Brodie and Nadelhaft are sympathetic toward Conrad's portrayal of women in the text, while Smith and Strauss view women's position as "out of it" as the bedrock that upholds the ideology of imperialism.

40. Jacques Lacan, "Seminar on 'The Purloined Letter,'" in *The Purloined Poe,* ed. John P. Muller and William J. Richardson (Baltimore: Johns Hopkins Univ. Press, 1988), pp. 28–54.

41. Important feminist analysts of the Victorian and early modern period include Elaine Showalter, *The Female Malady: Women, Madness, and English Culture, 1830–1980* (New York: Pantheon, 1985); and *Sexual Anarchy* (New York: Viking, 1990); Deborah Gorham, *The Victorian Girl and the Feminine Ideal* (London: Croom Helm, 1982); Barbara Ehrenreich and Deidre English, *For Her Own Good: 150 Years of the Experts' Advice to Women* (New York: Doubleday, 1978); and Martha Vicinus, ed., *Suffer and Be Still* (Bloomington: Univ. of Indiana Press, 1972).

42. My references to *Falk* are from Joseph Conrad, *Tales of East and West,* ed. Morton Dauwen Zabel (New York: Hanover House, 1958), p. 234.

43. John Carlos Rowe has pointed out to me that "old wine" is the sign of aristocracy for the Victorian gentleman, a trace of the landed gentry to which the professional bourgeois gentleman aspired. The wine cellar that preserves the wine is a sign of the firstborn son's inheritance. That this group drinks the "old wine" and refuses "execrable" food is no doubt linked to class pretensions, just as anorexia was originally a disease of the upper class. At the turn of the century, noneating was a sign of refined, upper-class status.

44. "Eating the other" is on my mind from the Jacques Derrida seminar on "The Rhetoric of Cannibalism" (Univ. of California, Irvine, 1990–91).

45. On this metaphor, see Caroline Walker Bynum, *Holy Feast and Holy Fast: The Religious Significance of Food to Medieval Women* (Berkeley: Univ. of California Press, 1987), pp. 260–77; as well as Margaret Atwood, *The Edible Woman* (New York: Warner Books, 1969).

46. Sigmund Freud, *Three Essays on Sexuality,* in *The Standard Edition of the Complete Psychological Works of Sigmund Freud,* vol. 7, trans. James Strachey (London: Hogarth Press, 1955), p. 159.

47. In the later *Totem and Taboo,* of course, Freud makes a similar historical argument.

48. The best example of this is Albert Guerard, *Conrad the Novelist* (Cambridge: Harvard Univ. Press, 1966). See also Meyer, *Joseph Conrad.*

4. Missing Persons

1. Arthur Kroker and Marilouise Kroker, *The Last Sex: Feminism and Outlaw Bodies* (New York: St. Martin's, 1993), p. 12.

2. Judith Kegan Gardiner, "*Good Morning, Midnight;* Goodnight, Modernism," *Boundary* 2, nos. 11 and 12 (fall/winter 1982/83), p. 233.

3. Although inadequate for situating the subject within Rhys's cultural and historical context, some labels from psychology do apply to her life and some of her characters, and have a limited usefulness in explaining one strand of the logic that informs her texts. To explain them using only this vocabulary would be a mistake, however, for it would risk defining a pathological subject, rather than, as Rhys suggests, a subject that, if she is pathological, is made that way by the social forces impinging upon her. As Gardiner writes, "[P]sychological labels fit Rhys and her characters. Beaten as a child, molested as an adolescent, Rhys repeatedly involved herself in painful situations, and her characters share some traits with incest victims. She and her characters are also often depressed, even suicidal, and paranoid about their persecution by neighbors; they may appear as Laingian divided selves or as Horneyan neurotics whose insatiable demands for love drive people away. From the perspective of self-psychology, Rhys and many of her heroes manifest a 'narcissistic personality disorder' with weak sense of self and difficulties with self-esteem. Such people crave mirroring or idealizing relationships in which they feel merged with something more powerful than themselves. . . . Rhys has seemed paradigmatic of the way that social prescriptions make women 'mad'" (*Rhys, Stead, Lessing and the Politics of Empathy* [Bloomington: Indiana Univ. Press, 1989], p. 21). Carole Angier, author of the authoritative biography *Jean Rhys: Life and Work* (Boston: Little, Brown, 1990) also discusses the psychological diagnosis of Rhys when she reports on her consultation with analysts about her:

The analysts all agreed too on what she was. I put :n my list all her most permanent and most painful feelings. Her sense of being nothing, a ghost, already dead; or else twins, one docile, the other lost in a dark wood. Her constant anxiety . . . her constant battle against depression, which was what the make-up, the clothes, the treats, the drink were all for. Her absolute inability to be alone . . . her inability none the less to ever feel anything *but* alone: ever to feel any real connection to or understanding of another human being. Her wild changes of mood, hope to despair, exaltation to abasement. . . . her immediate and intense expression of her feelings in her face . . . her inability to contain her very worst feelings, so that her rage and violence burst out even against those she most needed, even to the extent of public humiliation. Her extreme passivity, and her extreme incompetence . . . her extreme emotional need and dependence—which could so suddenly change to extreme opposition and independence. . . . They recognized it all. Jean suffered, they said, from what is now called a borderline personality disorder. This disorder goes back to infancy, to a failure of the relation between mother and child. The child's needs are not met; from the start, therefore, it feels what Jean felt: hostility from the world, and deep, unassuagable rage towards it. And it fails to develop a complete, autonomous self. That is the key: the nothingness where the self should be. That is the nothingness Jean always felt. . . . the doctor's explanation of her personality is surely true; it is illuminating; but it doesn't touch the real mystery. If Jean was a borderline personality *of course* she couldn't be alone, of course she couldn't control herself or accept control, couldn't act or decide, couldn't do what was hard, above all couldn't accept the evil inside her. And yet she did. She should have been only a cripple, only a drunkard. But she was not. . . . The *nothing* she so feared, and saw behind and under everything was her own self. But in her writing she herself made it whole (pp. 657–58). I would add that in writing, Rhys made the connection to the social and historical forces—including literary ones—that define women as "nothing," so that while Rhys's "nothing" was a construction she projected upon the outside world, it also was projected on her— and she accepted it. The blame cannot go one way or the other. If Rhys suffered from "borderline personality disorder" (also known as "borderline syndrome"), she shares this with clinical anorexics, for borderline syndrome is one of the central features of anorexia. See Hilde Bruch, *The Golden Cage: The Enigma of Anorexia Nervosa* (New York: Vintage, 1979), p. 21.

4. I stress this point because as I have begun to circulate my work on anorexia among an academic audience, I have found that many of the young women, generally first- or second-year graduate students who were at some point anorexic themselves, have a strong emotional investment in claiming anorexia as a valid social protest. I empathize with their position and, having held that position myself, understand all too well the powerful feelings of frustration and need to claim agency that motivate it. It is, however, not a tenable position, since in an anorexic's "critique," she must first accept the rejection of the feminine that derives from the very standards she ostensibly questions. By taking "absolute control" of her own body, which the cultural matrix tries to define and label for her and uses to label her subjectivity as well, she may well develop anorexia as a protest against the social standards that designate her a "powerless woman." To the extent that this control can only be an agency of negation that ultimately destroys her, however, its political viability is severely limited and is usually cast in terms of individual pathology. Anorexia is a disease enacted in extreme isolation, and that often is part of a competition with other women. The anorexic derives feelings of superiority from her "greater control" and often has much contempt for those women "weaker" and more feminine than herself (see Bruch, *Golden Cage,* pp. 79–83). The anorexic acts out bodily the annihilation of female subjectivity she perceives and to this extent "protests" that annihilation, but it is a central feature of the disease that in her protest, she violently rejects those aspects of herself labeled "feminine," the aspects that in the cultural matrix put her in a position of disempowerment. In that rejection she merely

repeats the rejection of the feminine that created that position of disempowerment in the first place. This is the anorexic's double bind.

5. Molly Hite, *The Other Side of the Story: Structures and Strategies of Contemporary Feminist Narrative* (Ithaca: Cornell Univ. Press, 1989), p. 27.

6. See Susan Bordo, "Anorexia Nervosa: Psychopathology as the Crystallization of Culture," in *Feminism and Foucault: Reflections on Resistance*, ed. Irene Diamond and Lee Quinby (Boston: Northeastern Univ. Press, 1988).

7. Rachel Bowlby, "The Impasse: Jean Rhys's *Good Morning, Midnight*," in *Still Crazy after All These Years: Women, Writing, and Psychoanalysis* (New York: Routledge, 1993), p. 34.

8. This echoes William Faulkner's designation of himself on the map at the back of *Absalom, Absalom!* as "sole owner and proprietor" of the fictional universe he has created, Yoknapatawpha County (New York: Vintage, 1986). It is perhaps the same impulse, configured differently according to the subject's social relationship to power, that causes a male author like Faulkner to designate himself "sole owner and proprietor" of a fictional kingdom, while the anorexic designates herself "sole owner and proprietor" of her flesh, an ownership that is often taken away through medical treatments like force-feeding. Professor Gabriele Schwab emphasized the connections between force-feeding and rape (American Studies Group, Univ. of California, Irvine, March 12, 1993). This raises the important question that if, as an agency of negation, anorexia is a willed suicide, does the medical establishment have the right to intervene and force-feed patients, intravenously or otherwise? Poststructuralist assumptions aside, to be "sole owner and proprietor" of one's own text is very different than to be "sole owner and proprietor" of one's own body. The social machinery that allows males to express themselves poetically, while women are forced to express themselves physically, is undoubtedly part of what the anorexic expresses through an "agency of negation." In her book *Eating Disorders: Obesity, Anorexia Nervosa and the Person Within* (New York: Basic, 1973), Hilde Bruch highlights the ways in which anorexics have an underlying sense of themselves, what I describe as subjectivity as black hole, that is very similar to that expressed in Rhys's novels: "[Anorexics] experience themselves as acting only in response to demands coming from other people . . . as not doing things because they want to. . . . [This] is camouflaged by the enormous negativism and stubborn defiance with which these patients operate, and which makes personal contact so difficult. The indiscriminate nature of rejection reveals it as a desperate cover-up for an undifferentiated sense of helplessness" (p. 254). Anorexics are entirely dependent upon the perceptions of others for a sense of identity: "She felt she could not possibly be fat because nobody would respect her,

and she could not exist without respect from people" (p. 259). The underlying issue, Bruch explains, is not loss of weight to fit a particular ideal of beauty but rather "the urgent need to lose weight is a cover-up symptom, expressing an underlying fear of being despised or disregarded, or of not getting or deserving respect. . . . Karen would resort to complaints about her worthlessness and emptiness" (p. 262). Emptiness, which so characterizes the metaphysical horizon of characters in Rhys, characterizes the anorexic horizon as well. Bruch writes of an anorexic similar to Rhys, who in her life and novels expressed a belief in fate: "in Sharon's philosophy (and that of most anorexics) 'fate' directed everybody's life and all she had to do was fulfill it" (p. 263). Repeatedly, Bruch's patients express that "what [they were] afraid of is something [they] called 'emptiness'" (p. 271). Anorexics experience an unrelenting sense of "emptiness," Bruch writes, and their "drive for achievement . . . precedes the whole syndrome. The noneating and fear of being fat are resorted to after previous efforts at establishing a sense of 'being in control' have failed" (p. 275). Anorexia is a desperate attempt to control a life that feels empty and out of control, because of the lack of agency they sense (characterized by a belief in "fate").

9. Morag Macsween, *Anorexic Bodies* (London: Routledge, 1993).

10. Thanks to John Carlos Rowe for providing the concept "agency of negation." Rowe used the term to explain Sethe's action in Toni Morrison's *Beloved*. Sethe enacts an agency of negation when, confronted with the prospect of slavery—outright ownership of the body and soul—for her child, she negates that ownership by slitting the child's throat. It seems to me that this term also provides the most apt formulation of the anorexic position. Although anorexics are hardly in the position of slaves, the agency of negation combines the idea that the anorexic is enacting a protest against her socially determined position as devalued feminine flesh/emotions with the idea that, although such an act demonstrates a kind of agency, this agency is negative and self-destructive, and so ultimately falls back into the very terms that it protests, since those terms (Hegel's "impotent shadows") define the subject negatively.

11. Jean Rhys, *Quartet* (New York: Carroll and Graf, 1990), p. 186.

12. Mary Lou Emery, *Jean Rhys at "World's End": Novels of Colonial and Sexual Exile* (Austin: Univ. of Texas Press, 1990).

13. Susan Bordo, *Unbearable Weight* (Berkeley: Univ. of California Press, 1993), p. 24. See also Teresa de Lauretis, "Upping the Anti (sic) in Feminist Theory," in *The Cultural Studies Reader*, ed. Simon During (New York: Routledge, 1993).

14. The following studies are very powerful readings of Rhys, and I do not pit my own interpretation against them to discredit them. To do so would

follow the anorexic logic of literary criticism, which posits that to do a reading yourself, you must first eliminate everyone else's. I would rather situate my work in conversation. I document one particular tendency in Rhys—I do not claim to account for everything. Those studies that persuasively present alternative ways of knowing, reading, and writing in Rhys include Deborah Kelly Kloepfer, *The Unspeakable Mother: Forbidden Discourse in Jean Rhys and H.D.* (Ithaca: Cornell Univ. Press, 1989), which articulates the ways in which Rhys's writing "instinctively insists on subverting the premise of language—that to write means to relinquish the mother" (p. 22); Emery, *Rhys at "World's End,"* which argues that Rhys, through her use of Caribbean culture, "present[s] an alternative to European concepts of character and identity. . . . an isolated and alienated female protagonist vies . . . with a more communal satirical laughter that derives from the Caribbean carnival . . . an exploration of subjectivity that seeks an alternative to that of the European novel" (pp. xii, xiv); Nancy R. Harrison, *Jean Rhys and the Novel as Women's Text* (Chapel Hill: Univ. of North Carolina Press, 1988), which argues that Rhys "both disrupts the framework of masculine discourse and fills in the gaps in that discourse to expose her own language—our language—and theirs. In this process of exposure she places the 'silent' speech, the 'unsaid things,' center stage. Her writing speaks out loud what is left unsaid, showing us, allowing us to hear, the full resonance of our speech through the gaps, the spaces, the 'holes' in masculine discourse" (p. 53); and Hite, *The Other Side of the Story,* who shows how "Rhys continually places a marginal character at the center of her fiction and in doing so decenters an inherited narrative structure and undermines the values informing this structure. In particular the novel, a form that emerged with the bourgeoisie and embodies the ethical priorities of this ascendant class, privileges agency" (p. 25). Hite shows that Rhys shows how those "inherited narrative structures" grant agency to some through the designations of others as "other"—a designation that makes their agency possible.

15. The hunger striker position has been associated with the anorexic position most thoroughly in Susie Orbach, *Hunger Strike: The Anorectic's Struggle as a Metaphor for Our Age* (New York: Norton, 1988). Orbach's argument, echoed by many others, is that anorexia is a form of female self-expression that the culture has denied them:

the individual woman's problem—for which anorexia has been the solution—is that despite a socialization process designed to suppress her needs, she has continued to feel her own needs and desires intensely. . . . her anorexia is the daily, even hourly, attempt to keep her needs in check, to keep herself and her desires under wraps. . . . Whenever a woman's spirit has been threatened, she has taken the control of her body as an avenue of self-expression. The anorectic refusal of food is only the latest

228   *Notes to Pages 150–151*

in a series of woman's attempts at self-assertion which at some point have descended directly upon her body. If woman's body is the site of her protest, then equally the body is the ground on which the attempt for control is fought. (p. 19)

The problem with the parallel between the anorectic's "self-expression" and the hunger striker's is that the hunger strike is a temporary state, a specific strategy with specific goals and is usually undertaken as part of a larger political community vying for change, as with the British suffragettes. The anorexic, by contrast, is obsessively alone, cutting herself off from all contact with others. Her struggle, and I agree it is a political struggle, is directed toward herself, not at the system that has produced the necessity to protest in the first place. Unlike the hunger striker who openly questions the standards of the dominant culture, the anorectic has internalized those standards to a radical degree. Even if she makes use of an agency of negation and defies the powerless woman position the cultural matrix has assigned her, in her defiance of that position she accepts the pejorative definition of the feminine and attempts to excise it, to distance herself from it—precisely the opposite of the suffragettes who struggled to empower women through the vote.

16. Elaine Showalter, *The Female Malady: Women, Madness, and English Culture, 1830–1980* (New York: Pantheon, 1985), p. 162. In *Fasting Girls: The History of Anorexia Nervosa* (Cambridge: Harvard Univ. Press, 1988), Joan Jacobs Brumberg points out that the problem with this statement is that it "obscures the real distinctions between conscious political strategies involving refusal of food until a goal is reached and forms of food refusal that are unrelentingly self-destructive" (p. 293). Since the anorexic position accepts the pejorative definition of the feminine/female body and protests an identification with that body, rather than the definition that defines it pejoratively, it is very different from the hunger strike, which protested the definitions of women and the infringement upon their rights that the definitions created.

17. For an excellent reading of the ways in which Rhys makes the relationships between gender and genre clear, exposing who is and who is not authorized as a "proper" subject for literature, and whose voices the literary tradition erases, see Hite, "Writing in the Margins: Jean Rhys," in *Other Side of the Story*, pp. 19–54.

18. As representative of the first, more critical view, see A. Alvarez, "Down and Out in Paris and London," *The New York Review of Books* 37, no. 15 (October 10, 1991). Enthusiastic feminist readings include Nancy R. Harrison, *Jean Rhys and the Novel as Woman's Text*, which argues that "it matters not if what her heroine narrators say is unsuitable for today's more 'liberated' woman: the recording of a woman's unspoken response within the set framework of masculine speech or discourse is the point. . . . Rhys shows

us the conversation, the dialogue, between the powerful and the powerless. She displays the use of language as a tool of repression" (pp. 63, 68). Harrison's point is that the female half of the dialogue or conversation, usually equated with the personal, is what is usually cut out of literature, since traditional literary standards do not value the inclusion of her voice. Rhys, she argues, is a pioneer in breaking those traditions and restoring the female voice to literature.

19. To unproblematically conflate Rhys with her heroines, as well as to assume that the heroines are all the same woman and that this woman is Rhys, has been a problem in Rhys criticism. As Hite writes, "[M]any feminist critics have salvaged [Rhys's] characters by identifying them with the author, and in the process have turned Rhys's writing into compulsive self-revelation, a by-product of therapy. . . . to make biography the principle that governs interpretation of her works is to make Rhys unable to control the form and ideology of her own text. . . . Rhys in no way wrote five novels about the *same* woman; she did write about five women in analogous situations" (*Other Side,* p. 22). Despite the tendency in recent feminist criticism to attempt to go beyond the notion of agency, critics always return to this idea. To make Rhys able "to control the form and ideology of her own text" is to grant her a form of agency. Agency is a notion that, at this particular time, I think it is important to retain, since the "real" of the social and political relations we negotiate daily is still very much informed by it.

20. Angier writes,

I think Jean was the baby they had to assuage their grief over the loss of her sister. Often, perhaps mostly, this works, and pulls the mother back into life. But sometimes it doesn't. Then there is a phenomenon which doctors also recognize: what can happen to a child with a mourning mother. It can be left with a lifelong sense of loss and emptiness, of being wanted by no one and belonging nowhere; of being nothing, not really existing at all. . . . It must go back to her mother, who mourned her dead sister and preferred the living one to her. . . . from the beginning she was unhealable, a stranger on the face of the earth and full of rage. (*Jean Rhys,* 11, 658)

While this is a possible explanation for some aspects of Rhys's life, it seems reductive and somewhat reactionary to attribute everything to failed mother love—blame it on the mother!

21. Kloepfer, *Unspeakable Mother;* and Lori Lawson, "Mirror and Madness: A Lacanian Analysis of the Feminine Subject in *Wide Sargasso Sea,*" *Jean Rhys Review* 4, no. 2 (1991), pp. 19–27. Emery offers a different interpretation than the dominant one that Rhys's writings express a longing for a nurturing, maternal influence: "Rhys's characters, especially Antoinette and Anna, discover new sources for identity and kinship through spiritual communities of women descended from Caribbean slave society. Rather than

centering their personalities, such kinship ties fulfill their characters by re-placing their multiplicitous selves within the folk history of a pluralistic cul-ture" (*Rhys at "World's End,"* p. 128).

22. Angier notes that, unlike the way Jean always told it, "when she defied her family, when she deceitfully, obstinately insisted on becoming a chorus girl, it wasn't because her mother didn't want her back, and was relieved she'd be earning her own living: it was because she wanted to, and her father let her (*Jean Rhys*, p. 52).

23. Alvarez, "Down and Out," p. 43. Alvarez's piece is a review of the Angier biography and demonstrates an extraordinary blindness to the ways in which gender affected Rhys's life. He writes, for instance, that "if you set [Rhys] against America's long line of alcoholic writers who managed to keep a canny grip on their careers, despite their bad habits, you begin to under-stand both the degree of Rhys's self-destructive rage and helplessness, and her lack of any sense of herself as an artist" (p. 42). "America's long line of alcoholic writers" is, of course, almost exclusively male. This statement completely disregards the ways in which the situation for women writers was drastically different—Rhys "lacked any sense of herself as an artist," because for most of her life, she was not treated like one. As Rhys put it herself in *Good Morning, Midnight* (New York: Norton, 1986 [hereafter cited as *GMM*]): "Thinking how funny a book would be, called 'Just a Cérébrale' or 'You Can't Stop Me From Dreaming.' Of course, to be accepted as authentic, to carry any conviction, it would have to be written by a man" (p. 161). Al-varez demonstrates a little anorexic logic himself: "Her prose was pure and self-denying and it kept very close to the facts of her life. In doing so, it distilled them, shaped them, made them seem inevitable. But the facts be-hind the art are shabby and demeaning" ("Down and Out," p. 43). "Art" is "pure and self-denying"; "life" (particularly a woman's life?) is "shabby and demeaning." Alvarez goes further: "Rhys was right when she said that only through writing could she earn death. In all other ways, her life was mon-strous" (p. 43). I'm reminded here of the prim, moralistic language used to describe Bertha Mason in Charlotte Brontë's *Jane Eyre* (New York: Bantam, 1987): "What it was, whether beast or human being, one could not, at first sight tell: it grovelled, seemingly on all fours; it snatched and growled like some strange wild animal: but it was covered with clothing, and a quantity of dark, grizzled hair, wild as a mane, hid its head and face" (p. 278). Desig-nated as a "monster" (many in Rhys's own time, as well as Alvarez, have fixed her with this label), Rhys turns to this "fellow monster," Bertha Mason of *Jane Eyre*, and tells her side of the story in *Wide Sargasso Sea*—a text that clearly shows where labels like "monster" come from, which have little to do with the "essence" of the one so called.

24. On Jean's imprisonment for an assault charge, see Angier, *Jean Rhys,* pp. 445–47. On Rhys and the lack of critical distance between her life and her fiction, see any of the critics cited above. Presence or absence of critical distance is an ongoing controversy in Rhys criticism.

25. The definitive biography is Carol Angier, *Jean Rhys: Life and Work,* cited above, n. 3. The letters are collected in Francis Wyndham and Diana Melly, eds., *Jean Rhys Letters* (London: André Deutsch, 1984). A feature of much recent criticism is an attack on the "autobiographical" argument. As Veronica Marie Gregg writes in "Jean Rhys and Modernism: A Different Voice" (*Jean Rhys Review* 1, no. 2 [spring 1987], pp. 30–46), "[O]ne consistent feature of much of the criticism is the obliteration of the dividing line between the author and the critics' interpretation of her characters and themes. Her work is seen as minor, narrow, personal, sordid even, with little connection to anything outside of itself and the author's reality" (p. 30). I contend that both critical traditions get it wrong. The first, in devaluing autobiography, is decidedly New Critical in orientation, but the second, represented here, is also problematic in that Rhys, more than many writers, *does* invite a collapse "of the dividing line between author" and her characters and themes. She writes almost exclusively from her own experience and makes little attempt to go beyond her interpretation of the events in her life. While this is not necessarily a basis for criticism, we cannot turn around and separate Rhys too much from her work. To do so is to mystify and elevate the author above "real life." Since the material effects of that life on a disempowered subject is Rhys's content, we run the risk of missing the real personal, emotional urgency that informs her texts and reducing them to the kind of formalistic study that excises the biography from the realm of criticism in the first place. My approach lies somewhere between these two.

26. Ford Madox Ford, preface to *The Left Bank,* by Jean Rhys (London: Jonathan Cape, 1927). The University of California library still carries this edition, and it may be out of print. Most of the stories in that volume are reprinted in Jean Rhys, *The Collected Short Stories* (New York: Norton, 1987), hereafter cited as *CSS.*

27. Alicia Borinsky, "Jean Rhys: Poses of the Woman as Guest," in *The Female Body in Western Culture,* ed. Susan Rubin Suleiman (Cambridge: Harvard Univ. Press, 1985), pp. 288–302.

28. Octavio Paz, "The Sons of La Malinche," in *The Labyrinth of Solitude* (New York: Grove Press, 1961); rpt. as *The Labyrinth of Solitude and Other Writings* (New York: Grove Press, 1985), p. 86.

29. Because the anorexic defines herself through a rejection of qualities conventionally named "feminine" and renounces the feminine subject position, she is usually male identified (see chapter 1). Not one of Rhys's heroines

is male identified, but several of her representations of the *femme convenable* are and to that extent share anorexic features, even though they don't starve themselves.

30. Jean Rhys, "Illusion," in *Left Bank,* p. 29. All text references to "Illusion" are from this collection.

31. Although this passage, taken out of context, seems to suggest a lesbianism in Miss Bruce, this does not seem the point of the story. The emphasis is on, as quoted earlier, Miss Bruce's ability, given her financial independence and chosen profession, to look at women from the perspective of the male gaze: "she would look appraisingly with the artist's eye and make a suitably critical remark" (*CSS*, p. 1).

32. Please see Bruch's comments on the anorexics' senses of emptiness in note 8 of this chapter. A black hole is defined as "a hypothetical invisible region in space with a small diameter and intense gravitational field that is held to be caused by the collapse of a massive star" (*Webster's Ninth New Collegiate Dictionary,* s.v., "black hole"). As such, the "black hole exists as a powerful vortex," waiting to suck anything and everything into its nothingness, its absence or lack that was once a powerful presence. By analogy the black hole functions as a persuasive metaphor for the traditional constitution of female subjectivity vis-à-vis the male, as analyzed in chapter 1.

33. Jean Rhys, *Smile Please: An Unfinished Autobiography* (New York: Harper, 1979), pp. 118, 131.

34. Jean Rhys, *After Leaving Mr. Mackenzie* (New York: Carroll and Graf, 1990), pp. 146–47.

35. See Emery, *Rhys at "World's End,"* who argues that the question of "where" instead of "who" emphasizes the importance of context or place in the constitution of the self in Rhys (p. 38).

36. Joseph Conrad, *Heart of Darkness,* ed. Robert Kimbrough (New York: Norton, 1988), p. 69.

37. Critics like Emery have also connected Rhys's sense of alienation with the loss of her Caribbean heritage. Emery's work suggests that the interpretive framework I employ here comes from "the mainly European aesthetic, moral, and psychological standards I believe have operated to misread . . . Rhys's writing [, which] challenges those standards." She argues that Rhys "moves away from European and toward Caribbean cultural values . . . presenting an alternative to European concepts of character and identity. From the vision of this alternative, evaluations of Rhys's protagonists as passive . . . no longer hold; instead, we can perceive their efforts at dialogue, plural identities, and community" (*Rhys at "World's End,"* p. xii). While I agree with Emery's analysis of the dialogic nature of Rhys's writing, which she relates to the carnival traditions of the Caribbean, I argue that the European

and Caribbean traditions are not as opposed in Rhys's work as Emery seems to suggest here. If the heroines, through their language, do present "an alternative to European concepts of character and identity," the latter presumably not defined by agency, then that "alternative" cannot be fully extricated from the terms of the European tradition, because it occurs in indisassociable relation with the European and struggles against that more dominant definition. There are moments, I agree, where the texts seem to envision an alternative and a possible way out, but those moments seem to operate like Julia's flame and "shoot up, having reached nothing." Most often the texts can envision no way out, as in Sasha's dream in *Good Morning, Midnight*:

> I am in the passage of a tube station in London. Many people are in front of me; many people are behind me. Everywhere there are placards printed in red letters: This Way to the Exhibition. But I don't want the way to the exhibition—I want the way out. There are passages to the right and passages to the left, but no exit sign. Everywhere the fingers point and the placards read: This Way to the Exhibition. . . . I touch the shoulder of the man walking in front of me. I say: "I want the way out." But he points to the placards and his hand is made of steel. I walk along with my head bent, very ashamed, thinking: "Just like me—always wanting to be different from other people." (p. 13)

Sasha is "different" because she "want[s a] way out," but neither she nor any of the other heroines ever find one, with the exception of Antoinette, who in destroying Thornfield Hall destroys herself. I argue that because Rhys shares an anorexic mode of thought, although she does protest "things as they are" and seeks alternatives, she is never very good at finding "the way out," because she is fully complicit with the terms she questions. It is, I think, very difficult to find any real sense of community, especially for the heroines, except in a limited way in *Wide Sargasso Sea*.

38. "Buy" in a literal sense as well, since a large part of the ability to construct oneself as a sexual object comes from the ability to purchase the commodities to create the right image: clothes, makeup, body, shoes, and so on.

39. Jean Rhys, *Voyage in the Dark* (New York: Norton, 1982), p. 76.

40. Camille Paglia is quoted in Kevin Sessums, "Stone Goddess," *Vanity Fair* 56, no. 4 (April 1993), p. 202. In a full-page photo featuring Sharon Stone's legs, the writing under the photo, which takes up a good deal of space, proclaims, "She has created a brand-new old-fashioned screen siren: a goddamn goddess for the postfeminist era" (p. 160). "Postfeminist"? It is almost as if feminism never happened, as if the devastating analysis of the mythology of women's "sexual power" had never taken place.

41. Race and class often exacerbate and further complicate the trajectory Rhys's story describes.

42. This material is quoted or paraphrased from Rhys's diary, the "Black Exercise Book," by Angier in her recent biography *Jean Rhys*, pp. 26–29.

43. Quoted in ibid., p. 27.

44. These passages from Rhys's diary are quoted in ibid., pp. 28, 29.

45. In spite of what would seem the nearly self-evident valence of this particular assertion, a number of women calling themselves "feminists" have recently resurrected the femme fatale as an empowering subject position for women. Disturbing assertions of "female power" include Naomi Wolf's new book, *Fire with Fire*, in which she refutes virtually all her insights in *The Beauty Myth: How Images of Beauty Are Used against Women* (New York: Morrow, 1991). In *Fire with Fire* (New York: Random, 1993) Wolf claims that the feminist critique of beauty and male power is part of the dated ethos of so-called victim feminism, and that we are now in a more progressive era of power feminism, where issues like sexual harassment are moot because American women are now "the political ruling class—probably the only ruling class ever to be unaware of their status" (p. xv). In an article dedicated to disarming "feminists [who] found *Basic Instinct* and [Sharon] Stone's role as the bisexual killer in it offensive," Wolf also argues that in this film, Stone is a "complex, compelling, Nietzschean Uberfräulein who owns everything about her own power" (Sessums, "Stone Goddess," p. 202).

46. The "postmodern body" was a feature in *Vanity Fair* (March 1993), pp. 196–99. The Guess? ads refer to a series that appeared in the *Los Angeles Times Magazine* every Sunday in the winter and spring of 1993.

47. *Webster's*, s.v. "bad."

48. A contemporary hard rock band headed by Courtney Love pokes fun at this old cultural designation of women as lack, biological and otherwise, by calling themselves Hole.

49. Another powerful example of the role that appearance and male attention plays in female identity construction is Antoinette in *Wide Sargasso Sea* (New York: Norton, 1982). Imprisoned in the attic, she says that "there is no looking glass here and I don't know what I am like now. . . . what am I doing in this place and who am I?" (p. 180). Without the mirror, to a certain extent it is impossible to know who she is, what she is "like," because that identity is dependent on reflection.

50. Of course, Rhys herself, through writing her stories and novels, was not in a position of silence. However, public response and the critical tradition that treated her for a long time in the same way—praising her style but condemning her "sordid subject matter"—repeated the same violent silencing enacted upon her by "Mr. Howard" or whoever the man really was. Since she was condemned for speaking about the relationships between power,

sex, violence, and gender, the critical tradition metaphorically repeated the original violation.

51. A good collection of scholarly essays on the Clarence Thomas hearings is Toni Morrison, ed., *Race-ing Justice, En-gendering Power: Essays on Anita Hill, Clarence Thomas, and the Construction of Social Reality* (New York: Pantheon, 1992).

52. Public attitude toward sexual harassment has recently become characterized by an almost violent ambivalence. There is the wave of so-called power feminist texts that claim sexual harassment is just another way to designate women as "victims" (Katie Roiphe's *Morning After: Fear, Sex, and Feminism on College Campuses* [New York: Little, Brown, 1993], which also deals with date rape, is a good example), and David Mamet's play *Oleanna* (New York: Random, 1993), on stages throughout the country, must be read as ambivalent. While the play is effective in conveying the clash in points of view that so often characterizes sexual harassment, it also seems fundamentally wrongheaded in that it neutralizes the sexual register, focusing on the power dynamic of the teacher-student relationship in such a way that sex, gender construction, and male and female identity construction aren't really part of the issue. This fundamentally misconstrues the problem, deflecting public attention from the real issues in all of their complications.

53. Many experiences of harassment are given voice in *The Lecherous Professor: Sexual Harassment on Campus,* ed. Billie Wright Dziech and Linda Weiner (Chicago: Univ. of Illinois Press, 1990). Furthermore, many contemporary women writers focus on experiences of sexual abuse, among them, Toni Morrison in *The Bluest Eye* (New York: Washington Square Press, 1970); and Jane Smiley in *A Thousand Acres* (New York: Fawcett Columbine, 1991).

54. In moving from Rhys's text to my own experience in order to construct a feminist frame, I am undoubtedly guilty of "misinterpreting [Rhys's] intentions," as Angier reports on the feminist "misuse" of Rhys:

America was ready now for [*Good Morning, Midnight*]: especially American women. No sooner had one critic suggested that [the book] might become a "strong weapon in the current and growing movement toward women's liberation" than another used it in exactly that way. Now the only thing Jean liked about feminists was teasing them. . . . She stood outside the women's movement as she stood outside everything. Nevertheless they were right to hail her as a champion. Her novels explored the pain (and pleasures) of female dependency with great insight and honesty. . . . from now on the women's movement would increasingly appropriate her and misinterpret her intentions. But though she meant only to explore her own alienation and oppression, not women's in general, despite herself she did have a great deal to contribute to that wider question. (*Jean Rhys*, pp. 596–97)

As Rhys's text stands as a cornerstone in an examination of the material ways in which female subjectivity becomes constructed pejoratively from within, I am willing to "misinterpret her intentions" and draw parallels between her experience and my own, with the assumption that similar incidents and subjectivities characterize the lives of many women.

Although it is beyond the scope of the analysis here, an examination of the issue of sexual harassment should also investigate the problem of the female professor and her relation to her students. The configuration is different, since a culturally disempowered person is placed in a position of authority, thus to some extent neutralizing her disempowerment in relation to a male student, but this doesn't grant her the freedom to abuse that power. The relation of a female professor to a female student is more complicated.

55. This dialogue interestingly echoes the exchange between Rochester and Antoinette in *Wide Sargasso Sea*. She asks him, "Why did you make me want to live?" and he responds, "[B]ecause I wanted to, isn't that enough?" (p. 92).

56. Coco the parrot in *Wide Sargasso Sea* has his wings clipped by Mr. Mason and is used later in the novel as a figure for both Antoinette and her mother, Annette.

57. Again, see Wolf's *Fire with Fire*, for an argument that could be used to accuse me of "whining" and making women look "weak." What I hope to show, however, is that it's a more complicated question that the simple binary of power/victim. It works both ways. In *Getting Personal* (New York: Routledge, 1991), Nancy K. Miller writes that "women on college campuses live in a climate of authorized sexual harassment" (p. 19), by which she means that harassment is usual, and I hope to have demonstrated that this is the case. Since harassment is so much a part of ordinary experience, questions of women's empowerment are more complicated than simply "taking control."

58. See, for instance, Angier, *Jean Rhys*, pp. 525–67; and Jane Neide Ashcome, "Two Modernisms: The Novels of Jean Rhys," *Jean Rhys Review* 2, no. 2 (spring 1988), p. 26. Hite asserts that "[i]f Antoinette Cosway in *Wide Sargasso Sea* has proved by far the most attractive and sympathetic of Rhys's protagonists, the attraction and sympathy are in many respects due to the historical documentation of the novel, to the fact that Antoinette is 'emblematic of an entire way of life,' as [Joyce Carol] Oates observes" (*Other Side*, p. 41).

59. On the difference between metaphoric and metonymic presentations in modernist style, see David Lodge, *The Modes of Modern Writing: Metaphor, Metonymy, and the Topology of Modern Literature* (Ithaca: Cornell Univ. Press, 1977).

60. Joyce Carol Oates, introduction to *Jane Eyre,* by Charlotte Brontë, p. xvi.

61. In *Wuthering Heights,* of course, both Catherine and Heathcliff starve themselves to death, but that is another chapter.

62. One of the provisional titles for *Wide Sargasso Sea* was *The Two Mrs. Rochesters.*

63. Just recently (April 1993), Fine Line Features released a film version of *Wide Sargasso Sea* directed by John Duigan, produced by Jan Sharp, with the screenplay by Jan Sharp, Carole Angier (Rhys's biographer), and John Duigan. The film stars the model Karina Lombard, in her first movie role, as Antoinette, and Nathaniel Parker as Rochester. The casting of Lombard seems, to me, at the center of everything that goes wrong in the movie. Because Lombard is, at least at this juncture, a model, not an actress, her performance is singularly wooden and lacking in motivation. Because any understanding of Rhys's text requires a heroine who is unusually spiritually alive, so that her spiritual death at Rochester's hands is that much more horrifying, Lombard was a bad choice. Her beauty is essentially decorative, with nothing to back it up. Furthermore, in the film, since the "death" conversations coincide with lovemaking, which they do not in the novel, their meaning is obscured. As Terrence Rafferty, a reviewer for the *New Yorker* writes, "*Wide Sargasso Sea* is so serenely paced and so envelopingly lovely to watch that you may not realize until the end that it is, in the deepest sense, a horror movie—a devastatingly intimate portrayal of the relationship between a monster and his victim. In Rochester the movie gives us a character who progresses from desire to terror to cold, repressive violence: we see the evolution of the impulse to enslave" ([April 19, 1993], p. 111). What the movie gets right is Rochester's sense of entrapment, visually enacted by dream sequences of underwater entanglement in the infamous sargasso that becomes, in his mind, a metaphor for Antoinette. What it gets wrong is the complexity of her character and the extent of her annihilation.

64. At points in this writing I have paused and considered whether I am committing the sin of a characterological analysis, making the fatal mistake of discussing characters as if they were people, rather than linguistic constructs. I have decided that the critical insistence on not talking about characters as if they were people is part of the anorexic logic that depersonalizes them and keeps us from learning the very human lessons they teach.

65. Susan Bordo, "Anorexia Nervosa: Psychopathology as the Crystallization of Culture," *Feminism and Foucault: Reflections on Resistance,* ed. Irene Diamond and Lee Quinby (Boston: Northeastern Univ. Press, 1988), p. 106.

66. Emery discusses an Amerindian legend about the fight between na-

tive Arawaks and Caribs. The Arawaks take refuge in a tree to which the Caribs set fire, burning the Arawaks but converting them to sparks that rise into the sky and become the Pleiades. Hence, Emery argues that Antoinette commits the crime "not of suicide, but of flight" (*Rhys at "World's End,"* pp. 58, 59).

67. Kaja Silverman, *Male Subjectivity at the Margins* (New York: Routledge, 1992), p. 4.

68. Quoted in Hite, *Other Side,* p. 33.

69. See Adam Begley, "The I's Have It: Duke's 'Moi' Critics Expose Themselves," *Lingua Franca* (April 1994), pp. 54–59.

Index

Women's Movement, 114; and the first wave, 13, 15, 214–15n.36, 219n.10; and hunger striking, 150, 152, 227n.15; and suffrage, 64, 215n.36
Wooley, Susan C., 204n.5
Woolf, Virginia, 118, 157

Wuthering Heights, 237n.61

Young, Elizabeth, 203n.1

Zach, Natan, 100–101
Zizek, Slavoj, 40, 75

Compositor:	Graphic Composition, Inc.
Text:	11/13.5 Caledonia
Display:	Caledonia
Printer and binder:	Thomson-Shore, Inc.